SQL/DS Performance

SQL/DS Performance
Techniques for Improvement

Dov Gilor

John Wiley & Sons, Inc.

New York • Chichester • Brisbane • Toronto • Singapore

The following terms used in this book are registered
trademarks of the International Business Machine
Corporation: IBM, AS/400, CICS/VSE, PS/2, SAA,
SQL/400 and Systems Application Architecture.

This publication is designed to provide accurate and
authoritative information in regard to the subject
matter covered. It is sold with the understanding that
the publisher is not engaged in rendering legal, accounting,
or other professional services. If legal advice or other
expert assistance is required, the services of a competent
professional person should be sought. *From a Declaration
of Principles jointly adopted by a Committee of the
American Bar Association and a Committee of Publishers.*

Library of Congress Cataloging-in-Publication Data

Gilor, Dov.
    SQL/DS performance : Techniques for improvement / Dov Gilor.
       p.   cm.
    Includes bibliographical references.
    1. Data base management. 2. SQL/DS (Computer program) I. Title.
    QA76.9.D3G524 1990
    005.75′6—dc20   90-45558
    ISBN 0-471-52624-X   CIP

Printed in the United States of America

10 9 8 7 6 5 4 3 2 1

To my dear wife, Barbara
To our three sons, David, Donny, and Avi
And to David's wife, Shira,
Who gave us our most precious possessions:
Ariel, Amiad, and Shilo.

Contents

7 Resource Contention   198

Preface

The professional user of SQL/DS must sooner or later learn to cope with the task of tuning SQL/DS systems and applications. This book is designed to help in that tuning process and should be read by the application programmer, the systems programmer, the database administrator, and the systems analyst. Each will learn how to properly tune that segment of the total environment for which he or she is responsible. Each of these professionals should be viewed as a member of the *Performance Tuning Team*.

Too often, each member of the *Performance Tuning Team* prefers to ignore what he or she can do to improve performance and shrugs off the problem by blaming the other members of the team. We have all heard the lament from application developers that the "*systems people do not provide adequate resources*," and from the systems staff complaining that the "*application developers write such resource-hungry and inefficient applications*." Everyone laments, "*We need more real storage, CPU power, and disk capacity*."

The goal of this book is to present **an alternative to blaming the other guy.** Each of the members of the performance team has a role to play and a job to do to improve the environment in which SQL/DS operates. Senior management should encourage (no, demand!) that the database administrator, systems programmers, and application developers work as a team to improve system response without necessarily increasing hardware capacity.

This book stresses those areas sensitive to resource strain and covers those elements and principles of tuning available to each user. For the experienced user of SQL/DS, this book serves as a concentrated repository of the knowledge and information gained as a result of many years of experience implementing and tuning SQL/DS systems. As the book was being written, however, it became apparent that the relatively new users of relational database have an even greater need for performance tuning information than do the experienced users. In order to accommodate the needs of both communities of users, some introductory explanations are included in many of the topics to assist the new user and to define the terms being used, but the emphasis remains on the needs of the experienced user. To derive full benefit from the recommendations in this book, the inexperienced user should have completed the basic SQL/DS courses.

There are those who might translate many of the chapters in this book into exact technical and mathematical terminology. It is possible to express the concepts scientifically and other authors have reached levels of exactitude that this book does not aim to reach. This book is written in non-mathematical terms so that all of the application developers, business analysts, database administrators and systems programmers can read and understand it. Not all of the SQL/DS concepts will be discussed. Some of the basic concepts will be mentioned in context in one chapter but discussed in greater detail in another chapter. This was done to improve readability and to reduce the reader's need to skip from chapter to chapter in order to understand a topic.

SQL/DS is such a powerful tool that with even simple transactions, developers of application programs can easily cause massive resource utilization that will result in disastrously poor performance for the entire system. Performance tuning is a delicate task that requires continuous monitoring to ensure that a modification to help one application does not negatively impact all of the other applications. There cannot, of course, be any guarantees that the solutions recommended in this book that were successful in some environments will be successful in all other environments, but the experience gained over the years by the author can definitely point to those items that require further investigation. The author has personally succeeded in reducing on-line applications **from a 2 to 5 minute** response **to a less than 1 second response.** Long-running SQL/DS batch applications were reduced from four to eight *hours* to less than 5 *minutes.* In all of the above instances, no changes were made to the hardware or the function of the applications.

Such cases may seem extreme but they are all too common in the world of databases. End-users have grown accustomed to 30 second response times and consider them *acceptable.* Such response times are **not acceptable** in the vast majority of cases. Some applications, of course, cannot be tuned any further but the database professional's motto must be "**A database transaction should not take forever.**"

The subject of improving SQL/DS performance, while mentioned in many texts, is generally not emphasized to the degree it should be. This book will provide an insight into those factors that play a prominent role in database performance and provide hints, tips, and rules of thumb on a level useful to both the novice and the experienced professional.

Each chapter will discuss performance from a different perspective and will touch upon the tasks of one or more of the members of the *Performance Tuning Team*. The major points made in the chapter will be covered by a review and a summary of the recommendations made. Every chapter will contain practical examples of commands and output to help the reader better understand the material being discussed.

Dov Gilor

Monsey, New York
November 1990

Acknowledgments

This book would have been impossible to write without the support of my spouse. I would like to thank my wife, Barbara—for her total support for this project, for allowing me to neglect her for the many months that it took to write the book, and mainly for the countless hours she spent reading and editing the manuscript. She is a true **Woman of Valor**.

I would also like to thank Sara and Norman Blaustein for providing us with the environment, facilities, and equipment with which to complete the manuscript. They are dear friends.

D.G.

CHAPTER 1

Introduction

SQL/DS FEATURES

Structured Query Language/Data System (SQL/DS) is a very powerful database system and it incorporates many features required of a relational database, for example:

- Data recovery and integrity
- Entity integrity
- Data security and independence
- On-line data administration
- Access via high-level languages and interpreters
- A powerful database utility
- A data dictionary (known as a catalog)
- Portability of applications and tables.

Each of these features can be tuned while improper use of a feature can negatively impact system performance.

Structured Query Language incorporates many features that make application development comparatively easy. The table structure is easy to comprehend and logical views simplify development even more. The SQL/DS system catalogs, with their wealth of data, are accessible using the SQL commands that give the database administrator (DBA) the capability of closely monitoring database activity. The ease of creating, altering, and dropping tables and indexes simplifies the task of the DBA. The many automatic features that do not require the knowledge or intervention of the programmer (locking, data access path, optimization, etc.) help make application development relatively simple.

The *forgiving nature* of SQL/DS makes it so user-friendly that if resources were unlimited, **the user would never have to learn anything about performance tuning.** SQL/DS does not require indexes or

1

sargable predicates. It does not require *normalization* or *denormalization*. Commands can all be executed ad hoc and do not have to be preplanned. *Joins* and *subqueries* are virtually unrestricted and *scalar* functions are acceptable both in *predicates* and in SELECT lists. Unfortunately, all of this freedom must be curtailed by the reality of limited resources and by the requirements of quick response. These resource limitations make it necessary for all of those involved in SQL/DS systems to learn the ABCs of performance tuning.

Performance is partially controlled by the automatic functions of the optimizer. The optimizer determines how data will be accessed but the user can help the optimizer make the best choices. The knowledge of how to make a *predicate sargable* and when to use dynamic commands can guide the optimization process to choose the best access path for efficient operation. When precompile parameter choice, space utilization, and buffer requirements are understood, the user can ensure that the applications will run more efficiently. When the user knows why it is essential to avoid mass updating, inserting, and deleting, or selecting or updating extra columns during peak processing periods, the entire environment will benefit.

Table design can have a great impact on transaction response. *Normalization* and *denormalization* and the judicious use of *joins*, *subqueries,* and *unions* can reduce input/output (I/O) and locking contention and central processing unit (CPU) utilization. Referential integrity is an extremely important feature in a database but its impact on processing must be understood so that disastrous response impact is not the result of its use. Primary and foreign keys ensure data integrity but the use of these keys and the importance of indexes to speed response and reduce access load must be understood by all developers.

The coding of *pre-planned* applications differs from the coding of *ad hoc* queries only in minor ways but understanding these differences is very important. There is a need to correctly define host variables and to precompile using the most suitable parameters for efficient transactions. It is of critical importance to understand when to avoid the impact of opening and closing *cursors* and of updating statistics. EXPLAIN tables will provide an insight into the way the optimizer chooses an access path and it is a powerful tool of the application developer and the DBA. Even the granting and revoking of authority can impact performance and must be analyzed and planned.

The powerful SQL commands can be used simultaneously by many users. When these users utilize the same resources, contention slows response. The developer and the DBA can control the environment and reduce this contention to a reasonable level. Part of the technique of contention control is the proper use of storage areas, buffers, and storage pools. A knowledge of how SQL/DS manages storage and what the developers can do to use storage more efficiently, can reduce locking and I/O and ensure that the automatic procedures to protect against running out of log and storage pool space are not initiated.

The DBA and systems programmer need to know how to protect data from accidental loss in an effective way. They also need the knowledge and tools to tune the operating system environment.

All of the subjects mentioned are covered in the chapters that follow. A review of many of the new SQL/DS functions and their impact on performance will be included. The tuning information in these chapters is vital to the effective operation of an SQL/DS system.

WHY TUNE?

In practice, errors in efficient design and operation can often be overlooked in the early stages of application implementation because some excess computing power is usually available. It becomes very rapidly apparent, however, that the insatiable appetite of end-users, once they become aware of the broad spectrum of SQL functional capabilities, will soon place enormous strain on system resources. As more and more users take advantage of SQL/DS functions, the developers regret their previous lax attitude. The best way to work with SQL/DS is to use it efficiently from the very beginning. This demands that the design, application, and system parameters be optimized and effectively tuned at the earliest stage possible.

Performance tuning concerns itself with the finding of system bottlenecks and the relieving of the pressure on the system by adjusting parameters or by adding resource capacity. Additional hardware is almost always helpful but not always necessary. There is no point in adding more disks, for example, when the bottleneck is CPU power, and it is wasteful to add hardware capacity when relatively simple application tuning will vastly improve response time. It is also important to keep in mind that SQL/DS does not execute in a vacuum. Adding a thousand data buffers to SQL/DS startup parameters executing in a storage constrained CPU is not only counter-productive to SQL/DS users but also to all other system users.

WHO CAN BENEFIT FROM THIS BOOK?

All of the users of SQL/DS can benefit from the information in this book. The systems analyst will gain an insight into the performance factors that need to be taken into consideration in the early design stages. The applications programmer will receive practical hints and tips as well as a solid basis in SQL/DS application performance. The database administrator (DBA) will gain an understanding of the many aspects of SQL tuning. The systems programmer or administrator will learn what impact the system parameters have on SQL performance and what impact SQL has on system performance. Non-IBM users and DB2 users might also gain a perspective into general SQL tuning factors and will find several chapters very helpful.

SQL/DS tuning is similar to tuning any other computer system. The process requires knowledge of the environment and of tuning techniques. With an understanding of the performance aspects of SQL/DS and the application of database and system tuning techniques, an SQL/DS application with a **five minute** response time can often be tuned until a **sub-second** response time is achieved. This book will help the reader gain this knowledge and technique.

WHAT WILL BE DISCUSSED

This book will discuss the role of each of the people involved in database usage and performance tuning. Readers should be able to gain a better understanding of the factors at work in an SQL/DS environment and the steps that they can take to improve system and application response. The DBA and the systems programmer must work together with the application developers to ensure that the entire environment is adequately tuned. Each member of the performance team has a role to play and a professional stake in the results. Working together for their mutual benefit will produce positive results.

In general, most chapters begin with an introduction to the topic, include concrete examples, and conclude with a summary of the recommendations and the contents of the chapter. Each will explain the impact of different aspects of the SQL/DS system on performance tuning.

THE IBM RELATIONAL FAMILY

SQL/DS is IBM's Relational Data Base Management System (RDBMS) for the VM/SP, VM/HPO, VM/XA, and VSE/SP environments. SQL/DS has become one of the most popular databases for these systems. The first version of SQL/DS was announced for VSE/SP in 1981 and, by 1983, the VM/SP version became available. SQL/DS is a member of the IBM family of relational databases (DB2, AS/400/SQL, and so on) which operate on almost all of IBM's hardware including: PS/2, AS/400, 9370, 4300, 3090, etc. SQL/DS is similar in many ways to other IBM and non-IBM relational products. In 1986, SQL was adopted by the American National Standards Institute (ANSI) and, in 1987, by the International Standards Organization (ISO) as a standard interface for relational databases.

SQL VERSUS SQL

The two major components in a database are the language that is used to express the actions that should be taken and the database management system (DBMS) that controls database I/O. The language is used in application programs, interactive communication, and utilities, to instruct the DBMS to take the action specified. The commands that are passed to the DBMS for execution might specify:

```
SELECT a record with a key 2134
DELETE all records for "Joe Smith"
UPDATE record 9362
```

When running under the MVS operating system, the two components have different names. DB2 is the DataBase Management System and SQL is the command language. In VSE/SP and VM/SP there is **only one name for both** components; **SQL** is the language and **SQL/DS** is the DBMS. Many users become confused when SQL is mentioned because they are not sure what is being discussed. Every attempt will be made in this book to specify whether the DBMS or the language element is meant. Since IBM products and many non-IBM products use Structured Query Language commands, **many of the suggestions found in this book to improve the performance of SQL/DS may also apply to DB2 and non-IBM SQL products.** The author, however, has not tested any of the suggestions under systems other than VSE/SP, VM/SP, and VM/HPO and cannot, therefore, make any claims concerning these other systems. Many of the recommendations and much of the information may also apply to the Double Byte Character Set (**DBCS**) but the subject is not directly covered in this book.

CRITERIA OF PERFORMANCE

Efficient performance does not happen, it must be planned, and planning means studying the current system response and activity and deciding the performance improvements that are desirable at the maximum acceptable cost. The performance level to be achieved must be explicitly stated as the *service level objectives* so that those involved in capacity planning and performance tuning will know what their goals are and when they have reached them. The absence of a set of objectives is similar to aiming at a continuously moving target and it is hard to determine whether or not tuning has been successful.

A *service level agreement* is needed to guarantee that the data processing department will provide a specified and stable level of service for a high percentage of the user's workload. The criteria for *acceptable* performance levels should normally be decided upon by the company-wide Computer Steering Committee and documented as the goals to be met in a service level agreement. It is inadequate to proclaim that *better performance is needed* without documenting what *poor performance* is.

This definition of acceptable performance levels will enable the DBA to determine what constitutes good or poor performance. It will enable him or her to prepare an estimate of the cost of good performance and to determine what additional resources have to be acquired to satisfy the performance levels desired. The steering committee can then adjust the requirements to an acceptable level of cost and the necessary trade-offs can be made by the DBA to arrive at the *best* performance possible at an affordable price. This will usually ensure that reasonable and achievable targets will be chosen.

The performance team should aim for an SLO of 90–95%. A lower SLO is impractical and a higher level doesn't allow much room for the imponderables. It is also important to track any modifications that are made to any SLO applications because changes often result in a degradation in performance. New applications need to be monitored to ensure that they do not impact production performance levels and standards need to be strictly enforced.

The best basis for *service level objectives* is usually response time. This emphasizes the need for monitoring before the implementation of a *service level agreement* to document what the current response is. In addition the criteria for improved performance might include all or some of the following:

- Expected response time of specific critical applications
- Estimated number of transactions to be run per time frame

- Acceptable variations of response time levels
- Estimated I/O per second on each channel and/or device
- Estimated permissible impact of SQL/DS on non-SQL applications and vica versa
- Estimated storage and CPU usage
- Batch run schedule and its assumed impact on on-line processing
- Acceptable recovery time from system failures
- Other installation specific criteria.

It is also important to measure and document response time rather than to depend upon *user impressions*. These measurements should be taken at various periods during the day and must include normal concurrent system activity. The current workloads should be measured using the available tools to check the stress on the CPU, DASD, real storage, and controllers. In addition, the transaction mix should be studied and sample workloads chosen for further observation so that tests will be representative and duplicatable.

It should be kept in mind that response time includes terminal display speed, line delay, VTAM processing, VM/SP or VSE/SP control programs, application initiation and processing, IUCV or XPCC data transfer, AGENT availability, SQL/DS processing, and I/O transfer. Transactions are also affected by the volume of data which is related to the time of day, month, or year.

Not everything can be accomplished at once and a timetable must be prepared and priorities established. When eventually the *service level objectives* are reached, tuning can be suspended but monitoring must continue until an indication is received that it is time to begin the entire tuning cycle over again.

SYSTEM RESOURCES INVOLVED IN TUNING

SQL/DS will perform poorly when adequate resources are not available. SQL/DS applications, for example, can be installed on an entry-level lightly loaded IBM/9370 but they may not be able to be added to a highly active, CPU and storage constrained IBM/3090. It is not the size of the computer that is important but it is the availability of adequate resources.

SQL/DS applications run in a total environment and it is this total environment that must be studied and improved. There are three major system resources available on the local system and there is an additional communication resource available for remote and distributed systems. The systems programmer must monitor all of the resources available to the total system including the:

- Disk I/O subsystem
- CPU utilization
- Real and Virtual Storage subsystem
- Communication subsystem.

The primary function of monitoring is to determine which resource is stressed to the point of becoming a bottleneck. When the bottleneck is found, steps can be taken to relieve the stress.

While the purpose of this book is to show how to reduce stress on resources caused by SQL/DS, it is important that the reader realize that each time a bottleneck is cleared and the stress on one resource is relieved, another resource may come under stress and become the new source of a bottleneck. Every tuning action has an impact on the system and this impact should be studied to ensure that the overall system performance has actually been improved. As an example, it is reasonable to assume that when an overloaded CPU is replaced by a more powerful CPU, throughput will increase thereby increasing the stress on the I/O subsystem and on real storage.

THE TUNING PROCESS

The tuning process can be compared to a circular stream with three dams. When increased throughput (*heavy rains*) stresses one of the dams and steps are taken to relieve the pressure on the first dam, the pressure on the second builds up. When pressure on the second is relieved, pressure builds on the third. When pressure on the third is relieved, the first again must cope with added pressure and the cycle repeats itself.

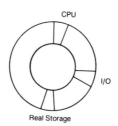

The first rule of tuning is to avoid increasing the use of a resource already under stress. When any new application is being readied for implementation, tests must be made to ensure that the system can handle the load. **Installations too frequently wait until an application is about to go into production before capacity planning is done** to ensure that the computer system can handle the new load. The recommended practice is to do the capacity planning checkup when the application is in the design stage.

The need to view performance monitoring and tuning as a **continuous process** cannot be overemphasized. Many times the improving of the performance of one application has led to the deterioration of performance in another application. This should not discourage the DBA or systems programmer but it should serve as a challenge and as a warning. I vividly recall the pleasure of finding the most efficient index for an application and noting the excellent improvement in its response time, only to discover that the optimizer chose (after access module re-creation) to also use the new index for another application. The other query involved a *nested loop join* and the new index reversed the inner and outer *join* tables. The result was an unacceptable degradation in response for that transaction. This served to emphasize the importance of checking every modification to an SQL/DS system.

Tuning Strategy

SQL/DS performance levels should not be decided upon in isolation of the rest of the environment. The performance level of non-SQL applications and of CMS or CICS and ICCF must also be considered and planned for.

Steps to improve the applications, index and table structure, and system resource availability should be taken **before** response time begins to deteriorate. When performance problems already exist, it is usually much too expensive to start searching for the causes, to rewrite applications, and to restructure SQL/DS tables. With production stalled, the easiest solution to justify is to pay the price to increase hardware capacity. This method is often unnecessary and is very wasteful. Performance should be planned for and taken into consideration at the application analysis and design stages and should be checked and rechecked throughout the coding, testing, and implementation stages.

All elements of the system need to be tuned but *only one element at a time should be modified.* Before any element is modified, it must be monitored using a planned strategy to document the current level of performance. The planning and strategy should include many of the following:

1. The frequency of system monitoring: daily, weekly, during peak hours, extended periods, or all of the above?

2. A plan that details the aspects of SQL/DS activity that should be monitored. Many of the following should be included: catalog contents, counters, lock activity, failures, specific applications, resource utilization, specific tables, and so on.

3. The tools to be used to measure resources, throughput, and SQL activity.

4. The load to be measured on-line, in batch mode, or as an exception load.

5. The procedure to review the reports. A chart of summary data should be prepared.

6. A procedure to record application and system modifications during the monitoring process.

7. A method to determine the expected growth in system activity during the coming year or years.

8. A checklist detailing the timetable of parameters and functions to be modified and tuned. This list might include:

   - The overall hardware utilization parameters

   - The operating system parameters

   - SQL/DS startup parameters

   - Division of EXTENTS among available disks (also VSAM parameters in VSE)

   - Table and row design for index usage, *normalization,* and redundancy

   - Program design and application usage of SQL/DS

   - SQL/DS command design and modification.

An important aspect of this process is to avoid over-tuning the system. Most professionals involved in tuning adhere to the **80/20 rule** which specifies that 20% of the effort should achieve 80% of the possible benefit. The other 20% of performance improvement should usually be ignored as too costly a process for too meager a benefit. Shaving 20 microseconds from the response time of a noncritical transaction may never be noticed and may not really improve overall performance. Experience has shown, however, that a 5 minute or a 5 second response time of an on-line transaction can often be reduced to sub-second response. **The key aspect of this entire tuning process is to identify the critical, highly utilized applications that have poor response and to concentrate on improving their performance** without impacting the performance of other applications.

There are no exactly right answers in tuning a system but when the concepts and critical factors of SQL performance tuning are understood, the **rules of thumb** can be intelligently applied. Such a **rule of thumb** value can be greatly exceeded with no ill effect on the system while at other times a low *acceptable* value results in serious degradation of performance. It is, however, more reasonable to first investigate those system values that exceed recommended levels before checking other values. Chapter 10 will outline the initial steps that can be followed to find system bottlenecks.

SQL/DS PERFORMANCE DATA

There are several sources where performance-related information can be found and modified so that the user can determine the SQL/DS system activity level and can tune it. The sources include:

- SQL/DS catalogs (covered in this chapter)
- EXPLAIN tables (covered in Chapter 6)
- COUNTER command output (covered in Chapters 6 and 8)
- SHOW command output (covered in Chapter 8)
- SQL/DS initialization listing (covered in Chapter 8)
- Accounting information
- SQL/DS trace facility output.

Each source contains important information. The first four are crucial to the DBA and to the application developer with access to ISQL, RXSQL, or the database utility (DBSU), while the other three are basically relevant to the DBA and to the systems programmer.

SYSTEM CATALOGS

The SQL/DS data dictionary elements are called *catalogs* and these catalogs are continuously referenced by the DataBase Management System. These catalogs contain information about tables, views, indexes, user authorization, referential relationships, and access module dependencies. The catalogs also contain statistics that are very important for performance tuning and are used by the optimizer to determine access paths. The SQL/DS catalogs are tables that may be accessed using standard SQL/DS SELECT commands. INSERT, DELETE, and UPDATE commands, while permitted to users with DBA authority, should not be used on system catalogs unless extreme care is exercised by someone who understands what is being done.

The catalogs are implicitly updated by data definition language commands (DDL) which define user application tables, views, and indexes and are explicitly updated by the UPDATE STATISTICS commands. They are **not** updated by INSERT, DELETE, or UPDATE commands. This explains why catalog statistics will not be accurate after modifications are made and before update statistics is executed.

The catalog data, **whether accurate or not,** is used by the optimizer to determine the best access path to the data. It is generally in the best interest of the users to invoke UPDATE STATISTICS periodically.

Each catalog contains valuable information but some catalogs are more important than others to the system tuning team. The most important include:

SYSDBSPACES	contains a row for each DBSPACE.
SYSCATALOG	contains a row for each table.
SYSINDEXES	contains a row for each index.
SYSCOLSTATS	contains a row for the first column of each index.
SYSKEYS	contains a row for each primary and each foreign key.
SYSKEYCOLS	contains a row for each column in each primary and foreign key.
SYSUSAGE	contains a row for each dependency of one SQL/DS object upon another.
SYSACCESS	contains a row for each access module and view definition.

This section will provide a brief description of several of the columns in the above tables that are useful for performance information gathering. The contents will be reviewed here and their impact upon performance will be discussed in other chapters.

1. **SYSDBSPACES**—Each public and private DBSPACE defined, even if not yet acquired, is represented by a row in this table. The columns of special interest are:

    DBSPACETYPE—Public or private. When the type is private only one user at a time may access the DBSPACE. Multiple users may access public DBSPACES simultaneously.

    NTABS—This column indicates the number of tables that are actually in the DBSPACE. It is usually recommended that each DBSPACE contain **only one** table.

    PCTINDX—The percentage of the DBSPACE pages potentially available for use as index space. Space is not actually allocated until it is needed.

    FREEPCT—This value specifies the percentage of each page that should be left free for future inserts. **The space will never be used if this value is not modified.** The space is not used until the FREEPCT value is changed to zero or to a lower value. This value is approximate as explained in Chapter 8 in the section on free space.

    LOCKMODE—The type of locking in effect for all of the tables in the DBSPACE. Row and Page locking are only available for public DBSPACES. DBSPACE locking is available for all three.

    NACTIVE—Indicates the number of active pages that have to be read for a DBSPACE scan.

2. **SYSCATALOG**—A row for each table or view. A *-1* in a column means that update statistics was not done for that table. **Many columns are used by the optimizer to help determine the best access path.** When no data is available because update statistics was not done, the optimizer uses a special set of default values.

    TABLETYPE—Indicates table or view.

    CLUSTERTYPE—Indicates whether rows are to be inserted in accordance with default rules or by using an index. This is a very important parameter. When the value is 'I', the FIRST index is used to determine where to insert new rows.

    CLUSTERROW—When the default insert rules are used, this is the address of the "last" row in the table known to

SQL/DS. The system tries to insert new rows near this address. This value is not updated automatically.

AVGROWLEN—Average size of the rows in the table. This value is not updated automatically.

ROWCOUNT—Total number of rows in the table. Updated by UPDATE STATISTICS and CREATE INDEX but not updated automatically.

NPAGES—When UPDATE STATISTICS is run, this field will indicate the number of active pages containing rows from this table. It will not include pages containing long columns. When only one table is in the DBSPACE, the total number of active pages can be found in the NACTIVE column in the SYSDBSPACES table which will indicate total active pages including those containing long columns.

PCTPAGES—This is the percentage of active pages containing rows from this table. It is calculated by dividing active pages (NPAGES) by the NACTIVE column in the SYSTEM.SYSDBSPACES table for the DBSPACE where this table is found.

NOVERFLOW—The number of rows which no longer fit in their original page. Overflow usually occurs when the row has VARCHAR fields that have expanded. The address of the row is not changed. A pointer in the original page points to the new page where the data is found. When this value is large, the table should be reorganized.

PARENTS—The number of parent tables (referential integrity associations) this table has.

DEPENDENTS—The number of dependents this parent table has.

3. **SYSCOLUMNS**—A row for every column in every table or view. When a column is the first column of an index, various columns (COLCOUNT, HIGH2KEY, LOW2KEY, AVGCOLLEN, ORDERFIELD) in this table are updated when the index is created or when UPDATE STATISTICS is executed. When UPDATE ALL STATISTICS is executed all of these columns are updated whether or not they are part of the first column of an index.

LENGTH—The size of the column. Blank if integer, date, time, timestamp, or smallint.

COLCOUNT—The number of unique values in the column. This column and ROWCOUNT in SYSCATALOG indicate what percentage of the column values are duplicates. The first column of an index should not be very non-unique.

ORDERFIELD—Indicates whether the rows are physically stored according to the sequence of this column.

COLINFO—'Y' indicates that additional information about this column is found in SYSCOLSTATS.

4. **SYSINDEXES**—Contains a row for every index.

COLNAMES—The names of the columns in the index. A '+' indicates ascending sequence. To view all of the columns using ISQL, SET VARCHAR 100 before SELECTing from SYSINDEXES.

INDEXTYPE—Unique (U) or not (D). If the index is unique, make sure to inform SQL/DS in the CREATE command. The optimizer prefers unique (and *clustered*) indexes.

CLUSTER—Type of index. FIRST ('F' or 'W'), *Clustered* ('C' or 'F'), *Unclustered* ('N' or 'W'), or an inactive primary key (blank).

FIRSTKEYCOUNT—The number of distinct values in the first column (only) of the index. Indexes should be designed so that the first column is as unique as possible. The optimizer uses this value when deciding whether or not to use this index when only part of the key is used in a *predicate*.

FULLKEYCOUNT—The number of distinct values when the full key is considered. The full key should be as unique as possible.

NLEVELS—The number of index levels.

IPCTFREE—The percentage of free space reserved in the index. After the index is created, this space is automatically made available for additional keys (unlike free space in the data pages).

CLUSTERRATIO—This new column is a measure of how *clustered* the index is. 10000 means that it is totally (100.00%) *clustered* and 0 means it is totally *unclustered*. It is a very significant factor in the optimizer's calculations on whether or not to use an *unclustered* index.

KEYTYPE—Indicates whether or not this is a primary index ('P' or 'I').

5. **SYSCOLSTATS**—Contains additional statistics on the **first column on an index.** This information is very useful to the optimizer when it has to decide whether or not to use an index. This table highlights the significance of the **first** column of the index and reemphasizes that this column should contain as many unique values as possible. If sensitive information is contained in this column, the public should **not** have access to this table.

VAL10

VAL50

VAL90—The value in the column where 10%, 50%, or 90% of the values in the column are less than or equal to this value.

FREQ1VAL

FREQ2VAL—The first and second most frequent values in the column.

FREQ1PCT

FREQ2PCT—The frequency that this value is actually found expressed as a percentage. This replaces the optimizer assumption in previous releases that the values were distributed evenly among the number of unique values in the column.

6. **SYSUSAGE**—Lists the dependencies of views on tables and other views and of programs access modules on views, tables, indexes, and DBSPACES.

BNAME—The name of the table, view, index, or DBSPACE.

BTYPE—Which type of object the BNAME refers to.

DNAME—The View or access module dependent on BNAME.

DTYPE—Whether DNAME is a view (V) or an access module (X).

7. **SYSACCESS**—Lists information about access modules and views

TNAME—The name of access module or view.

VALID—'N' if the access module is invalid. 'Y' if the access module is valid.

TABTYPE—'X' If it is an access module. 'V' If it is a view.

A FEW WORDS ABOUT SAA

System Application Architecture (SAA) is a collection of IBM standard conventions, interfaces, and protocols to provide an environment within which applications are portable between most IBM computer operating systems. IBM has defined SQL as the common database interface within SAA and SQL/DS is the VM/SP component of this interface. To date, while there has been some mention that VSE/SP may have some elements of SAA compatibility (CSP, CICS, SQL/DS) it is still not officially an SAA system.

SAA LIMITS

A vast majority of SQL/DS users do not approach the limits for size or number of any resource in SQL/DS. Some consideration, however, should be given when applications begin to approach SAA limits. Users planning to migrate to other systems should keep in mind that there are differences between the SQL/DS limits and the SAA limits and application designers should make every effort to remain within the SAA limits.

The SAA limit for LONG VARCHAR, for example, is 4,000 and an attempt should be made to keep within that limit. The maximum host variable size is ten while in SQL/DS it is 18 and the longest index key and the maximum length of a GROUP BY is 120 in SAA and 255 in SQL/DS. The SAA limits are fairly generous and should be observed.

SUMMARY

SQL/DS is a very powerful database system with many features that make application development easy. Each of the features can be tuned. The SQL/DS system catalogs are accessible using the SQL language commands which gives the DBA the capability of closely monitoring database activity.

The *forgiving nature* of SQL/DS makes it user friendly and it has few limits except for the reality of limited resources and the requirement for quick response.

Performance is controlled by the optimizer which determines how data will be accessed. The user can help the optimizer make the best choices. The user must learn how to use the system to control performance.

It is important to realize that end-users will soon place enormous strain on system resources. The best way to work with SQL/DS is to use it efficiently from the very beginning.

The installation management should determine the service level objectives, strategy, and goals of performance tuning, monitor system activity and growth, and save collected data for documentation of performance improvements and for future capacity planning. When monitoring the resources, a record of any new applications to be added must be kept. New applications can have a significant impact on performance levels.

Performance tuning concerns itself with the finding of system bottlenecks and the relieving of the pressure on the system. SQL/DS tuning is similar to tuning any other computer system. The process requires knowledge of the environment and of tuning techniques. Additional hardware is almost always helpful but not always necessary.

In VSE/SP and VM/SP there is only one name for both components; **SQL** is the language and **SQL/DS** is the DBMS. Suggestions found in this book to improve the performance of SQL/DS may also apply to DB2 and non-IBM SQL products but no claims concerning these other systems are made.

SQL/DS will perform poorly when adequate resources are not available. SQL/DS runs in a total environment and it is this total environment which must be studied and improved. Real storage is a critical resource. Adding real storage to improve throughput often tends to increases CPU and I/O utilization.

Performance monitoring and tuning is a continuous process. When performance problems already exist, it is usually much too expensive to start searching for the causes. With production stalled, the easiest solution is to increase hardware capacity. This method is often unnecessary and is very wasteful.

All elements of the system need to be tuned. Experience has shown that a five-minute or a five-second response time of an on-line transaction can often be reduced to sub-second response.

The sources of performance related information include: SQL/DS catalogs, EXPLAIN tables, COUNTER command output, SHOW command output, SQL/DS initialization listing, accounting information, and trace facility output.

IBM has defined SQL as the common database interface within SAA and SQL/DS is the VM/SP component of this interface. There are differences between the SQL/DS limits and the SAA limits.

RECOMMENDATIONS

1. Avoid increasing the use of a resource already under stress.
2. Do not wait until an application is about to go into production before performing capacity planning to ensure that the computer system can handle the new load.
3. Check every modification to an SQL/DS system.
4. Steps to improve the applications, index and table structure, and system resource availability should be taken before response time begins to deteriorate.
5. Performance should be planned for at the application analysis and design stages and should be checked and rechecked throughout the coding, testing, and implementation stages.
6. Only one element at a time should be modified. Before any element is modified it must be monitored.
7. Avoid over-tuning the system. Adhere to the 80/20 rule.
8. Identify the critical, highly utilized applications that have poor response and concentrate on improving their performance without impacting the performance of other applications.
9. Application designers should make every effort to remain within the SAA limits.

CHAPTER 2

Basic Concepts

Not every experienced user has had the time or opportunity to learn the performance implications of the basic SQL commands and how they affect the application and the system. This chapter should be of special interest to the inexperienced user but **it is strongly recommended that the experienced user also read it,** especially the section on the ALTER TABLE command that describes the manipulation of primary and foreign keys. This chapter concentrates basic SQL/DS concepts and performance tuning information in one location and will serve as the basic building blocks for all of the other chapters in this book.

The chapter will start with a short introduction to basic SQL/DS concepts *with an emphasis on their impact upon performance* so that all of the readers will use the same terminology to refer to the same facilities of SQL/DS. Many of the subjects covered in this chapter will be discussed in much greater detail in other chapters.

Structured Query Language (SQL) has become the industry standard for relational database languages because of its versatility and power. It has three component parts that provide the user with facilities for data definition, control, and manipulation:

- **Data Definition Language** (DDL) is used to create physical table definitions, logical view definitions, and indexes. It is also used to alter tables and define *referential integrity* relationships.
- **Data Control Language** (DCL) controls who can use the data and facilities via GRANT and REVOKE authority commands. It also controls when data is committed to the database or rolled back via the COMMIT WORK and ROLLBACK WORK commands.
- **Data Manipulation Language** (DML) is used to read, write, insert, update, and delete rows to and from the database.

The data definition commands and data control commands of SQL/DS are executable on-line, from application programs, or via the

Data Base Services Utility (DBSU). These commands, however, usually issue exclusive locks on the data dictionary (catalog) tables and their execution should be carefully planned to take place after peak processing time.

The data manipulation commands are very powerful; for example, with one command:

```
SELECT * FROM very_large_table ORDER BY 1
```

the user can cause 100,000,000 rows or more to be accessed, sorted, and readied for presentation. The user could also have requested that the data be grouped into categories, summed, counted, averaged, or acted upon in a number of other ways within the same one command. It is no wonder that a good knowledge of the potential results of the various language elements is so important to developers and end-users. Knowing how SQL/DS handles its language elements and how to avoid careless use of the commands is essential in order to avoid performance degradation. SQL/DS provides the EXPLAIN facility to help the application developer test the DML commands to determine if they will execute efficiently.

DATA FORMATS

The formats used to define SQL/DS data is one of the first topics learned by a new developer and the performance impact of even this basic topic must be stressed.

Character Data

Not every data format is acceptable to SQL/DS and all data placed in tables must conform to one of several specific formats. Alphabetic and alphanumeric data may be variable or fixed in length. Fixed-length string data may be from one to 254 bytes in length and is defined with the CHAR parameter during table creation. Once defined, a column's attributes may not be changed (unless the table is dropped and re-created). To define a fixed data format column with 39 bytes, for example, the table creator would specify:

```
columnname CHAR(39)
```

SQL/DS handles fixed-length character data more efficiently than it does variable length data. Even when columns should logically be variable in length, when small amounts of data are involved or the average differences in size are less than fifteen bytes, they should be defined as fixed character (CHAR).

Variable-length string data can be from one to 32K bytes in length and is defined as VARCHAR or LONG VARCHAR. To define a variable column with a maximum length of 207 bytes, the DBA would specify:

columnname **VARCHAR(207)**

Newer versions of SQL/DS no longer require the use of LONG VARCHAR for columns larger than 254 bytes. When the VARCHAR column is defined as being greater than 254, it is automatically treated as a LONG VARCHAR column. There are several limitations on LONG VARCHAR column types and they should be avoided whenever possible.

The LONG VARCHAR columns are not stored with the other columns of the table but are held in separate tables in the same DBSPACE. *There is a performance advantage to defining LONG VARCHAR columns as VARCHAR data types.* The defined length of a LONG VARCHAR column is fixed at 32K. When the same column is defined as a VARCHAR column, its **real** defined maximum length can be made available to the application. The VARCHAR column type will allow an application to use the actual defined maximum length to request storage for the size needed rather than for a fixed length of 32K. If a column is 300 bytes, for example, it is wasteful to acquire 32K of storage to hold the column.

Variable size data can save huge amounts of storage and should be used where needed. Its use, however, should be evaluated against the potential performance degradation. SQL/DS requires additional processing to bypass variable length rows in its search for the specific columns selected. When variable fields are stored in a row, only the number of bytes necessary to hold the column and the length bytes are reserved. When, at a later point, the column is updated and more bytes are needed for the new value, an overflow condition may occur which will result in additional I/O and processing.

Numeric Data

Numeric data may be defined in one of five formats. A SMALLINT column can contain a numerical value from −32,768 to +32,767 (15 bits plus a sign bit) and an INTEGER can contain approximately +2 billion to −2 billion. Four-byte, single precision, floating point numbers (defined as COMP-1 in COBOL) and eight-byte, double precision, floating point numbers (defined as COMP-2 in COBOL) are represented in either of two formats:

Single Precision	Double Precision
FLOAT(21)	FLOAT(53)
REAL	DOUBLE PRECISION

The fifth numeric datatype format is DECIMAL where the number of integers and the scale are specified in the definition. To specify a nine-digit column of which three appear after the decimal place, for example, the DBA would specify:

columnname DECIMAL(9,3)

SQL/DS handles numeric data more efficiently than character data and fixed character data more efficiently than variable character data. This implies that numeric data should not be defined in character format, as has been done in the past.

Date and Time Data

DATE, TIME, TIMESTAMP, and TIMEZONE are new data types that permit date and time arithmetic. While the DBA may define private formats for these datatypes, most installations use one of the standard formats described in Chapter 5. These column types are stored in a compact internal format in the tables but are always presented to the user in the format specified by the user or by the DBA. The DATE column is usually a 10-byte field written:

('1992-01-01')   or   ('01/01/1992')

The TIME column is usually 8 bytes and is written:

('24.00.00') or ('12:00 PM')

The TIMESTAMP column is usually 26 bytes long and includes the date, the time and microseconds:

('1992-01-01-24.00.00.000000')

The DATE, TIME, TIMESTAMP, and TIMEZONE column data is always presented to the user or application as character data but is not stored in the table nor is it accessible as character data.

SQL/LDS TABLES

SQL/DS uses a table structure to maintain all of the user data and all of its own catalog information. A table has two dimensions: a column and a row.

ROWS	COLUMNS		
	USER_ID	USER_NAME	BIRTH_DATE
1	1034	Joseph Cohen	03/04/1937
2	1862	Ross Wolf	09/22/1943
3	2035	Max Daniels	12/10/1940

The column is the smallest addressable data element. A row is a group of related columns and a table is a group of related rows where each row has the identical format as every other row.

Indexes may be created on one or more columns of a table and they make access to specific rows in the table much more efficient. Every table should have at least one index. More than one index may be created on every table but care should be taken to ensure that the creation of too many indexes on a table does not negatively impact performance. It is also important to carefully choose the first index created on the table and the first column of each index.

Tables that are often modified need to be reorganized. SQL/DS provides utility functions to facilitate this reorganization. The reorganization of tables has both a very positive and a very negative impact on performance and should be carefully planned.

SYSTEM TABLES

The use by SQL/DS of tables to hold the catalog data ensures that, through the use of simple SQL commands, all of the information available to the system is also accessible by the DBA. The system catalog tables and the indexes on these tables are created during system generation and they serve as a primitive data dictionary.

These system tables cannot be dropped by the DBA and, unfortunately, there is also no way to reorganize these tables. The number of rows in these catalogs, however, is often very low and the catalogs usually do not require reorganization. The DBA can, however, reorganize the catalog **indexes,** should it become necessary. In VM/SP, for example, the catalog indexes are reorganized using the SQLCIREO EXEC. The DBA would specify, in single-user mode, the database name and use the standard startup parameters:

```
SQLCIREO DBPROD PARM(PARMID=STRTFLE)
```

The DBA may also create additional indexes on system tables, create views and synonyms, and update or insert data into any system table. It cannot be emphasized too strongly, however, that modifications to the catalog tables should never be done in haste and should be carefully thought out but is best usually avoided. **Modifying the SQL/DS catalogs is unhealthy.** There are, however, instances where modification of the SQL/DS catalogs can prove very useful, especially in a test system, as will be discussed in Chapter 6.

CREATING AND ALTERING TABLES

The application tables are created, modified, and deleted using the CREATE, ALTER, and DROP table commands. These commands are usually utilized by the database administrator and are presented here for the general information of the reader. The inexperienced SQL/DS user may derive maximum benefit by reading this section, then reading the explanation of *referential integrity* in Chapter 4, followed by a re-reading of this section.

The CREATE command ascribes attributes to each of the columns of the tables, indicates the DBSPACE in which the table will be created, and designates primary and foreign keys. To create a seven column table called PERSONNEL_TBL in a DBSPACE owned by PUBLIC and named PERSPACE, for example, the DBA would specify:

```
CREATE TABLE PERSONNEL_TBL (EMPID SMALLINT NOT NULL,
    DEPT_NUM SMALLINT NOT NULL, PHONE_NUM CHAR(10) NOT
    NULL, BASE_SALARY DECIMAL(8,2) NOT NULL, SEX CHAR(1) NOT
    NULL, FAM_NAME CHAR(20) NOT NULL, FIRST_NAME CHAR(15)
    NOT NULL) IN PUBLIC.PERSPACE
```

Tables should generally be loaded with initial data before any indexes are created so as to avoid the constant updating of the index for each individual row. It is also usually more efficient not to specify primary and foreign keys in the CREATE command. The table should be loaded with the initial data before the primary and foreign keys are defined so as to avoid the constant checking for every row inserted that contains a foreign key.

The ALTER TABLE command enables the user to modify several parameters specified in the CREATE TABLE command. It has become a very powerful command in newer versions of SQL/DS. In previous versions the command was only used to add a column to a table. In the newer version it can be used to define and manipulate primary and foreign keys. When a primary key is designated, a unique index is created automatically by the system. If the primary key were only definable on the create index command, there would be no way to prevent performance degradation during the load. It would also, despite the user's plans to the contrary, always make the primary key index the *FIRST* index (the significance of which will be explained in Chapters 3 and 8). With the ALTER command and the capability to add a primary key, the table can be created and loaded and other indexes created before the primary key is designated and before the special unique index is created. To define a primary key and a foreign key on the PERSONNEL_TBL, the table creator would specify:

```
ALTER TABLE PERSONNEL_TBL
    ADD PRIMARY KEY (EMPID)
    ADD FOREIGN KEY DEPT_KEY (DEPT_NUM)
        REFERENCES DEPT_TBL
        ON DELETE RESTRICT
```

In the example, when the PERSONNEL_TBL is altered and a primary key added, a unique index on the EMPID column will automatically be created by the system. If additional indexes are desired, on the foreign key (DEPT_NUM), FAM_NAME, for example, the user can issue the CREATE INDEX commands as follows:

```
CREATE INDEX INDX1_PERSONL ON PERSONNEL_TBL (DEPT_NUM)
    PCTFREE = 3
CREATE INDEX INDX2_PERSONL ON PERSONNEL_TBL (FAM_NAME)
    PCTFREE = 3
```

The CREATE INDEX command will require the reading of every page in the DBSPACE (a DBSPACE scan) and a SORT. For large tables many resources will be used and **the CREATE INDEX command should not be issued during peak processing time.**

Primary and foreign keys may also be dropped using the ALTER TABLE command as is shown in the following example:

```
ALTER TABLE PERSONNEL_TBL
    DROP PRIMARY KEY
    DROP FOREIGN KEY DEPT_KEY
```

When a primary key is dropped all of the *dependent* foreign keys that reference this primary key are automatically dropped. The *referential relationship*s will no longer be checked by the system.

ALTER TABLE is also used to deactivate and activate primary and foreign keys. Deactivating a key will suspend the *referential constraint* restrictions, which are described in Chapter 4 and is used to facilitate mass inserts by the avoidance of the continual referential checks made on the data inserted. If the restraints were active the system would execute internal SELECTS to check the *referential integrity* for each insert. This technique is also useful for mass deletes of a primary key. Without the deactivation, the system would check every table *dependent* on this primary key to ensure that no matching referential values exist as foreign keys in the other tables. *Deactivation has a serious effect on performance,* however, because it makes the *parent* table and the *dependent* table unavailable to end-users other than the creator of the tables or to the DBA. To deactivate the primary or the foreign key of the PERSONNEL_TBL, the table creator would use one of the following commands:

```
ALTER TABLE PERSONNEL_TBL
    DEACTIVATE PRIMARY KEY

ALTER TABLE PERSONNEL_TBL
    DEACTIVATE FOREIGN KEY DEPTKEY
```

If these were the only two keys on the table, both would be deactivated by the **ALL** parameter, as shown below:

```
ALTER TABLE PERSONNEL_TBL
    DEACTIVATE ALL
```

When the required processing is completed, the ALTER TABLE command would again be used to activate the primary and foreign keys. Keep in mind that the re-activation of a primary key results in the creation of the unique index and the verification of all of the foreign keys *dependent* on this primary key. The re-activation of a foreign key results in a verification of all foreign key values in every row to insure that a matching primary key exists. These activities seriously impact performance and should be carried out after peak on-line hours. Examples of the command to activate a primary or a foreign key would specify:

```
ALTER TABLE PERSONNEL_TBL
      ACTIVATE PRIMARY KEY

ALTER TABLE PERSONNEL_TBL
      ACTIVATE FOREIGN KEY DEPT_KEY
```

For additional information and a thorough discussion of *referential integrity,* please refer to Chapter 4.

SQL/DS VIEWS

When it is preferable that a specific application or user should not have access to all of the columns or rows of a table, a logical table or VIEW may be created. This VIEW will be application specific and will only reference that portion of the table that should be available. To create a view of the PERSONNEL_TBL, the table owner might specify:

```
CREATE VIEW PERSONNEL_VIEW (EMPLOYEE_NUMBER,
      DEPARTMENT_NUMBER, PHONE_NUMBER, SEX, FIRST_NAME,
         FAMILY_NAME) AS
      SELECT EMPID, DEPT_NUM, PHONE_NUM, SEX,
            FIRST_NAME, FAM_NAME
         FROM PERSONNEL_TBL
         WHERE DEPT_NUM > 4
```

The above view does **not** allow the user to display salary information or to retrieve the phone number and other data about personnel in departments 1, 2, 3, or 4. It also renames several of the columns and reorders the family and first names columns. The WHERE conditional clause could have been written:

```
WHERE Dept_num NOT IN (1, 2, 3, 4)
```

but for performance reasons the "> 4" was used, as will be discussed in Chapter 3.

A view may also be used to simplify complex joins that need to be used by multiple applications or end-users. The following example creates a view of a three table join:

```
CREATE VIEW USERINFO_VW (EMPLOYEE_NUMBER, CODE,
      CODE_VALUE, DEPT_NUMBER, DEPT_NAME, MANAGER,
      FIRST_NAME, FAMILY_NAME) AS
      SELECT P.EMPID, C.CDNUM, C.CDVAL, D.DEPT_NUM,
      D. DEPTNME, D.MGRNME, P.FIRST_NAME, P.FAM_NAME
      FROM PERSONNEL_TBL P, DEPT_TBL D, CODE_TBL C
            WHERE P.DEPT_NUM = D.DEPT_NUM AND
                  P.EMPID = D.EMPID AND
                  P.CODE = C.CDNUM
```

The application developer could then retrieve the result table from this view and even add additional conditions by specifying:

```
SELECT * FROM USERINFO_VW
      WHERE DEPT_NUMBER = 24
```

During access module generation (or precompile), SQL/DS will check the SYSCATALOG and find that Userinfo_VW is a view. It will extract the full definition of the view from the access module table where view definitions are stored and translate the simple SELECT into the complex one.

Views may also be used to reorder the default sequence of the columns, to rename columns for specific users, to view a view, or to add virtual columns to a table. Virtual columns are columns that contain expressions such as the three examples in the following SELECT statement:

```
SELECT (SALARY * MONTH_WORKED), (SALARY * 1.1),
                  (TOT_SAL/10)
      FROM PERSONNEL_TBL
```

To simplify this query and to label these *virtual* columns, the application developer or DBA should define a view:

```
CREATE VIEW SALARY_VAL_VW (USER_ID, DEPT, ANNUAL_SAL,
      SALPLUS_TENPCT, ONE10_SAL) AS
SELECT SALARY * MONTH_WORKED, SALARY * 1.1, TOT_SAL/10
      FROM PERSONNEL_TBL
```

The application developer can also create a view of this view to, for example, summarize the total information and to define a name for each *virtual* column, by using the SUM built-in function:

```
CREATE VIEW SAL_TOT_VIEW (DEPARTMENT, TOT_DEPT_SALARY,
      TOT_DEPT_INCR, TOT_DEPT_ONE10) AS
SELECT DEPT, SUM(ANNUAL_SAL), SUM(SALPLUS_TENPCT),
            SUM(ONE10_SAL)
   FROM SALARY_VAL_VW
         WHERE TOT_DEPT_SAL > 30000
   GROUP BY DEPT
```

To use this view the user might specify:

```
SELECT * FROM SAL_TOT_VIEW
   ORDER BY DEPARTMENT
```

Views are basically overhead-cost free and are very useful for security and for making the query more user-friendly. There are several restrictions on using views for updating, deleting, and inserting but there are also many advantages to using views, especially when the table definitions are not yet stable.

USING THE DBSU

For documentation purposes and for use when re-definition is required, it is recommended that all data definition commands (especially in a test system where they are redone many times) should be executed using the **DataBase Services Utility** (DBSU). In VM/SP, for example, a CMS file (CREATABLE DBSU) could be prepared to contain all of the SQL commands used in this chapter:

```
CREATABLE DBSU A1
```

```
SET AUTOCOMMIT ON;
CONNECT SQLDBA IDENTIFIED BY SQLDBAPW;
      CREATE TABLE PERSONNEL_TBL (EMPID SMALLINT NOT NULL,
            DEPT_NUM SMALLINT NOT NULL, PHONE_NUM CHAR(10)
            NOT NULL, BASE_SALARY DECIMAL(8,2) NOT NULL, SEX
            CHAR(1) NOT NULL, FAM_NAME CHAR(20) NOT NULL,
            FIRST_NAME CHAR(15) NOT NULL) IN PUBLIC.PERSPACE;
      ALTER TABLE PERSONNEL_TBL
            ADD PRIMARY KEY (EMPID)
            ADD FOREIGN KEY DEPT_KEY (DEPT_NUM)
               REFERENCES DEPT_TBL
               ON DELETE RESTRICT;
```

```
ALTER TABLE PERSONNEL_TBL
    DEACTIVATE PRIMARY KEY;

ALTER TABLE PERSONNEL_TBL
    DEACTIVATE FOREIGN KEY DEPT_KEY;

ALTER TABLE PERSONNEL_TBL
    ACTIVATE PRIMARY KEY;

ALTER TABLE PERSONNEL_TBL
    ACTIVATE FOREIGN KEY DEPT_KEY;

CREATE INDEX INDX1_PERSONL ON PERSONNEL_TBL (DEPT_NUM)
    PCTFREE = 3;

CREATE INDEX INDX2_PERSONL ON PERSONNEL_TBL
    (FAM_NAME) PCTFREE = 3;

CREATE VIEW PERSONNEL_VW (EMPLOYEE_NUMBER,
    DEPARTMENT_NUMBER, PHONE_NUMBER, SEX, FIRST_NAME,
    FAMILY_NAME) AS
    SELECT EMPID, DEPT_NUM, PHONE_NUM, SEX, FIRST_NAME,
        FAM_NAME FROM PERSONNEL_TBL
        WHERE DEPT_NUM > 4;

CREATE VIEW USERINFO_VW (EMPLOYEE_NUMBER, CODE,
    CODE_VALUE, DEPT_NUMBER, DEPT_NAME, MANAGER,
    FIRST_NAME, FAMILY_NAME) AS
    SELECT P.EMPID, C.CDNUM, C.CDVAL, D.DEPT_NUM, D.
    DEPTNME, D.MGRNME, P.FIRST_NAME, P.FAM_NAME
    FROM PERSONNEL_TBL P, DEPT_TBL D, CODE_TBL C
        WHERE P.DEPT_NUM = D.DEPT_NUM AND
            P.EMPID = D.EMPID AND
            P.CODE = C.CDNUM;

CREATE VIEW SALARY_VAL_VW (USER_ID, DEPT, ANNUAL_SAL,
    SALPLUS_TENPCT, ONE10_SAL) AS
    SELECT SALARY * MONTH_WORKED, SALARY * 1.1, TOT_SAL/10
        FROM PERSONNEL_TBL;

CREATE VIEW SAL_TOT_VIEW (DEPARTMENT, TOT_DEPT_SALARY,
    TOT_DEPT_INCR, TOT_DEPT_ONE10) AS
    SELECT DEPT, SUM(ANNUAL_SAL), SUM(SALPLUS_TENPCT),
        SUM(ONE10_SAL)
        FROM SALARY_VAL_VW
        WHERE TOT_DEPT_SAL > 30000
        GROUP BY DEPT;
```

This CMS file can be used as the input to the utility command and it would reduce re-typing and provide documentation for future use.

SYNONYMS

SYNONYMS simplify the use of ISQL, dynamic commands, and applications by negating the need for fully naming a table or view. A table or view name consists of a creator name and a table name. If a table name, for example, was PRODSYS.PERSONNEL_TBL, the user could create a synonym where the default userid.tablename would be equivalent to the real name. If the user was DOV1, the synonym could be defined as:

CREATE SYNONYM DOV1.PERSONNEL_TBL AS
    PRODSYS.PERSONNEL_TBL

After this synonym was created, if DOV1 were to precompile an application or run ISQL and issue the command:

SELECT * FROM **PERSONNEL_TBL**

the system would use the full default name of PERSONNEL_TBL which is **DOV1**.PERSONNEL_TBL. The system would automatically check the synonym table and find that a synonym on that name existed. The name in the synonym table would be substituted for the name in the command and the result would be:

SELECT * FROM **PRODSYS**.PERSONNEL_TBL

CREATE SYNONYM has little impact upon performance because the synonyms are resolved during precompile time or when an access module is created. Synonyms can only be dropped explicitly and will **not** be dropped automatically when the table is dropped.

SUMMARY

Data Definition commands provide a facility to allow the user to create tables, indexes, views, and synonyms and to alter several parameters of the table definition. Both CREATE and ALTER may be used to add, drop, deactivate, and activate keys that are used to form *referential relationship*s.

Tables contain two dimensions: columns and rows. A column is the smallest addressable element and values are retrieved from rows. SQL/DS stores its dictionary data in tables called catalogs. The DBA can reorganize the catalog indexes, should it be necessary. Views are used for system security, to simplify complex selects, and to make a table more user specific.

SQL/DS handles numeric data more efficiently than character data and fixed character data more efficiently than variable character data. SQL/DS requires additional processing to bypass variable length rows in its search for the specific columns selected.

DATE, TIME, TIMESTAMP, and TIMEZONE are new data types that permit date and time arithmetic. These column types are stored in a compact internal format in the tables but are always presented to the user in the format specified by the user or by the DBA.

The application tables are created, modified and deleted using the CREATE, ALTER, and DROP table commands. The ALTER TABLE command has become a very powerful command in later versions of SQL/DS. It is used to define, drop, and manipulate primary and foreign keys. When a primary key is designated, a unique index is created automatically by the system. CREATE INDEX requires the reading of every page in the DBSPACE and a SORT.

Deactivating a key suspends the *referential constraint* restrictions and is used to facilitate mass inserts and deletes. Deactivation has a serious effect on performance because it makes the *parent* table and the *dependent* table unavailable except to the creator of the tables or to the DBA. Re-activation of a primary key results in the creation of the unique index and the verification of all of the foreign keys. The re-activation of a foreign key results in a verification of all key values in every row.

The DBSU can provide documentation and simplify the process of issuing the same commands multiple times.

Views are basically overhead-cost free and are very useful for security and for making the query more user friendly.

RECOMMENDATIONS

1. Data Definition commands and data control commands should be executed after peak processing time.
2. To avoid performance degradation resulting from careless use, the EXPLAIN facility should be used.
3. Every table should have at least one index.
4. It is important to carefully choose the first index on a table and the first column of each index.
5. Tables which are often modified need to be reorganized.
6. Tables should be loaded before indexes are created.

7. Columns should be defined as CHAR rather than VARCHAR.

8. Use VARCHAR rather than LONG VARCHAR.

9. Any modification to the SQL/DS catalogs should be done with great care.

10. Primary and foreign keys should not be specified in the CREATE table command. They should be specified in the ALTER TABLE command.

11. Indexes on primary keys are not needed. They are automatically created by the system.

12. Referential relationships should not be activated or deactivated during peak processing periods.

13. Referential relationships should be deactivated prior to processing mass inserts or deletes.

14. Views should be used in application programs, where possible.

15. Indexes should not be created during peak processing periods.

16. The database utility (DBSU) should be used to create or modify tables, views, indexes, and synonyms.

17. Columns containing numeric data should not be defined as character data types.

DATA CONTROL LANGUAGE (DCL)

The data control commands provide a means of granting authority to or revoking authority from other users to access a table or to run an application program. DCL commands will also control when the data will be committed or not committed (COMMIT WORK, ROLLBACK WORK) to the database. They also allow the DBA to GRANT specific or DBA authority to other SQL/DS users or to REVOKE authority from users.

The GRANT and REVOKE commands have little effect upon performance except that they lock the authorization table when executed. These commands may be executed on-line, via the DBSU, or from an application and the GRANT or REVOKE take effect immediately. It is recommended that for documentation purposes, GRANTs be executed via the DBS utility. The database does not have to be halted to issue these commands. To grant authority to several users to run the PERSAPPL program or to use the PERSONNEL_TBL table, for example, the application developer should specify:

GRANT RUN ON PERSAPPL TO DOV1, MOSHE2, DONNY
GRANT SELECT, INSERT, ALTER, REFERENCES ON PERSONNEL_TBL
    TO DAVID2, ABE5 WITH GRANT OPTION

The above GRANT gives DAVID2 and ABE5 the authority to use the PERSONNEL_TBL, to use the table's primary key in a *referential relationship* with another table, and to grant other users permission to perform these tasks. When a user leaves the department, the DBA or the table or application owner can REVOKE the authority given as shown in the following examples:

REVOKE RUN ON PERSAPPL FROM MOSHE2
REVOKE ALL ON PERSONNEL_TBL FROM ABE5

The REVOKE command will cause any views created by the user who lost authority on a table to be dropped.

When modifications are made to any table, they do not take effect until they are explicitly or implicitly committed to the table. The application developer or the user have the option of undoing any changes made by issuing the ROLLBACK WORK command. When SET AUTOCOMMIT OFF is specified, the user may change the database tables, create new tables, prepare reports using the modified data, and then exercise the option to restore all of the tables to their original contents with this one command. *It is important to note that this type of processing ties up many resources and should usually be avoided during peak transaction processing.*

LOGICAL UNIT OF WORK (LUW)

The ROLLBACK process just described utilizes the concept of a *logical unit of work* (**LUW**) which will be summarized here and fully discussed in Chapter 7. The user can start an LUW, make any modifications and print any reports needed, and only then make the decision as to what should be done with the changes. To keep the changes, the user would issue the COMMIT WORK command and to remove or undo the changes, the user would issue a ROLLBACK WORK command. This undo is possible because when a change is made to a data page, the system maintains a copy of the unchanged page in a *shadow page* and in the log and can easily restore the original data before the data is committed.

A *logical unit of work* is started when the first SQL/DS command is issued and terminates when a COMMIT WORK or a ROLLBACK WORK is implicitly or explicitly issued. The default in ISQL, for example, is that after each SQL/DS command is executed, an implied COMMIT WORK is issued. The user can change this default at any time by issuing the command:

SET AUTOCOMMIT OFF

From that point on, all commands are considered as part of the same *logical unit of work* unless an explicit COMMIT WORK is issued or the session ends.

Each application program is considered one *logical unit of work* unless the application developer explicitly includes COMMIT WORK in the code. In most cases, when an application ends, an implied COMMIT WORK will be issued. If an error were to occur in the application, an implicit ROLLBACK WORK would usually be issued. The application developer should **not** allow the system to implicitly decide what to do but should explicitly code a COMMIT WORK or a ROLLBACK WORK.

Long *logical units of work* tie up locked resources for long periods of time. The logic of an application program usually requires that all of its commands be executed before a COMMIT WORK may be issued, but if this is not the case, the work should be committed as soon as possible. This is true for all applications **unless** the application runs in single-user mode. In single-user mode multiple COMMIT WORK commands should be limited or avoided because in single-user mode, **each** such command triggers a CHECKPOINT. In multiple user mode, COMMIT WORK commands **are** needed as often as possible to free resources for other users. When there is no need to free resources for other SQL/DS users, COMMIT WORK is wasteful.

The ROLLBACK WORK command may take a very long time to execute. Each update must be individually undone. After many deletes, a ROLLBACK WORK will have to re-insert all of the rows and this may take hours of time. This type of processing should **not** be allowed during peak transaction processing.

CONNECT

The CONNECT command allows a user to sign on to the database using the password and identification of another user. For example, User DOV1 might specify:

CONNECT SQLDBA IDENTIFIED BY Sqldbapw;

Once the connect has been executed, the system treats the DOV1 user as if he were SQLDBA without considering what the original connect was. The system has no way of knowing that this user is not SQLDBA. The command has no direct performance impact.

Many installations use one user ID for all table creations and program precompiles. The administrative convenience of this procedure is understandable but it seems to negate the entire authorization structure of SQL/DS. It also makes the CREATOR columns of various system tables very non-unique and makes it more difficult to establish who the real creators and owners of application tables, indexes, and views are.

The concept of *one user* for all production precompiles and all production table creations seems to also defeat the purpose of qualified names and table ownership. It bypasses much of the built-in security and makes only one level of GRANT RUN on the applications necessary. There is no need to GRANT privileges on the tables because the creator of the applications is the creator of the tables. In a small installation this does not seem to be too much of a problem but it is not recommended in larger installations. The procedure also may reveal the ID and password of the owner of all of the tables and applications to all application developers, which may result in a gaping hole in system security.

LOCK TABLE OR DBSPACE

LOCK is a control command which allows an application program or an on-line user to lock an entire table or DBSPACE despite the regular level of locking specified when the DBSPACE was acquired. This command may either have a significantly **negative or** a significantly **positive** effect on performance and should be used with care. The negative impact would occur when a table or DBSPACE is exclusively locked and there are other users trying to access it. The positive effect would be the minimizing of lock overhead, contention, and possible deadlock, as will be discussed in Chapter 7. The commands to lock the PERSONNEL_TBL, for example, or the PERSDBSP DBSPACE should specify:

LOCK TABLE PERSONNEL_TBL IN EXCLUSIVE MODE
LOCK DBSPACE PERSDBSP IN SHARE MODE

UPDATE STATISTICS

UPDATE STATISTICS and UPDATE ALL STATISTICS refresh the data in the columns of the system tables that contain statistical information and the command should be executed periodically. This command should never be run during peak on-line activity because it locks system resources and requires at least one DBSPACE scan to gather the needed data. This is an extremely important command directly tied to system performance. The statistics are critical to optimizer calculations. When the statistics are not up to date, the optimizer may not make the most efficient decisions. UPDATE ALL is usually not recommended as explained elsewhere. To update the statistics for the PERSONNEL_TBL or the PERSDBSP DBSPACE specify:

> **UPDATE STATISTICS** FOR **TABLE** PERSONNEL_TBL
> **UPDATE ALL STATISTICS** FOR **DBSPACE** PERSDBSP

DATA MANIPULATION COMMANDS

The data manipulation commands, SELECT, INSERT, DELETE, and UPDATE perform most of the functions in applications.

Select

The SELECT command retrieves specific column data in the sequence listed in the command from one or more SQL/DS tables. The SELECT command is used more than any other command in SQL/DS and is therefore the target of many of the recommendations in this book. This emphasis is to ensure that the SELECT command operates under the best conditions for its proper and efficient use. The power of the SELECT command is one of the basic strengths of the SQL language. Even when other commands are requested, a SELECT is often involved. When a row is to be updated, for example, it must first be selected implicitly or explicitly.

The SELECT command not only can retrieve column data but can also perform various arithmetic operations on the retrieved column data before presenting it. A column value, for example, can be added, divided, multiplied, or subtracted. The following command, for example, will multiply GROSS by 10%, subtract 120 from NET, divide FICA by 100 and add 12 to TOT before presenting the data to the user:

```
SELECT (GROSS * 1.1), (NET - 120), (FICA/100), TOT + 12
    FROM SALARY_TBL
        WHERE EMPID = 13412
```

The conditional WHERE clauses can also have basic mathematical expressions. The following condition will be true when the GROSS is less than (NET * 1.1):

```
WHERE GROSS < NET * 1.1
```

SELECT statements can be very complex although **simple queries are usually the most efficient.** The command allows the use of built-in functions, GROUP BY clauses, sorts (ORDER BY clause), the UNION of two or more SELECT commands, SELECTs within SELECTs (subquery), and conditions checked after all other conditions are checked (HAVING). The following example of a SELECT was taken from an application program. It is by no means the most complex one noted:

```
SELECT SALE_DOLLAR, C.STORE_CODE, S.SALE_CODE, L.MAIN_STORE,
    C.ST_RATE
FROM COMMERCIAL_TBL C, SALES_TBL S, LIST_TBL L, WAREHOUSE_TBL W
WHERE (C.STORE_CODE = L.BRANCH_CODE AND
        (L.MAIN_STORE = :SQL_STORE OR
        L.MAIN_STORE IN (SELECT BRANCH_CODE
                FROM STORE_LIST WHERE
                MAIN_STORE = :SQL_STORE)))
    AND (C.DATE_SWITCH BETWEEN :SQL_START_DTE AND
            :SQL_END_DTE) AND
        (C.STORE_CODE = W.STORE_CODE AND
        W.INDEX_FLAG IS NULL OR W.INDEX_FLAG = ' ')
        AND (C.SALE_CODE = S.SALE_CODE OR
        C.SALE_CODE = BRANCH_CODE_S) AND
        C.SALE_CODE NOT IN ('2153', '3777', '5773',
                'SHRT', '3778', 'SKIP')
        AND SALE_FLAG = 'N' AND C.ST_RATE ^ = 2
        AND C.CLERK_ROLE = 'K'
ORDER BY C.MAIN_STORE, SALE_DOLLAR
GROUP BY C.MAIN_STORE
HAVING (SALE_DOLLAR < SELECT AVG(SALE_DOLLAR)
        FROM COMMERCIAL)
```

The only limits to the SELECT command are the imagination of the application programmer and various system-imposed and practical limits. **The application developer should restrain his or her imagination and keep queries simple,** when possible.

Some Right and Not So Right Queries

The following are examples of SELECT commands that demonstrate how the command can be written with different conditional clauses which achieve the same results, but which turn out to be quite different from a performance perspective.

1. Select all the employees who will still earn less than $21,000 after everyone receives a $200 increase.

```
          SELECT EMPLOYEE DATA
                 FROM PERSONNEL_TBL
NO ⟹             WHERE SALARY + 200 < 21000

          SELECT EMPLOYEE DATA
                 FROM PERSONNEL_TBL
YES ⟹            WHERE SALARY < 20800
```

2. SELECT all employees in the sales department whose salary is not = :WRKERSAL.

```
          SELECT EMPLOYEE DATA
                 FROM PERSONNEL_TBL
NO ⟹             WHERE NOT SALARY = :WRKERSAL AND
                       DEPT = 'SALES'

          SELECT EMPLOYEE DATA
                 FROM PERSONNEL_TBL
YES ⟹            WHERE SALARY NOT EQUAL :WRKERSAL AND
                       DEPT = 'SALES'
```

3. SELECT all employees whose salary is not > or = :WRKERSAL.

```
          SELECT EMPLOYEE DATA
                 FROM PERSONNEL_TBL
NO ⟹             WHERE NOT SALARY > :WRKERSAL OR
                       NOT SALARY = :WRKERSAL

          SELECT EMPLOYEE DATA
                 FROM PERSONNEL_TBL
YES ⟹            WHERE SALARY :WRKERSAL
```

4. SELECT all employees earning $10,000 or $20,000.

```
          SELECT EMPLOYEE DATA
                 FROM PERSONNEL_TBL
NO ⟹             WHERE SALARY = 10000 OR 20000
```

```
        SELECT EMPLOYEE DATA
            FROM PERSONNEL_TBL
YES ⇒           WHERE SALARY IN (10000, 20000)
```

5. SELECT all employees earning $10,000 who have more than two children or $20,000 and have more than 3 children.

```
        SELECT EMPLOYEE DATA
            FROM PERSONNEL_TBL
NO ⇒           WHERE (SALARY = 10000 AND CHILDCNT > 2)
                OR (SALARY = 20000 AND CHILDCNT > 3)

        SELECT EMPLOYEE DATA
            FROM PERSONNEL_TBL
            WHERE (SALARY = 10000 AND CHILDCNT > 2)
YES ⇒          UNION

        SELECT EMPLOYEE DATA
            FROM PERSONNEL_TBL
                WHERE (SALARY = 20000 AND CHILDCNT > 3)
```

The rule is

(a) Determine what the user really wants.
(b) Translate the user's request into efficient SQL/DS queries.
(c) Test the query using the EXPLAIN facility.

Insert

The INSERT command adds one or more rows to a table. One row or an entire table may be inserted with one command. The first INSERT command, below, adds a row to the PROJECT_TBL and the second INSERT command adds an entire series of PERSONNEL_TBL records to the NEW_PERS_TBL:

```
INSERT INTO PROJECT_TBL (PROJ_NAME, WORKER, ACCT_NUM)
    VALUES('INITIALIZE', 7, 4582)

INSERT INTO NEW_PERS_TBL
    SELECT * FROM PERSONNEL_TBL
        WHERE DEPT_NO > 4
```

This command may affect performance in many ways. If many indexes exist, for example, each index has to be individually updated with the new keys. When *referential relationships* exist, they will have to be checked for each inserted row. The INSERT command issues exclusive locks which prevent other users from accessing the row, page, table, or DBSPACE, depending on the locking scheme used. COMMIT WORK should be executed as soon as possible to release the locked resources.

The physical page on which each new row will be inserted will depend upon the INSERT RULE. If a *FIRST* index exists, the system will try to maintain its *clustered* property (whether or not it really is clustered) and may require many additional directory reads. This topic will be discussed in greater detail in Chapter 3. The INSERT command should be used with caution during peak on-line periods.

Update

One row or many rows can be updated with one UPDATE command. Every modified row is locked with an exclusive lock until the end of the *logical unit of work* (LUW). The following command, for example, will UPDATE the record(s) for EMPID 10345 and will set SALARY to zero:

```
UPDATE PERSONNEL_TBL
    SET SALARY = 0
        WHERE EMPID = 10345
```

When the conditional clause is omitted, **all** of the rows in the table will be updated. To grant all workers an across-the-board 10% raise, for example, the following command can be used:

```
UPDATE PERSONNEL_TBL
    SET SALARY = SALARY * 1.1
```

The careless coding of an update application is often a major cause of resource locking and will result in poor performance. The application developer should keep in mind the need to minimize the number of rows that have to be updated and the need to issue a COMMIT WORK or a ROLLBACK WORK as soon as possible. Work not committed will cause delays.

In a program that has to update many rows, the application developer can declare a placeholder (*cursor*), which will be discussed later in this chapter, as follows:

```
DECLARE CURSORNAME CURSOR FOR
    SELECT ... FOR UPDATE OF SALARY
```

When the row to be updated is selected this way the user will specify:

```
UPDATE PERSONNEL_TBL
SET SALARY = SALARY * 1.1
    WHERE CURRENT OF CURSORNAME
```

A *cursor* may also be used for INSERT and WHERE CURRENT OF *cursor*name may also be used for DELETE as will be discussed in Chapter 6.

When only one row is to be updated in a program, for example, the application developer can code:

```
UPDATE PROJECT_TBL
    SET STARTDATE = '1992-01-02'
    WHERE STRIP(TASK_NAME) = 'WRITE-BOOK'
```

The Update command will cause the acquisition of a new page (if one doesn't already exist) to hold the changed page and the old page will become a *shadow page*. This need for a new data page will apply to any modification (UPDATE, DELETE, or INSERT) of a row. An exclusive lock is held on the page and the *before* and *after* image of the modified row are written to the log. **Each of these activities impacts performance and all modifications should be carefully controlled.**

It is also very important to update only those columns that are actually modified. The following example of a partial UPDATE command shows that among the columns updated is the EMPID:

```
UPDATE . . . .   SET EMPID = :EMPLOYEE
        WHERE EMPID = :EMPLOYEE
```

This type of update is often used when the application developer updates every column in the table whenever one or more of the columns needs to be updated. **Many instructions must be executed for each column that is updated and the number of columns modified should be kept to an absolute minimum.** When columns that are part of an index key are updated, the index usually cannot be used to find the row. When there are many columns being modified and the application cannot (and should not) write a separate update for each combination, then, in an attempt to minimize the number of columns updated, the developer should consider coding two or three standard combinations of columns that are usually updated together. Each time the application is executed it would then choose the combination that needed to be updated.

A suggested method of updating columns contained in index keys is to DELETE the row and then re-INSERT the row after modification. Both the DELETE and the INSERT may use an index, while the update would not.

DISCARDING DATA

Deleting Data Rows

Table and index design decisions made in the early stages of application development will have an impact when data or tables have to be discarded from the database. The simplest way to remove data is to delete rows from a table. For example, to delete all of the rows for userid 3479, the user would specify:

```
DELETE FROM PERSONNEL_TBL
    WHERE USERID = 3479
```

To delete a row, SQL/DS must acquire an exclusive lock on the page or row and a lock on the index. These locks prevent other users from accessing the data. (Locking will be fully discussed in Chapter 7.) An additional data page must also be acquired to store the modified page and the old page is saved and is designated the *shadow page* to be used in case of a ROLLBACK.

Be aware that if the row to be deleted contained a primary key associated in a *referential relationship* with other tables where the *referential constraint* rule is CASCADE or SET NULL (see Chapter 4), the deletion of just this one row could automatically result in the modification of thousands of rows in other tables. **The deletion of a row with a primary key should be handled with careful consideration and should never be performed during peak processing periods.**

When the WHERE clause of the delete statement is omitted, all of the rows in the table are deleted:

```
DELETE FROM PERSONNEL_TBL
```

This is one method of emptying a table of data so that it can then be reused. The advantage of this process is that indexes and views are **not** dropped, tables do **not** have to be re-created, and access modules are **not** invalidated. The disadvantages are that:

1. An extra data page is required in the storage pool for every page containing a row to be deleted.

2. Index entries must be individually deleted for every key in every index on this table (this DELETE could run for hours).

3. Empty pages are **not** returned to the storage pool but remain assigned to the DBSPACE.

4. The modified entries may fill the LOG and trigger a checkpoint or an ARCHIVE.

When many rows have to be deleted and the entire table or DBSPACE cannot be dropped **it is recommended** that the indexes be dropped and data be deleted a few rows at a time followed by a COMMIT WORK. This process should not be executed during peak processing periods.

An alternative to deleting all the rows might be to use the DATAUNLOAD command of the DBS utility to unload only the data that needed to be saved. Other tables in the DBSPACE can be unloaded with the unload table function and the DBSPACE can be dropped and re-acquired. The table would then be re-created and the saved data reloaded. The indexes and views would be re-created and the other tables re-loaded. While this seems complex, it may prove more efficient than the mass deleting of individual rows. The dataunload would be in the format:

```
DATAUNLOAD
    SELECT * FROM PERSONNEL_TBL
        WHERE CONDITIONS FOR DATA TO BE SAVED
    etc.
```

The DELETE command is fairly straight forward and efficient but there are several performance stumbling blocks which may create inefficiencies. The command is efficient unless one or more of this partial list of disrupting elements is true:

1. Another user is locking the row or indexes to be updated. This may also be caused by SQL/DS's use of a *HASH key* scheme for locking indexes.

2. The row has a primary key which will generate the modification of thousands of other rows because of a referential restriction of SET NULL or CASCADE.

3. There is an insufficient number of pages in the storage pool for all of the pages to be modified.

4. No index exists on the key column and a DBSPACE scan of every page in the DBSPACE will be required to find the row or rows to be deleted.

5. The table has many indexes that all have to be updated.
6. A checkpoint or an archive will be triggered by the DELETE.
7. No AGENT is available to service this request.
8. The catalog tables are exclusively locked by another user.
9. Contention for system resources is very high.

Many of these disrupting elements apply equally as well to the other SQL/DS commands and should provide an insight into the potential complexity of *simple* database commands. The general user, of course, does not have to be concerned about these problems but they will help make him or her be more aware of what to look for when searching for the cause of poor performance.

Dropping Tables

The advantage of dropping the table is that the indexes and *referential relationships* are automatically dropped and each key does **not** have to be individually deleted. The disadvantage is that the indexes, views, and *referential relationships* are also dropped, GRANTs are revoked, and access modules are marked invalid. In many ways it is similar to deleting all of the rows in the table and every page modified will require an additional page and the log may be filled or a checkpoint and archive triggered. When there is an insufficient number of pages available in the storage pool, the DROP TABLE will fail as it would for a DELETE of all of the rows. If the DBSPACE cannot be dropped because there is more than one table in the DBSPACE, the DBA or user should drop the indexes and delete a few rows at a time and COMMIT WORK, as suggested earlier.

The pages in the DBSPACE are **not** returned to the storage pool when a table is dropped. The pages remain assigned to the DBSPACE. If other tables exist in the DBSPACE, the other tables are the only ones able to use the released space.

Drop DBSPACE

The most efficient way to discard data is to drop the DBSPACE. This is one reason why it is recommended that large active tables be placed in their own DBSPACE. Additional pages are not required because *shadow pages* will **not** be saved. The entire DBSPACE, tables, and indexes are destroyed, all data pages are returned to the storage pool, and the DBSPACE becomes available for re-acquiring.

Views, *referential relationships*, and grants no longer exist and access modules using any of these objects are marked invalid.

When the DBSPACE is dropped, a DBSU should be used to re-acquire the DBSPACE; to recreate the table, *referential relationships*, and indexes; and to ensure that the steps are carried out in the proper sequence for good performance as shown in the following example of pseudo–commands:

```
DROP DBSPACE
ACQUIRE DBSPACE
CREATE TABLE
LOAD TABLE
CREATE VIEWS
CREATE INDEXES
ALTER TABLE
ISSUE GRANTS
REPREP the application programs
```

DROP PROGRAM

DROP PROGRAM drops an access module from the system table. It does not have the same function as marking an access module invalid. When an access module is tagged invalid, it can be regenerated from the information contained in the access module table the next time it is used. When the program is dropped, the data needed to recreate the access module is deleted from the SYSACCESS table and SQL/DS no longer has any record of the application program's existence. A new precompile of the application will be required to restore the data in the SYSACCESS table and to create an access module. To drop the PERSPROG access module, for example, the creator could specify:

DROP PROGRAM PERSPROG

ACQUIRE DBSPACE

Tables are stored in DBSPACES as will be explained in Chapter 3. Before a DBSPACE can be used to store a table, it must be acquired. The ACQUIRE DBSPACE has several parameters with default values that should **not** be used unless they are calculated to best fit the needs of the installation. This command determines the minimum size of the DBSPACE, the potential size limits, the free space to be set aside during data load, the amount of index space to be reserved, the storage pool to be used, and whether the DBSPACE will be private, or public and all of the tables locked by row, page, or DBSPACE. The following is an example of the acquisition of a public DBSPACE:

```
ACQUIRE PUBLIC DBSPACE NAMED PERSDBSP (PAGES = 256,
    PCTINDEX = 20, LOCK = ROW, PCTFREE = 0,
    STORPOOL = 2)
```

The number of pages specified in the command is the **minimum required** but not necessarily the number of pages that will actually be acquired. When the smallest DBSPACE in storpool 2 is 1024 pages, for example, that will be the actual size of the DBSPACE acquired in the above example even though only 256 pages were requested.

The default of 33% of the pages to be reserved for indexes **is much too large** (or much too small). When the DBSPACE will contain one read-only table with many indexes, the PCTINDEX should be greater than 33. If a few small indexes will be defined, the value should be smaller. The potential pages reserved for indexes, even when not used, are not available for data. The same is true of potential data pages which will not be freed for index usage if they are not needed for data. If, for example, the DBSPACE contains 256 pages and PCTINDEX is 50 then a maximum of only 128 pages will be available for data. **These values should be examined and calculated.** The only way to modify the size of index and data space is to back up the DBSPACE, drop the DBSPACE, and re-acquire it.

If the STORPOOL = 2 parameter is omitted, the DBSPACE will be acquired from any recoverable storpool that has the specified size and type of DBSPACE available.

The LOCK = ROW parameter will apply to all of the tables in the DBSPACE. The LOCK parameter will only apply to public DB-SPACES because private DBSPACES are **always** locked with a DB-SPACE lock. The LOCK parameter and the PCTFREE parameter are the only two parameters that can be overridden by the ALTER command. The following command will modify the lock level to page and will specify that 10% of the data space should remain free:

```
ALTER DBSPACE PERSDBSP (LOCK = PAGE, PCTFREE = 10)
```

EXPLAIN IT

Each of the data manipulation commands is a very powerful command and can process a large volume of data in one instruction but it can also be the cause of serious performance degradation. The EXPLAIN command should be used to examine data manipulation commands that are to be used in application programs, EXECs, or ad hoc queries. **The EXPLAIN command will store the data which explains how the optimizer will create the access path for the command in up to four tables.** The application developer and the DBA can use the contents of the EXPLAIN tables to understand which factors were considered by the optimizer and to improve the queries in the application.

EXPLAIN can be executed using ISQL, the DBSU, or the precompile of an application program, as detailed in Chapter 6. An application program does **not** have to be executed in order to store the results of the EXPLAIN command in the EXPLAIN tables. The preprocessing step which creates the access module will also insert the data into the EXPLAIN tables. The follow example requests the details of the optimizer's access path choices for the SELECT command:

```
EXEC SQL
     EXPLAIN ALL SET QUERYNO = 10 FOR
         SELECT * FROM PERSONNEL
             WHERE GROSS > NET AND SALARY < 10000
END-EXEC
```

Many of the rules of thumb and performance hints mentioned in this book stem from the experience gained by the author while using the EXPLAIN tables to test data manipulation language instructions.

APPLICATION PROGRAMMING

Almost all of the commands covered up until this point may be used in application programs. There are several additional SQL commands used during application coding to conform with application programming language restrictions. This topic will be covered in much greater detail in Chapter 6. This section will serve as an introduction to the basic concepts of application development.

Every language has a DECLARE *host variables* section where those variables that will be used to store data values in an application program for SQL statements, are declared. The precompiler will make these variables known to the SQL/DS access module. These variables should be written very carefully to conform **exactly** to the definitions required by the host language. When they do not exactly match, there is often a serious degradation in performance because the optimizer cannot utilize an indexed column that should match the field to access the desired rows.

High-level programming languages like COBOL can only process one row at a time. When the SQL/DS *result table* contains more than one row, a place holder (*cursor*) is initialized which moves from row to row as it is fetched and read into, or PUT and written out of, program memory. Each FETCH command will read one row from the result table into the *host variables* specified in the FETCH command. Each PUT command will insert one row from the *host variables* in memory into the designated table.

Many *cursors* for many different tables may be opened in one application program. Two or more *cursors* may also be opened against the same table from the same application program. This technique can provide different views of the data for comparison processing. The relational system, however, does not consider the sequence of rows to be significant. If more than one row has the same key value, the sequence of the rows fetched with the second *cursor* may be different from that of the first *cursor* unless a SORT was requested with an ORDER BY clause. Rows will be in a different sequence when changes have occurred after the first FETCH was preprocessed and the optimizer chose a different path for the second *cursor*.

These *cursors* used by the application programs can have a severe impact upon system performance. When the application is written in such a way that for every row retrieved from one table, a parameter of a SELECT command is modified and a *cursor* to execute that command must be closed and reopened, the impact on response and performance is significant. Each time a *cursor* is opened, the SELECT command is re-executed and the data is prepared to match the criteria of the conditions (which might involve a SORT, a DBSPACE scan, etc.). **The opening and closing of** *cursors* **should be controlled and minimized.** The following pseudo-code, for example, of a **poorly written code segment,** might describe part of an application where the salary of each employee is to be calculated and printed:

```
EXEC SQL DECLARE CURS1 CURSOR FOR
SELECT EMPNO, OTHER INFORMATION
      FROM PERSONNEL_TBL END-EXEC.

EXEC SQL DECLARE CURS2 CURSOR FOR
SELECT SALARY, OTHER INFORMATION
      FROM SALARY_TBL
            WHERE EMPID = :EMPLOYEE
END-EXEC.
EXEC SQL
OPEN CURS1
END-EXEC.
```

```
         PERFORM FETCH-LOOP UNTIL NO MORE RECORDS.
         RETURN.
FETCH-LOOP.
*                  READ A ROW FROM THE PERSONNEL TABLE
*                  INTO THE HOST VARIABLE EMPLOYEE.
*                  THIS VARIABLE IS USED IN THE CONDITION
*                  CLAUSE OF CURS2 SELECT
         EXEC SQL
         FETCH CURS1
             INTO :EMPLOYEE AND OTHER HOST VARIABLES
         END-EXEC.
*                  THE CURS2 CURSOR HAS TO BE OPENED BECAUSE
*                  THE HOST VARIABLE VALUE HAS CHANGED
         EXEC SQL
         OPEN CURS2
         END-EXEC.
         EXEC SQL
         FETCH CURS2
             INTO :SALARY AND OTHER HOST VARIABLES
         END-EXEC.
         EXEC SQL
         CLOSE CURS2
         END-EXEC.
         END-PERFORM.
```

Cursor CURS2 will be opened and closed for every row in the PERSONNEL_TBL and performance may be very poor. A join, of course, would have been better in this case, as shown in the example below, but a join is not always possible:

```
EXEC SQL DECLARE CURS1 CURSOR FOR
SELECT P.EMPNO, S.SALARY OTHER INFORMATION
    FROM PERSONNEL_TBL P, SALARY_TBL S
        WHERE P.EMPID = S.EMPID
END-EXEC.
```

It is also possible to reference a table two or more times in the same SELECT command. This can obviate the need for extra *cursor*s, as shown in the following example:

```
SELECT A.EMPID, . . . , B.EMPID, . . . . ETC
    FROM PERSONNEL_TBL A, PERSONNEL_TBL B
    WHERE . . . . .
```

Precompile Parameters

Several parameters can be specified during the precompile of an application program. Each parameter has an impact upon performance and will be discussed in greater detail elsewhere in the book (see Index). There are, for example, two isolation levels that can be chosen: **Repeatable Read** and **Cursor Stability**. When the *Repeatable Read* option is specified, every row accessed by the application is locked until the end of the program or until a COMMIT WORK or ROLLBACK WORK command is issued. BATCH application programs that process large numbers of rows without ending the LUW and improperly written on-line applications which do not release their locks, tie up system resources. On-line application programs can usually be modified to release resources quickly but batch programs often need to complete all of their processing before the logical unit of work can be committed or rolled back. This is because a COMMIT WORK command closes **ALL** of the *cursors* in the application program and there is no way to selectively close just some of the *cursors*. Batch applications should usually not be run during on-line processing hours unless they are designed to release resources quickly.

When isolation level *Cursor Stability* is used, only the last row or page in each block or request will be locked. This will prevent one user from locking out the other users and improve concurrency. Most production applications, however, cannot use *Cursor Stability*.

When the *blocking* and the *Repeatable Read* parameters are specified during the precompile step, all of the rows in the blocks are locked for each *cursor* and the CLOSE *cursor* does not release the locks (only COMMIT WORK or ROLLBACK WORK does). When *BLOCKing* is specified every data manipulation command in the program uses blocking, even those requesting the return of only one row. The application designer must decide whether *BLOCKing* is really needed for on-line applications. Do not always default to *BLOCK*. Blocking, however, significantly improves performance when multiple rows are accessed or inserted and as such is a valuable feature.

The PUT command inserts rows using a *cursor* either one row or one block at a time. When *BLOCKing* is in effect, the row is placed in a buffer until the block is filled. It should be remembered that when using *BLOCKing* with inserts, the return codes are not received by the program until an attempt is made to write it to the database when the block is filled.

Single User Mode

Batch application programs often run much faster in single-user mode with LOGMODE = N to avoid I/O's to the log. **Do not, however, issue multiple COMMIT WORK commands in this mode** because each ROLLBACK WORK or COMMIT WORK forces an SQL/DS checkpoint. If there is an explicit COMMIT WORK at the end of each transaction, the checkpoints will significantly increase run time.

SUMMARY

Discarding data that is no longer needed can be accomplished by either deleting individual rows, dropping tables, or dropping DBSPACEs. Mass deletions or insertions can take many hours when indexes are not dropped first. Deleting rows with primary keys may result in the modification of many rows in other tables. When a table is dropped, the indexes, views, *referential relationship*s, and GRANTs are dropped and the access modules referring to the table will be marked invalid. The SYNONYMS are not automatically dropped.

When a DBSPACE is acquired, the DBA specifies the locking scheme, the percent of free space, and the percentage of space to leave available for indexes. Authority may easily be granted or revoked. When authority is revoked, any views depending upon this authority will be dropped. *Logical units of work* can be used to insert and study potential changes in data values without actually modifying the data. Long LUWs tend to tie up many resources. Applications or on-line users may lock tables and DBSPACEs to reduce locking overhead. Updated statistics are required by the optimizer to calculate the most efficient access method.

The bulk of all applications utilizes the Data Manipulation Language commands (SELECT, INSERT, DELETE, and UPDATE). These are very powerful commands. SELECTed columns and condition values may contain arithmetical expressions. When rows containing foreign keys are inserted, *referential relationships* are checked. Careless coding of UPDATE commands is often a primary cause of poor performance. Old copies of modified data pages become *shadow pages*. In an update, an index usually cannot be used if one of its columns is being updated. The EXPLAIN command provides the application developer with information on how and why the optimizer chose a particular path to access the data. Application programs use *cursor*s as place-holders to access one row at a time. When many rows are selected or inserted, *BLOCKing* significantly improves performance.

RECOMMENDATIONS

1. DROP DBSPACEs rather than DROP TABLE.
2. DELETE rows with primary keys during non-peak periods.
3. When mass deletes or inserts are necessary, drop indexes and delete/insert in stages by issuing COMMIT WORK as often as possible.
4. Avoid mass deletes/inserts during peak processing periods.
5. An alternative to mass delete might be to DATAUNLOAD on the data that should be saved and DROP and recreate the DBSPACE and table.
6. For documentation purposes, use the DBSU to GRANT authority .
7. Keep LUWs short and end them explicitly.
8. Do not issue COMMIT WORK in applications running in single user mode.
9. It is NOT recommended that all of the tables, programs, etc. in the database have the same creator name.
10. Statistics should be updated periodically. Avoid using UPDATE ALL unless really needed.
11. Carefully plan and choose the parameters that will be specified with the ACQUIRE DBSPACE command.
12. Keep SELECT statements simple.
13. Inserts, updates, and deletes should be curtailed during peak processing periods.
14. SELECT and UPDATE only those columns that are actually needed.
15. DELETE and INSERT rather than UPDATE when key columns are being updated.
16. EXPLAIN all data manipulation commands.
17. Avoid excessive opening and closing of *cursors*.
18. Avoid BLOCKing one row retrievals and inserts.
19. BLOCK to significantly improve performance when multiple rows are selected or inserted.
20. Avoid COMMIT WORK in application programs running in single user mode.

CHAPTER 3

The Optimizer

The optimizer is that element of the SQL/DS database management system that determines, among its other functions, the most efficient, "cheapest" access path to the data. The result of optimization is the creation of access modules that are stored in table format, in an access module DBSPACE, specifically created to hold them. An access module may be used once and then discarded (when processing is dynamic) or may remain stored and used repeatedly until replaced or deleted (when processing is static or extended dynamic). The objective of this chapter is to explain the access alternatives available to SQL/DS, to suggest ways to influence the optimizer's choice, and to verify that the optimizer made a wise choice.

When the user, for example, issues the SELECT command to read the PERSONNEL_TBL:

```
SELECT *
      FROM PERSONNEL_TBL
          WHERE (LOCATION LIKE '%NYC%' OR LOCATION
                      = 'MONSEY') AND CHILDREN > 3
          GROUP BY LOCATION
          ORDER BY LOCATION, NAME
```

The optimizer can choose one of three possible ways to access the data. It may choose, for example, to use an index to directly retrieve only those pages that contain rows that match the conditional (WHERE) clauses. The index will contain the key and a direct address (TID) that will specify the DBSPACE page and the slot pointer number. The optimizer may decide that none of the indexes is suitable and that every page in the DBSPACE should be read in order to find the rows that satisfy the search conditions. The optimizer also has a third alternative—use one of the indexes, but only to determine which data pages contain rows belonging to the PERSONNEL_TBL table. This alternative is used when more than one table exists in a DBSPACE and the optimizer concludes that every row in the DBSPACE will have to be read because none of the indexes matches the conditions. This *nonselective* use of the index is designed to avoid reading pages that only contain rows belonging to other tables.

The optimizer may choose only one of these alternatives and that is why this basic decision of the optimizer is the most important aspect of performance tuning. When a table contains 500,000 rows on 100,000 pages and the response to the query should contain 100 rows, it is far better to require the database system to read a maximum of 100 pages rather than to require it to read all 100,000 pages and to examine all 500,000 rows.

The optimizer makes its decision based upon its calculation of the "cost" of retrieving, updating, or deleting the requested data. This cost is derived from the estimated number of I/Os and the quantity of CPU time required for each or many of the possible access paths. One of the objectives of performance tuning, therefore, is to ensure that this "cost" estimate is kept to a minimum by providing proper indexes, correct statistics, sufficient buffers, and suitable search arguments.

To help the user know how and why the optimizer will choose a particular access path for an SQL/DS command, SQL/DS provides a tool which will EXPLAIN the decisions that the optimizer will make and will detail what the basis for the decision was. This EXPLAIN tool will be discussed in Chapter 6.

SQL/DS SYSTEM COMPONENTS

Optimization is the process that endeavors to use the SQL/DS system components in the most efficient manner possible. A review of the functions of the three main components should help the reader better understand the optimization process. In order to communicate with application programs and to perform the database access function, SQL/DS utilizes the components described below:

1. **Data System Control** (DSC) is the component that contains the code to manage system functions. It serves as the dispatcher and task manager, controls the agents, and is the interface with application programs. It handles the RDIIN control block created during precompilation and communicates with the resource managers in the user machines or partitions.

2. **Data Base Storage System** (DBSS) is the file management component responsible for the accessing of the physical data. It handles the locking facility and the recovery function. DBSS is the first level of access to the database and it tries to

be "*Lean and Mean*" which implies that **it only handles basic** *predicate***s.** The most efficient means of accessing the data is to give the DBSS component sufficient data in a usable format to enable DBSS to make the final decision as to whether or not a row meets the criteria of the conditional clause. The DBSS component does only simple comparisons and does not do calculations of expressions or evaluations of different sized comparators. It accesses the data via VSAM (in VSE/SP) or Block I/O (in CMS) and each call returns only one row of data.

3. **Relational Data System** (RDS) is the SQL processor that is used during preprocessing and during execution. It does the optimization, generates the access module, checks authorization, loads and executes the access modules, and creates and maintains the system catalogs. RDS is the component that tests the row to see if it matches the conditional criteria when DBSS cannot complete the testing. When the DBSS component does not have sufficient information in an acceptable format, DBSS will read all of the rows that it assumes might meet the conditional criteria and will pass the rows to RDS. The RDS component contains the code to enable it to do all of the needed additional testing of the conditions. This process is wasteful because the DBSS will usually have to read many extra rows and will have to transfer the rows using its *one row at a time interface* to RDS. RDS will then examine the rows passed to it and will reject those rows that do not meet **all** of the criteria.

OPTIMIZED COMMANDS

Not all SQL/DS commands will be optimized. Only the data manipulation language (DML) commands (SELECT, UPDATE, INSERT, and DELETE) are optimized. Data definition and data control commands are not optimized. The optimizer will convert the access path chosen and the DML statements into a set of control blocks that will be stored in the access module.

OPTIMIZER ALTERNATIVES

The first step in understanding the alternatives available to the optimizer is to examine how the optimizer will reach its decision. One of the following three ways to access data will be chosen by the optimizer:

1. A DBSPACE scan that will access every page in the DBSPACE.
2. A TABLE scan that will use an index in a nonselective manner to access only the data pages containing rows from the table.
3. A SELECTIVE scan that will use an index to access only the specific data pages that contain rows with keys that match the search arguments.

The optimizer makes its calculations and decisions as to which method to use based upon the available statistics and data in the SQL/DS catalogs. The following paragraphs will detail each of the possible access methods along with several of the basic concepts of optimization. It may help explain why an index cannot, at times, be used and why the optimizer finds it more efficient sometimes to do a DBSPACE scan even when an index does exist. The three access methods will be examined first.

The DBSPACE Scan

When SQL/DS has to perform a DBSPACE scan, it will read each directory block only once and will access all of the active pages in the DBSPACE only once. When the optimizer's calculations determine that most of the rows in the table must be read, a DBSPACE scan may be the most efficient way to access them. The rows will be read in the same sequence as they are physically stored.

Nonselective Table Scan

When a DBSPACE scan is required for a DBSPACE containing more than one table, some pages may not contain any rows from the table queried. If an index exists on the table, the optimizer will have the option of using the index to point to all of the data pages which contain rows belonging to this table with the use of an index; pages that only contain rows belonging to other tables will be bypassed. To reach its decision, the optimizer will use the available statistics to determine if a nonselective table scan would be more efficient than a DBSPACE scan.

For *nonselective scans,* the optimizer will prefer an index, if one exists, in the same sequence as that in which the data is physically stored (*clustered* index). This does not imply that only a *clustered* index will be chosen, but *it is preferred.* The reason for this preference is that when an index is used, rows are accessed in index sequence. If the data is not stored in index sequence, SQL/DS may be forced to re-access several of the data pages. When a data page is read with a *nonclustered* index, for example, the page may contain keys corresponding to several entries in the index. SQL/DS will access the page but will **only** SELECT that row that is pointed to by the current index entry. The other rows will be ignored until needed. When a row with a higher key is needed, it may have appeared in a page previously read but the page may have already been purged from the buffer. This will result in an additional I/O to re-access the data page. This additional I/O can usually be avoided when a *clustered* index is used.

In a *nonselective* scan, the index has to be accessed only once and *every* row has to be accessed only once but individual data pages may need to be accessed more than once. The advantage, however, is that those pages that only contain rows from other tables will not be accessed. It is important, therefore, that if a DBSPACE scan may be needed, each table should be placed in a separate DBSPACE and/or *clustered* indexes should be created on the tables. Small tables should not be placed in the same DBSPACE as large tables. When tables are very small, the optimizer may assume that it is inefficient to access them via an index or the application designer may assume that an index is not needed (especially, for example, for a one-row table). SQL/DS may have to read every active page in the DBSPACE to find this one row table and performance will suffer.

The DBA may view the list of DBSPACEs and check the number of tables (and other interesting information) in each DBSPACE by issuing the following SELECT:

```
SELECT DBSPACENO, NTABS, NPAGES, NACTIVE, FREEPCT, LOCKMODE,
    PCTINDX
FROM SYSTEM.SYSDBSPACES
    ORDER BY 1
```

DBSPACENO	**NTABS**	NPAGES	NACTIVE	FREEPCT	LOCKMODE	PCTINDX
1	18	7168	1140	0	T	59
.						
7	**33**	33024	4653	15	P	33
8	1	3072	-1	5	P	50
44	1	33024	22105	15	S	33

Note that there are several questions about the above statistics that the DBA might find it hard to answer. Why are there 33 tables in DBSPACE 7? (There are 18 catalog tables in DBSPACE 1 but that is no excuse for the user not to distribute the tables.) Why were the statistics on DBSPACE 8 not updated (as shown by a −1 in NACTIVE and in other columns)? Why is there 15% and 5% free space? (The values may be reasonable but chances are that the DBA neglected to ALTER the PCTFREE value to zero after the data was loaded).

A DBSPACE scan may take place even though there is more than one table in a DBSPACE. There may be many small tables in a DBSPACE or there may be no index on the small table or there may not be any *clustered* index on a large table and the optimizer may assume that a DBSPACE scan is less expensive than a *nonselective* index scan.

Selective Index Scan

The most efficient method to access data, if available, is usually via a selective scan (using a *clustered* index). Using this method, SQL/DS will search the index in index key sequence, and will use the data address (TID) associated with the key to be read. The keys at the lowest index level (leaf pages) are not compressed but for VARCHAR columns the keys are coded. An index search will use the Compare Logical Character (CLC) command logic. A significant saving is achieved because only a small subset of the directory blocks and the table pages which contain the rows with keys matching the condition clauses in the query will have to be accessed.

When an index is used and all of the information requested is contained in the index, it should be noted that it will not be necessary for SQL/DS to read the data pages and the query will require a minimum of I/O. Unless the table contains only a few small columns, however, it rarely pays to specifically construct indexes to contain all of the columns needed for queries. This technique, however, can be used for special real time transactions that require high speed response.

If, for example, an index exists on PERSONNEL_TBL which contains EMP_NAME and STRTDATE and the SELECT reads:

```
SELECT EMP_NAME, STRTDATE
    FROM PERSONNEL_TBL
        WHERE STRTDATE > '12/11/1989'
        AND EMP_NAME LIKE 'SAM%'
```

SQL/DS may only read the index because it contains all of the data needed to satisfy both the query and the conditions.

CHOOSING A JOIN PATH

The optimizer will **not** check every JOIN path and the following discussion about a three table JOIN will demonstrate why. Assume that each of the three tables had only two indexes. If all paths had to be checked, the optimizer would have to consider the following:

1. Which table will be the first table? There are three choices and three ways to access each of the three tables (index scan, table scan, and DBSPACE scan) for a total of **nine** possible choices.
2. Which table will be the second table? There are two remaining tables and three ways to access each of them and two possible JOIN methods for a total of **12** (2 * 3 * 2) possible choices.
3. Which table will be the third table? There is one remaining table and three ways to access it and two possible JOIN methods for a total of **six**.

The optimizer would have to check (9 * 12 * 6) **648 different paths** and compare 648 different cost estimates to arrive at the correct decision. To avoid this excessive number of estimations, the optimizer eliminates all of the obviously *unreasonable* access paths.

PREDICATES

The SQL conditional clauses (WHERE clause) contain one or more search arguments known as *predicates*. The most efficient means of determining whether a particular row satisfies the condition criteria of a *predicate* is if the condition can be examined in an index record thereby allowing the *predicate* to be used as a key. When this condition is satisfied the *predicate* is called indexible or *index matching*. For example:

```
SELECT *
    FROM PRICE_LIST_TBL
        WHERE PRICE = 15
```

If an index were created on PRICE, the *predicate* might be *index matching*. It is important to keep in mind that there may be many *predicate*s in a query and more than one may be *index matching*. Only one index, however, can be used to find the row and the optimizer must choose the best index to use.

Sargable Predicates

Sargable means that the *predicate* is in a format so that the DBSS component can use it as a *Search* **ARG**ument without having to pass it on to the RDS component for further evaluation. The *sargable predicate* is used to determine whether or not the condition exists in the data row. In other words this means that when a WHERE clause (*predicate*) is written in such a way that the DBSS component can read the retrieved pages and compare them to the *predicate,* it is *sargable.*

Not every *predicate* can be used by SQL/DS for *index matching* purposes. The following *predicate,* for example, cannot be used to search the PRICE index to determine whether or not a particular row satisfies the criteria:

WHERE PRICE > (**COST * 1.5**)

because the value of COST * 1.5 cannot be determined until after the row is retrieved.

Predicates are *sargable* when the data type of both sides of the compare are **identical** or compatible. Each data type has a level and when, for example, the format of the *predicate* is:

Column   operator   variable

the identical column and variable data types are the most efficient, but if they cannot be identical, the column data type should at least be on as high a level as the variable data type. The variable can be a *host variable* or a literal.

The following chart will describe whether or not the *predicate* is *sargable* when the column type, as defined in the CREATE TABLE, and the *variable* type, as SQL/DS *views* it, are different. The hierarchy in the chart is shown from low to high:

Character ══════⟹ Varchar
Smallint ⟹ Integer ⟹ Decimal ⟹ Float1 ⟹ Float2

This implies that a *predic*ate with a column type of VARCHAR may be *sargable* when its variable type is fixed character. When, however, the *predicate* column type is CHAR (fixed character) and the variable type is variable character, the *predicate* will not be *sargable.* It also implies that a *predicate* with a double precision FLOAT column will be *sargable* with any numeric data type variable. Keep in mind that when a *predicate* is not *sargable* it is also not index matching.

Data Type Size

The following table will serve to further clarify another of the factors influencing *sargability:*

Column Type	Variable Type	Will It Be Sargable?
Character(5)	Character(5)	Yes
Character(5)	Character(3)	Yes
Character(5)	Character(6)	No
Character(5)	VARCHAR(5)	No
VARCHAR(8)	Character(5)	Yes
VARCHAR(8)	VARCHAR(7)	Yes
VARCHAR(8)	VARCHAR(9)	No
NUMERIC		
Smallint	Smallint	Yes
Smallint	Any other	No
Integer	Integer	Yes
Integer	Smallint	Yes
Integer	Any other	No
Decimal(5,1)	Decimal(5,1)	Yes
Decimal(m,n)	Decimal(r,s)	if $m > r$ and $n = 1$ Yes
		if $m < r$ No
		if $n <> 1$ No
Decimal(5,0)	Smallint	Yes
Decimal(m,n)	Smallint	if $n > 0$ No
		if $m < 5$ No
Decimal(10,0)	Integer	Yes
Decimal(m,n)	Integer	if $n > 0$ No
		if $m < 10$ No
Decimal(6,9)	Float	No
Float-single	Float-single	Yes
Float-single	Float-double	No
Float-single	Any other	Yes
Float-double	Float-double	Yes
Float-double	Float-single	Yes
Float-double	Any other	Yes

The general principle should be readily apparent. **The important factor in sargability is the size of the column type.** When the column type is equal or larger in size and higher or equal in type, then the *predicate* is *sargable;* if these conditions are not met, it is not. When literals are used, the optimizer tries to make the *predicate sargable* by converting the literal to the same data type as the columntype (when possible) as shown in the following examples:

Integercol > 2 (The 2 is treated as an integer and the *predicate* is *sargable.*)

Integercol > 2.0 (The literal can**not** be treated as an integer and the *predicate* is not *sargable.* The 2.0 implies a Dec(1,0) value.)

Decimalcol $(3,2) = 2$ (The literal is treated as a (3,2) Decimal column and the *predicate* is *sargable.*)

Decimalcol (3,2) = 2.1   (The literal is treated as a (3,2) Decimal
column and the *predicate* is *sargable.*)

Residual Predicates

When a *predicate* is not *sargable* it is RESIDUAL. This simply means
that the condition must be evaluated by the RDS component and
cannot be evaluated by the DBSS component and cannot be used as an
index key.

SARGABILITY is so very important to improved performance
that it would be useful to review some of the characteristics that make
a *predicate* not *sargable*.

A *predicate* is **NOT** *sargable* when:

- It contains an expression.

  WHERE GROSS = (NET + TAX + PROFIT)

- It contains a constant value with a length or data type which
  ca**nnot** be converted to match the length and data type of the
  column.

  WHERE *SIXBYTECOL* = *'TWELVEBYTEFLD'*

- The *predicate* is ORed with a *residual predicate*.

  WHERE (NAME = 'NYC' **OR** (**VALUE1** > **VALUE2** + **VALUE3**))

- It references a subquery.

  WHERE CITYCODE = (**SELECT** CODE FROM CITY_TAB WHERE
      POP > 1000000)

- It references more than one column from the same table.

  WHERE **A**.SALARY > **A**.EXPENSES

- It references columns from more than one table at the same
  level.

  WHERE **A**.NAME = **B**.NAMEOF

- It uses a NOT modifier.

  WHERE **NOT** SALARY < 10000
  WHERE **NOT** BETWEEN 25 AND 200

- It uses **ANY, ALL, EXISTS,** or **NOT EXISTS.**

Predicate Operators

Predicates can come in several formats. Some examples include:

```
COLUMNAME OPERATOR LITERAL
COLUMNAME OPERATOR COLUMNAME
COLUMNAME OPERATOR :HOST VARIABLE
COLUMNAME OPERATOR (SUBSELECT)
SCALAR FUNCTION(COLUMNAME) OPERATOR KEYWORD PAIR
```

The following operators are usually *index matching* and *sargable* unless they are disqualified by other conditions. **These operators are the ones to use,** where possible:

```
BETWEEN
=, >, <, <=, >=
IS NULL
LIKE 'XYZ%'   'ABCC---'
IN (LITERAL1, LITERAL2, . . . )
```

The following operators are *sargable* but not *index matching*:

```
NOT EQUAL
IS NOT NULL
```

The above operators are stated simply but their use may be very complex as will be noted later in the chapter. When several *predicates* in the query are *index matching,* the optimizer will choose the one which will have the lowest cost in I/O and CPU utilization. When it chooses to use an index, the optimizer will usually prefer a unique and *clustered* index.

Host Variables

In an application program, the data type and length of a *host variable* are as defined in the program data definition division. The most efficient way to insure that a *predicate* will be *sargable* is to ensure that the *host variable* **exactly** matches the column definition. If the application were written in COBOL, for example, the following sample definitions would exactly match the column definitions:

Column Definition	COBOL Definition			
DATE	01	DATEFLD	PIC	X(10)
TIME	01	TIMEFLD	PIC	X(8)
TIMESTAMP	01	TIMESTMP	PIC	X(26)
SMALLINT	01	SMALLFLD	PIC	S(4) COMP
INTEGER	01	INTFLD	PIC	S(9) COMP

Non-Sargable Operators

Not all operators enable a *predicate* to be *sargable*. The *predicate* will be *residual* and/or non-index eligible if any of the following operators is used:

```
ANY, EXISTS, ALL
IN (SELECT .... subquery)
LIKE   '%SUFFIX'
LIKE   '-XYZ'
```

When IN is specified with literals, SQL/DS translates the *predicate* into a BETWEEN command. Even though IN is not *sargable* it may be a candidate for *index matching* because of this translation process. The IN command is only partially efficient because after the DBSS component has completed its selection, the RDS component must complete the comparison process based on the IN list. When the IN list, for example, is:

```
WHERE Anyfld IN ('NYC', 'CON', 'CAL')
```

The command may be converted by SQL/DS to a BETWEEN command of the lowest and highest values and will state:

```
WHERE Anyfld BETWEEN 'CAL' AND 'NYC'
```

All of the values in the table between 'CAL' and 'NYC' will be read by the DBSS component and the RDS component will have to weed out those values that do not match the conditional criteria, such as: 'COL', 'GEO', 'FLO', etc.

When *host variable*s are used in an IN command list, the *predicate* is always *residual*. It is best to use literals whenever possible.

The LIKE operator may also be a candidate for *index matching* even though it too is not *sargable*. When the prefix or initial letters are specified, SQL/DS will translate the LIKE *predicate* into a BETWEEN *predicate* by using low and high values. Here, too, DBSS must choose all of the BETWEEN values and RDS must weed out those that do not match. The following example:

WHERE LIKECOL **LIKE** 'BROOK%N'

will be converted into a BETWEEN command which will contain the following values:

WHERE LIKECOL BETWEEN '**BROOK** *low value*' AND '**BROOK** *high value*'

and the RDS component will have to complete the comparison.

As mentioned earlier, index matching *predicate*s are the most efficient type because fewer rows will have to be read and they will require, therefore, less I/O and CPU resources. When a *predicate* is *sargable* but not *index matching* many additional rows have to be accessed but they do not have to be transferred from the DBSS component to the RDS component for further evaluation. The DBSS component will process the comparison without passing the rows to the RDS component. This will reduce CPU usage but not I/O activity. When there is no alternative, SQL/DS will use *residual predicate*s to at least reduce as much as possible the number of rows that have to be transferred from the RDS component to the application. The DBSS component will still have to pass a larger number of rows to the RDS component because DBSS cannot check *residual predicate*s.

Logical Operators

Care is needed in constructing queries because the logic of a query may transform an *index matching predicate* into a *residual predicate.* When there is more than one *predicate* in a query the simple *predicate*s are connected to each other via logical operators. In the following example, four *predicate*s are connected to each other using the AND connector:

```
SELECT COLX, COLB, COLA
     FROM PRICE_TBL
          WHERE PRICE > 750 AND
               PRICE > COST * 1.5 AND
               (COST = SELLAMT OR COST > 500)
               AND PRODUCT NOT EQUAL 'SHOES'
```

There are many ways to write the same query and the application developer can often make a complex query more efficient. For a *predicate* to be an *index matching* candidate, for example, it must be connected to the entire WHERE clause by an AND connector. In the above example, PRICE > 750 is connected to the entire WHERE clause by an AND connector. The other clauses are also connected by AND connectors and may be *index matching* candidates if not otherwise disqualified.

When two *sargable predicate*s are connected via an OR connector they remain *sargable* but may not be *index matching*:

SARGPREDA **OR** SARGPREDB (may not be index matching)

In general, when the *predicate*s are not *sargable* the logical connectors do not make them *sargable* and they remain *residual*. When a *sargable predicate* is connected via an AND to a *residual predicate,* the *sargable predicate* remains *sargable*. When a *sargable predicate* is connected via an OR to a *residual predicate* the clause becomes *residual:*

NONSARGEA OR SARGPREDB (may not be index matching)

The NOT *predicate* is **always** *residual*:

NOT *PREDICATE* A AND (PREDICATEB OR **NOT** PREDICATEC) AND
     PREDICATED

In the above case, only *predicate* D might be *sargable*.

The way a *predicate* is written can sometimes have a profound effect upon the response time and the resources needed to satisfy the query. It is very important that the application developer be logical and that he keep the rules of sargability in mind. NOT should be avoided, whenever possible:

USE COLA > = COLB *RATHER THAN* NOT COLA < COLB
USE COLA <> COLB *RATHER THAN* NOT COLA = COLB
USE (COLA <> COLB) AND (COLA <> COLC)
     RATHER THAN COLA NOT IN (COLB, COLC)

The AND connector should always be used as the outer operator, when possible. Use:

PREDICATEA **AND** (PREDICATEB OR PREDICATEC)

rather than

(PREDA **AND** PREDB) OR (PREDA **AND** PREDB)

The SQL/DS optimizer will, at times, perform conversions on the logic of the query to try to make a non-*sargable predicate sargable.* The condition:

NOT((NOT(COLA = COLB)) OR (NOT(COLC = COLD)))

will usually be converted to the *sargable predicate*:

(COLA = COLB) AND (COLC = COLD)

The optimizer, however, cannot and should not be relied upon to convert all of the poorly constructed queries. The non-*sargable predicates* connected by an OR, for example:

((COLA = COLB) AND (COLC > COLD)) OR ((COLA = COLB) AND (COLE <
    COLF))

will **not** be converted to the equivalent *sargable predicates*:

(COLA = COLB) AND ((COLC > COLD) OR (COLE < COLF))

It is assumed, of course, that the optimizer never transforms a well-constructed *predicate* into a poorly constructed one.

WHEN DOES OPTIMIZATION OCCUR?

Optimization will take place whenever a command requires a decision on how to access data. If this optimization and creation of an access module were required every single time a command was executed, as it is for ISQL, DBSU, and QMF transactions, it would greatly impact performance and be very wasteful. SQL/DS provides, therefore, a means of preprocessing the static commands found in application programs. Precompilors are available for application programs written in COBOL (or COBOL II), Assembler, FORTRAN, PL/I, or *C*. This preprocessing has positive and negative consequences that will be discussed later in this chapter.

The access authorization and *view* resolution will be done by the precompiler. This implies that using *views* in precompiled applications is just as efficient as using tables. *Views* will very slightly increase precompile time but will be cost-free in precompiled applications at run time.

ISQL, QMF, and the database utility (DBSU) commands cannot be preprocessed and will be less efficient than commands issued by preprocessed programs. In a production environment, ISQL, QMF, and the DBSU should only be used for special purpose applications and one-time runs, while application generators (CSP) and programming languages should be used for repeated applications.

INFLUENCES ON THE OPTIMIZER'S CHOICE

When there is more than one index on the table, **only one of the indexes can be used by any command** to access one table. When the index used selectively is *clustered,* the minimum number of pages has to be accessed. When the index is un*clustered,* some pages may have to be re-accessed as explained previously in the section on *nonselective* table scans. The optimizer will prefer, therefore, unique indexes to non-unique indexes and *clustered* indexes to non*clustered* indexes because it will assume that fewer rows and pages will have to be read. A FETCH of one row using a unique index is very efficient because only one row will be returned and only one index leaf page and one data page will have to be read.

The CLUSTER column of the SYSTEM.SYSINDEXES table would contain 'F' or 'C' for *clustered* tables and 'W' or 'N' for non*clustered* tables. The DBA could check if the index is *clustered* by issuing the SELECT:

```
SELECT ICREATOR, INAME, CLUSTER
    FROM SYSTEM.SYSINDEXES
    WHERE TNAME = 'PERSONNEL_TBL' AND CREATOR = 'DOV1'
```

The result of this query might look like this:

ICREATOR	INAME	CLUSTER
DOV1	PERSONNEL_INX	F
DOV1	PERSONNEL_IX	N
DOV1	PERSONNEL_I2	N
DOV1	PERSONNEL_I3	C

The optimizer, based on its assumptions and calculations, may even decide on occasion to use a *clustered* index *nonselective*ly rather than use a non*clustered* index selectively. Application developers using the EXPLAIN commands may at times be very surprised at the choices made by the optimizer.

UPDATES AND INSERTS

Updates, inserts, and deletes exclusively lock resources, require the use of the *shadow page* mechanism, and save "before" and "after" images on the log. They require special consideration and care to ensure acceptable performance levels and to prevent performance degradation. A row must be located before it can be updated or deleted so many of the usage rules and performance tuning suggestions made for SELECTS are applicable to these commands. In addition, they have several specific rules that must be also be considered.

Optimizing Updates

Update commands follow a special rule which states that when a column appearing in an index will be modified, that index cannot usually be used to locate the row. Application developers should be aware that **frequently updated columns are not efficient candidates for indexes.** When there is no alternative to using an updatable column in an index, more than one index should be defined for the table and it should contain non-updated columns. In that way, when a specific index that has to be modified cannot be used, the optimizer may choose to use one of the other indexes.

Care should also be used when the FOR UPDATE clause is invoked:

DECLARE CURSOR FOR SELECT ... **FOR UPDATE OF** ...

Its only purpose is to inform the optimizer **not** to use an index containing any of the columns in the FOR UPDATE clause. Where many SELECTs are done and few UPDATEs are actually executed, this feature should **not** be used. The application developer might design the application to read the row using *cursor stability* (CS), verify that it is the one to be updated, and then re-read it specifying *repeatable read* (RR). When RR is specified, the row is not released and no other user can update it. It should be reiterated that the application developer should always design programs to only SELECT those rows and columns that are absolutely needed, as discussed later in this chapter.

Optimizing Inserted Data

When the optimizer plans an INSERT it is only concerned with one index, the *FIRST* index created. The optimizer will assume, whether or not it is correct, that the *FIRST* index is or was *clustered* and it will attempt to maintain this *clustering*. To determine if a *FIRST* index exists, the DBA could use the following SELECT and check the CLUSTER column for an 'F' or a 'W'. The 'W' would indicate *FIRST* but not *clustered*. The fact that the *FIRST* index is not *clustered* does **not** prevent the system from treating it as the *clustering* index:

```
SELECT TNAME, INAME, CLUSTER
    FROM SYSTEM.SYSINDEXES
        WHERE TNAME = BUDGET_TBL AND
            CREATOR = USER
```

The output might look like this:

TNAME	INAME	CLUSTER
BUDGET_TBL	BUDGET_INDX	W
BUDGET_TBL	BUDGET_INDX1	N

The ability of SQL/DS to maintain clustering is dependent on the existence of sufficient free space which, as Chapter 8 explains, may not be at all efficient. The inefficiency is usually a result of the nonrandom nature of most inserts. Should the use of a *FIRST* index be inefficient, the DBA should drop the *FIRST* index and re–create it. If other indexes exist, no other index will become the *FIRST* index and neither will the one being dropped and re–created be designated the *FIRST* index.

When *clustering* is not possible or desirable and no column (TID) *FIRST* index exists, the optimizer uses the value in the CLUSTERROW in the SYSTEM.SYSCATALOG table to determine where in the table to start searching for available space. The CLUSTERROW is, assuming that statistics were updated, the address of the data page containing the *last* row in the table. If statistics have not been updated, additional directory I/Os may be required because the system will begin its search at the *last* row and will search all subsequently added directory entries.

In those tables where free space is allocated, ensure that:

- Statistics are current.
- The *FIRST* index is *clustered*.
- Sufficient free space exists for the inserts.

When *clustering* and free space allocations cannot be maintained. it will usually be more efficient to force SQL/DS to place inserted rows at the end of the table by dropping and recreating the *FIRST* index.

The *FIRST* index is also used by the UNLOAD / RELOAD DBSU function. If data is loaded in a specific sequence and then indexes are created, the *FIRST* index created will be used to sequence the data during unload. This process may resequence the data without the user being aware of it. **The *FIRST* index is important.**

THE NEED FOR OPTIMIZATION AND EXPLAIN

There are many ways to write an SQL/DS query and each application developer has his or her own method. For example, students were asked to determine which stocks on the New York and Chicago Stock Exchanges had an average cost of more than $25 a share. The following examples of queries written by the students all produce the same answer set but the level of efficiency and the response time of some of them varies significantly:

```
Q1. SELECT S.STOCK_NAME, S.S_AVG_COST
       FROM STOCK_COST_TB S, EXCHANGE_LIST_VIEW E
          WHERE S.STOCK_NAME = E.STOCK_NAME AND
             E.EXCH_NAME IN ('NYSE', 'CHIC') AND
             S.S_AVG_COST > 25

Q2. SELECT STOCK_NAME, S_AVG_COST
       FROM STOCK_COST_TB
          WHERE S_AVG_COST > 25 AND
             STOCK_NAME IN (SELECT STOCK_NAME
                FROM EXCHANGE_LIST_VIEW WHERE
                EXCH_NAME IN ('NYSE', 'CHIC'))

Q3. SELECT STOCK_NAME, S_AVG_COST
       FROM STOCK_COST_TB S
          WHERE S_AVG_COST > 25 AND
             EXISTS (SELECT STOCK_NAME
                FROM EXCHANGE_LIST_VIEW E WHERE
                EXCH_NAME IN ('NYSE', 'CHIC')
                S.STOCK_NAME = E.STOCK_NAME))
```

As an example of some of the factors that the optimizer will take into consideration, assume the following four indexes exist for the selected tables above:

Label	Index Name	Columns	Clustered
S1	STOCK_COST_N	STOCK_NAME	Yes
S2	STOCK_COST_C	S_AVG_COST, STOCK_NAME	No
E1	EXCH_LIST_N	STOCK_NAME	No
E2	EXCH_LIST_E	EXCH_NAME, STOCK_NAME	Yes

The optimizer must decide which one of the indexes, if any, will be used to access each table to satisfy the above queries. The decision is not clear cut partly because of the following reasons:

1. S1 and E1—these indexes match the potential join columns for the above queries but are un*clustered*.

2. S2—contains the information for STOCK_COST_TB but the join column is not the first and it is un*clustered*.

3. E2—contains all of the information for the Exchange list table but it is not in the join sequence. Its first column is also very non-unique.

The optimizer will use the available statistics to check the possible access paths and will estimate which would be the cheapest method. In the above example for STOCK_COST_TB table, the optimizer could do a DBSPACE scan, use index S1 selectively, use S2 selectively, use S1 *nonselective*ly, or use S2 *nonselective*ly. The EXPLAIN command, described in Chapter 6, will detail exactly which path the optimizer will choose.

If statistics are not available because the UPDATE STATISTICS command has not been executed, the optimizer will have to use default values. The default values, however, may or may not be suitable for the table. Even when the statistics do exist they may be inaccurate when, for example, many changes were made to the table after the statistics were updated. In both of these cases the optimizer may choose an access path which would not be the optimal choice.

RETRIEVING EXTRA COLUMNS

It is always correct, even in ISQL, to retrieve or update **only** those columns that are needed. Many queries are written like this partial query:

```
SELECT USER_NAME, USER_ID, SOC_SEC_NUM, . . . . . . . .
    INTO :HOSTUNAME :HOSTUID, :HOSTSOC
```

```
FROM PERSONNEL
    WHERE USER_ID = :VARUSERID AND
        SOC_SEC_NUM = :HOSTSOCS AND . . . . .
```

The above query is wasteful because both the user id and the social security number are known to the program and should not be requested. Each column in every row retrieved requires approximately 200 instructions. When the following is used by many clerks:

```
SELECT *
    FROM PERSONNEL
        WHERE . . . . . . .
```

and an average of 10,000 rows are accessed and the user only requires 10 of the 40 columns, the performance of the entire system can be impacted. For this one query where 30 extra columns are retrieved in 10,000 rows the number of wasted instructions will be significant. The calculation of the extra instructions for each user would be:

	Extra		
	Columns	Rows	Instructions
(200 instructions *	30) *	10000 * users	= 60 million * users

Sixty million extra instructions are processed for each user. When there are five users, the system must process **300 million unnecessary instructions** for this one query. It is, therefore, important to be specific and selective.

When coding an application program, performance is just one of the reasons:

```
SELECT *
```

should, despite its convenience, **never** be used. This rule is especially true in an environment where the design is not frozen and columns may be added via the ALTER TABLE command. The applications with SELECT * commands would all have to be modified. The application developer should SELECT only the columns needed.

UPDATING EXTRA COLUMNS

There are many instances when a table has to be updated from the inputted screen information and the application developer does not know exactly which columns the end-user will want to update. To avoid writing many update statements—one for each updatable column—the application saves all of the original data, modifies the fields that were changed, and updates all of the columns in the table in one instruction, as shown in the following example:

```
UPDATE PERSONNEL
      SET SALARY = :HOSTSAL
      SET USER_NAME = :HOSTNAM
      SET USER_ID = :HOSTUID
      SET SOC_SEC_NUM = :HOSTSOCS
      SET STARTDTE = :HOSTSTRT
      SET ENDDTE = :HOSTEND
          etc. etc.
          WHERE USER_ID = :HOSTUID
              AND SOC_SEC_NUM = :HOSTSOCS
```

This is very wasteful. Those identification and key columns that never change should **not** be automatically updated. It may prevent the optimizer from choosing an index as the access method. If the table has several columns that are rarely updated, it might pay to prepare two update commands: one containing the usually updated columns and one specifying the rarely updated columns. A flag could be used to indicate when both have to be executed.

Performance considerations such as these impact the entire system and the application developer must complete the analysis and know how the applications will use the data and tables so as to be able to design an efficient system.

USE AN INDEX

Care should be taken to insure that an index is used when it is available. The following is an example of how the user can write a query in such a way that SQL/DS may **not** be able to use an index that exists. If the user, for example, wanted to retrieve data based upon the starting employment date and wanted the report to include all employees who began work after December 31, 1987 and before January 1, 1990, the user might issue:

```
SELECT SALARY, NAME, STARTDTE
      FROM PERSONNEL_TBL
          WHERE STARTDTE > '1987-12-31' AND
              STARTDTE <    '1990-01-01'
```

The optimizer can only choose one of the *predicate*s to be *index matching*. If it were to choose:

WHERE STARTDTE < '1990-01-01'

every page with a row satisfying this condition would have to be selected and tested by DBSS for the second *sargable* condition. Only those rows with dates that are also greater than '1987-12-31' would be returned. The optimizer would, most probably, decide not to use the index for this query because too many rows might have to be initially selected and subsequently rejected by DBSS. To ensure that the index is used, the command should state:

WHERE STARTDTE BETWEEN '1987-12-31' AND '1990-01-01'

The EXPLAIN feature should be used to ensure that the index is being used as desired.

HOW MANY INDEXES?

Do the benefits of an index imply that an index should be created on **every** column accessed in a table? The answer, obviously, is **no!** Careful planning is needed before an index is created. Every table should usually have at least one index but creating too many or too few indexes on a table can disastrously impact performance. The question of *"How many?"* is **"too** *many"* is application specific. The **rule of thumb** that three or four indexes are optimum is not really correct in many cases. Two indexes, for example, are much too many when the data is continuously updated on-line by many users (a stock bid table, for example). Ten indexes, however, may not be enough for a read-only table continuously used to statistically study business or population trends.

MULTI-COLUMN INDEX USAGE

When a multi-column index is available the optimizer can choose to use the index only if the search conditions of the *predicate* exactly match the **beginning** of the index key.

PREPROCESSING PROCEDURE

To ensure that the optimizer chooses the optimum access path, the following operations should be performed in the sequence specified:

Load data into tables.

Create indexes.

Update statistics.

Run EXPLAIN function.

Preprocess the program.

A description of preprocessing and its parameters can be found in Chapter 2.

PREPROCESSING DRAWBACKS

Both the advantage and the drawback of preprocessing is that it need only be done once. When SQL/DS preprocesses static commands in a program, the optimizer uses the data and statistics found **currently** in the catalogs. When conditions change, the preprocessing is **not** automatically redone and the following rules apply:

1. Creating a new index does **not** guarantee that previously precompiled application programs will use it. The programs will **not** use the new index unless the access module is re-created.

2. Precompiling an application when the data or system parameters are different than they will be in the full production system may result in the optimizer choosing an access path that it would not have chosen in the full production system. This condition will have consequences both for the EXPLAIN command and for access module creation when the access modules are not re-created after the tables have been loaded.

3. Precompiling will require exclusive locks on several system catalogs (SYSUSAGE, SYSPROGAUTH, SYSACCESS, SYSTABAUTH, and SYS0002 access modules). Precompiling production applications should be avoided during peak on-line hours.

4. Preprocessing an application prior to being GRANTed authorization to use a table or a view accessed by that application will result in a dynamic authorization check every time the application is run. This may significantly increase response time.

This list of drawbacks is not meant in any way to imply that dynamic commands should be used instead of static commands. It comes to reiterate the need to continually monitor the system and to re–create the access modules when necessary.

EXPLAIN FEATURE

The EXPLAIN function will allow the application developer to test the performance of specific commands in an application program. To receive results similar to those in the production environment, the EXPLAIN command must execute in an environment that duplicates the production system. It is not, however, always possible to duplicate the production environment. **An alternative to loading production data into test tables might be for the DBA to UPDATE the test catalog statistics values for the application tables to match those of the production catalog table values.** This must be carefully planned and executed to avoid errors. Any change to a system catalog, even in a test system, is a serious matter and requires good backup. A DBSU procedure should be used, when catalog values are modified, to document the changes that were made and to have a way to backout the changes.

DYNAMIC SQL/DS STATEMENTS

Dynamic statements are useful in application programs when static SQL commands using *host variables* cannot be optimized correctly. When the values in the *host variables* are not known and the optimizer is required to use default values, the defaults may be very inaccurate and the optimizer may choose a less selective access path. Dynamic SQL/DS statements will be optimized at execution time and the optimizer will know what the values in the *host variables* are and will be able to choose the best access method. This is the only time dynamic statements may be preferable over static statements. The dynamic commands should only be used if a check of the application using static SQL commands by the EXPLAIN facility shows that performance will be poor.

Assembler language extended dynamic commands are available that enable the writing of precompilers for other SQL/DS products. With a precompiler, optimization will only occur once and the application can be executed many times without any need for re-optimization.

The life of a prepared statement in dynamic SQL/DS is a *logical unit of work.* Once the LUW is completed, the application may no longer reference the statement. With extended dynamic commands, however, a user may dynamically build a statement, store it in an access module, and repeatedly execute the command even from another application. This assembler language feature can be used by developers to write their own preprocessors and database interface routines that will operate like standard SQL/DS preprocessors for pre-planned transactions. It may also be used to create a package of SQL statements to be shared by a group of users. This type of package can also be written to reduce preprocessor-generated code.

DDL AND DCL IN APPLICATIONS

Avoid creating views, tables, indexes, or *referential relationships* from an application program because these commands exclusively lock system catalog resources until the LUW is released. Avoid issuing GRANT and REVOKE commands from applications because these, too, lock out other users. If any data definition commands must be used, COMMIT WORK or ROLLBACK WORK as soon as feasible.

WASTED SPACE

When more than one table is stored in a DBSPACE, each data page may contain rows from more than one table. When pages are read and only 50 percent of each page contains rows from the queried table, it will require twice as many I/Os to read all of the rows of the table. This waste can be avoided by placing each (large) table in its own DBSPACE and by specifying a low value or zero for free space (PCTFREE).

DATA BUFFER CONSIDERATIONS

During the optimization process the optimizer calculates the number of I/Os needed and it takes into consideration the number of buffers available. These buffers help to minimize the actual I/O operations required to retrieve data. Upon completion of a database I/O, the data page retrieved is placed in a data buffer. SQL/DS carefully manages its buffers and maintains an index of the pages found in its buffers. If a page found in a buffer is required at a later time, even by another transaction, a database I/O will be avoided and SQL/DS will retrieve the page from the buffer. That is why **a large number of buffers usually improves performance.**

When there is an insufficient number of buffers, the calculations and decisions of the optimizer may be incorrect. When a buffer is needed to store data pages belonging to the same or to a different transaction, SQL/DS will write the buffer to disk, if it was modified, and will use the now empty buffer to store the new page. When the discarded page will again be needed, it must be re-read into a different buffer. When this buffer "contention" occurs in one transaction, it may cause this transaction to be even more costly than the optimizer had assumed because the optimizer may have assumed that there would be enough buffers to hold the entire query. For addition information, please refer to Chapter 7.

SUMMARY

The optimizer chooses the access path to the data. It tries to choose the most cost effective path. The optimizer may decide that a DBSPACE scan, a *nonselective* (table) scan, or a selective index scan is needed. Statistics must be up-to-date for the optimizer's choice to be correct.

Optimization and access module creation occur prior to command execution. Preprocessing an application is preferable to ad-hoc type queries via ISQL, DBSU, or QMF. Providing sufficient *predicate*s to allow DBSS to isolate the rows requested is preferable to having DBSS pass many extra rows to RDS for further evaluation. The application developer can help the optimizer by careful coding and simplicity. *Clustered* and/or unique indexes are preferable to un*clustered* indexes.

Predicates which compare identical data types are always *sargable* and are the most efficient to use. They will reduce conversion time and will ensure that the optimizer does not consider the comparison values incompatible. It is usually more efficient to carry out the conversion of a non-identical datatype in the host program coding rather than to have SQL/DS do the conversion. Make sure that the variable is hierarchically an equal or lower level type than the column data type in the *predicate*.

It is important to ensure that the literals do not make the *predicate residual*. If the literal is coded with a decimal place, for example, even if the decimal value is zero, the literal will be considered a decimal value and will have to be converted in order to be compared to a non-decimal:

```
WHERE INTEGERCOL > 435.00 (RESIDUAL)
WHERE INTEGERCOL > 435. (RESIDUAL)
WHERE INTEGERCOL > 435 (SARGABLE)
```

Residual *predicates* should be avoided. They waste multiple resources. Modify queries and indexes so that *sargable predicates* can be *index matching* (also known as KEYDOMAIN). Allow the optimizer to choose the most efficient *index matching predicate* by offering as many as possible.

The BETWEEN command is more selective than '>= AND <='. OR is not selective. Use IN because it may generate a BETWEEN. Evaluate the use of dynamic statements when *host variable* defaults are not efficient.

Special care must be taken with Updates, Inserts and Deletes which exclusively lock resources. When columns used as (part of) the key in an index are updated, the index usually cannot be used to locate the data. Update only those columns actually requiring updating. Rows are inserted using the *FIRST* index, when one exists. When an index is used and all of the requested data is in an (multicolumn) index, the data pages will not be accessed. Selecting or Updating extra columns may result in much higher overhead and poorer response. The ability of tables to be modified precludes the use of SELECT * in application programs.

RECOMMENDATIONS

1. Make as many *predicates* as possible *sargable*.
2. *Host variables* should exactly match the length and data type attributes of a column.
3. Use IN or UNION instead of OR.
4. Do not prefix *predicates* with NOT.
5. Drop the *FIRST* index (and re-create it) when free space is not allocated in the DBSPACE.
6. Updating key columns in an index should be avoided.
7. Keep indexes small by including only the minimum of columns needed.
8. Use BETWEEN instead of greater than and less than.
9. Retrieve or update only those columns absolutely required.
10. SELECT * should rarely be used on-line and never used in application programs.
11. Avoid creating *views,* tables, indexes, or referential relationships from application programs.
12. Frequently modified columns are not efficient candidates for indexes.

PERFORMANCE ENHANCEMENTS

Several enhancements have been made to recent versions of SQL/DS to improve the optimization process. These new features provide additional statistical data that is used as input to the optimizer routines. They improve the probability that the optimizer will choose the optimal access path.

CLUSTERRATIO

In the past, an index was either *clustered* or not *clustered.* The preference of the optimizer for *clustered* indexes often resulted in a suitable index not being used when it was un*clustered.* When new rows were inserted into a table, the index would become un*clustered* at an accelerated pace because *clustered* meant that at least 90 percent of the data was in the sequence of the index.

When an index fell to 89 percent *clustered,* SQL/DS immediately tagged it as un*clustered,* yet it was almost as *clustered* as other *clustered indexes.* In order to help the optimizer make a more informed decision as to whether or not to use an index, the SQL/DS developers added the new CLUSTERRATIO column to the SYSTEM.SYSINDEXES catalog. This column will give a more precise degree of clustering value by indicating a percentage value of clustering where 10000 = 100%, 8999 = 89.99% and 0 = completely un*clustered.* The DBA can check the CLUSTERRATIO value by issuing the following SELECT command:

```
SELECT ICREATOR, INAME, CLUSTER, CLUSTERRATIO
    FROM SYSTEM.SYSINDEXES
        WHERE TNAME = 'PERSONNEL_TBL' AND CREATOR = 'DOV1'
```

The result of this query might look like this:

ICREATOR	INAME	CLUSTER	CLUSTERRATIO
DOV1	PERSONNEL_INX	F	**10000**
DOV1	PERSONNEL_IX	N	**371**
DOV1	PERSONNEL_I2	N	**8672**
DOV1	PERSONNEL_I3	C	**9995**

This new value gives the optimizer additional information and increases the probability that the most suitable index will be chosen as the access path.

SYSTEM.SYSCOLSTATS

A new table has been added which will be used to maintain column statistics for the **first column** specified in every index. To view the column statistics on the first columns of the indexes of the system catalog tables, the DBA might issue the following command:

```
SELECT TNAME, CNAME, FREQ1VAL, FREQ1PCT, VAL10, VAL50
    FROM SYSTEM.SYSCOLSTATS WHERE CREATOR = 'SYSTEM'
```

TNAME	CNAME	FREQ1VAL	FREQ1PCT	VAL10	VAL50
SYSCATALOG	TNAME	DEPT_TBL	1	CF_SAC_T	M_PABDI
SYSCOLAUTH	CREATOR	SQLDBA	21	SQLDBA	SQLDBA
SYSINDEXES	INAME	PERS_INDX	1	PE_SEC_IX	MON_IDX

First Column of Index

This again emphasizes the importance of choosing a column with few duplicate keys as the first column of an index. In a conglomerate with five companies, for example, every inventory part number is composed of:

A one byte prefix number indicating company   1 - 5

A seven byte part number   1000000 - 9999999

The standard approach is to create an index:

```
COMPANY_NUMBER, PART_NUMBER
```

and the query would read:

```
SELECT needed data
    FROM CO_INVENTORY_TBL
        WHERE COMPANY_NUMBER = :HOSTCOMP
        AND PART_NUMBER = :HOSTPART
```

With up to nine million rows in the table, for example, and only **five** different companies, the first column will be almost totally non-unique and the optimizer may often choose to do a DBSPACE scan rather than use this non-unique index.

When most of the access is by company (IE: list all the parts in Company 1) there is little choice. Most situations, however, will benefit from making the index:

```
PART_NUMBER, COMPANY_NUMBER
```

This will now make the first column much more non-unique and will not change the output. The query will still read:

```
SELECT needed data
    FROM CO_INVENTORY_TBL
        WHERE COMPANY_NUMBER = :HOSTCOMP
        AND PART_NUMBER = :HOSTPART
```

and will provide the same results. The only difference in the query results will be the sequence and if the output is desired in company sequence, a sort may be required. Here again there is a trade-off and the designer must decide which is more efficient. It is wrong to permit inertia or habit make this decision. The designer's default decision in SQL/DS should be:

```
PART_NUMBER, COMPANY_NUMBER
```

unless it is proven wrong. The default should usually **not** be Company_number first.

Filter Factor Calculation Input

The optimizer uses the statistics available in the catalogs to estimate the number of rows that have to be read (*filter factor*). When the *filter factor* of an access via an index is low, the optimizer is more prone to choose that index for the access path. The *filter factor* is a very important value and the **only** statistics available to help determine the number of rows that need to be accessed are the statistics on the **first column** of each index.

In the past, SQL/DS only had three columns in the SYSTEM.SYSCOLUMNS table to help estimate the *filter factor.* HIGH2KEY contained the first eight bytes of the second highest value in the column and LOW2KEY contained the first eight bytes of the second lowest value in the column. COLCOUNT contained the number of distinct values in the column. The optimizer assumed **a uniform distribution** of values which was often very incorrect and which could result in the choosing of less efficient access paths.

The SYSTEM.SYSCOLSTATS table now provides the optimizer with additional information to enable it to more accurately calculate filter factors. The new columns, each with up to 12 bytes of data, include:

VAL10 ⟹ 90 percent of the values in the column are higher than this value, less than 10 percent are lower or equal.

VAL50 ⟹ 50 percent of the values are lower or equal to this value.

VAL90 ⟹ 90 percent of the values are lower or equal.

FREQ1VAL ⟹ The value found most frequently in the column.

FREQ1PCT ⟹ The actual percentage of frequency of FREQ1VAL.

FREQ2VAL ⟹ The second most frequently found value in the column.

FREQ2PCT ⟹ The actual percentage of frequency of FREQ2VAL.

This new table enables the optimizer to check **constants** against the most frequent values in the first column of an index. It specifies in which range the value lies. The assumed distribution is more exact so that the optimizer can calculate a more accurate *filter factor.*

The SYSCOLSTATS catalog table can be queried to determine if an index has a first column that can be used effectively by the optimizer:

```
SELECT CNAME, FREQ1VAL, FREQ1PCT, FREQ2VAL, FREQ2PCT
    FROM SYSTEM.SYSCOLSTATS
```

A sample output might list:

CNAME	FREQ1VAL	FREQ1PCT	FREQ2VAL	FREQ2PCT
NEW_USER_NUM	15	0	108	0
CUST_TYPE	M	82	G	7
ACTIVE_CUST	Y	95	N	5
PREFIX_ID	3	92	7	6

The first columns in the sample, except for NEW_USER_NUM are very non-unique. To be unique and effective, the FREQ1PCT value should be zero or close to zero. When the sum of FREQ1PCT and FREQ2PCT is 100, there are most probably only two values in the column. The ACTIVE_CUST column, for example, contains only a Y (yes) or N (no) and is not a good candidate for an index.

The ADDRESS table with an index on CITY will further explain the effect of these new statistics:

CITY

—————

CHI
NYC
NYC
NYC
NYC
SFC
SFC
TOR

In the SYSTEM.SYSCOLSTATS table, the entries for CITY would read:

```
CNAME      ⟹ CITY
TNAME      ⟹ ADDRESS
CREATOR    ⟹ DOV1
VAL10      ⟹ CHI
VAL50      ⟹ NYC
VAL90      ⟹ TOR
FREQ1VAL   ⟹ NYC
FREQ1PCT   ⟹ 50
FREQ2VAL   ⟹ SFC
FREQ2PCT   ⟹ 25
```

This will enable the optimizer to more accurately calculate the *filter factor* of the following queries:

```
SELECT * FROM ADDRESS WHERE CITY = 'NYC'
SELECT * FROM ADDRESS WHERE CITY = 'TOR'
```

The calculations before and after the recent SQL/DS versions might be:

	Before	**After**
NYC ⟹	4 values, each = .25	.5 (from FREQ1VAL)
TOR ⟹	4 values, each = .25	.125 (half of the .25 remaining after subtracting the two high values known)

The results of the calculations now, more accurately reflect the actual filter factors of the two queries.

INDEX USED ON UPDATE

To avoid the possibility that an updated index key would be reposi-
tioned ahead of itself in the index and found again later during the
continuation of the index scan, prior versions of SQL/DS did not
allow an UPDATE command to use an index if the command was
updating any column in the index key. Newer versions of SQL/DS
allow the use of an index where (part of) the key is to be modified, on
condition that one and only one row will be updated by the command.
If this condition does not apply, the index will not be used.

ADDITIONAL PERFORMANCE ENHANCEMENTS

In early versions of SQL/DS, the **resource manager initialization** was
executed each time an external sub-routine with SQL statements was
called. This added significantly to application overhead. The newer
versions execute the initialization only once.

The **logical optimizer** will try to improve the use of local *predicate*s. When the following two conditions are found in a JOIN query:

```
WHERE A.USERID = B.USERID AND
    A.USERID = 5296
```

the optimizer will add the local *predicate* on the other table:

```
WHERE B.USERID = 5296
```

The optimizer will also remove some unnecessary conditions. If
the query states:

```
SELECT DISTINCT AVG(SALARY)
```

the DISTINCT is extraneous and will be omitted by the optimizer to
avoid a SORT.

In newer versions of SQL/DS, **access modules** contain control
blocks rather than code. This reduces the size of access modules and
reduces the number of buffers needed to load the access module.

EXIST and NOT EXIST now stop after one matching row is
found. In early versions, the command would continue the search until
all of the rows were examined.

The newer versions make more efficient use of *unique* indexes. If
an index is unique, it is important that it be defined as unique.

SUMMARY

To provide additional information for the optimizer, newer SQL/DS versions incorporate a new column in SYSTEM.SYSINDEXES and a new table, SYSTEM.SYSCOLSTATS. The CLUSTERRATIO column added to SYSINDEXES provides an indication of the level of clustering and allows the optimizer to determine how *unclustered* an index really is. SYSCOLSTATS provides distribution statistics on the values in the first column of the index and uses the data to calculate the *filter factor*. This usage stresses the importance of choosing the first column of an index wisely.

RECOMMENDATION

1. Carefully choose the first column of an index.

CHAPTER 4

Table Design Considerations

Despite what is written in many texts, table design is not and should not be an art but rather a straightforward analysis and design function by an analyst who understands both the requirements of the business and the way SQL/DS performs best. To determine what data to place in a table, relational theory maintains that after classifying the data into individual subjects on which data will be collected (*entities*), the *elements* describing these entities should be placed into a table. How to choose the best set of elements for each table and how to decide which columns of data belong in which tables, requires an analyst familiar with the way the data will be used.

Unfortunately, tables are rarely created strictly according to a careful study of data usage, business needs, and performance requirements. Old file structures are often simply copied field by field into columns or all of the data is listed and tables are created in accordance with artificial logical relationships of data. Neither of these techniques is the way to design SQL/DS tables for efficient operation. This does not mean that the NAME and the ADDRESS of an employee do not belong in the same table. They do, unless the name is used for many daily queries while the address is used once a month for special mailings or once a year for holiday greetings. When it is rarely used, ADDRESS definitely does **not** belong in the same table as NAME even though relational theory might place it there. The result of placing a rarely used piece of data in the same row as a highly used piece of data is degraded response and excessive I/O.

Any table design decisions made by the application developer or the DBA will have a significant impact upon system performance and they should be carefully evaluated. When making the decision, the designer will often be determining what the relationships will be between the tables, the data they contain, and the ways they will be used.

DATA RELATIONSHIPS

A *data entity* is any subject about which data is gathered. It could be an employee, a company, an account, or any similar *entity*. An SQL/DS table is usually made up of *data elements* describing the data entity. An early step in table design, therefore, is to determine what *data elements or items* are to be placed in each table. The *elements* chosen for a particular table should usually be related to each other. In a table containing information about an employee, for example, the following *elements* might be found:

Employee Name	Employee Number
Department Name	Department Number
Date of Birth	Spouse's Name
Salary Rate	Annual Salary
Children's Names	Equipment Used
Job Classification	Job Code
Courses Attended	Responsibilities

The data element names used in a particular SQL/DS table must be unique and should be meaningful. When a data *element* name is used in more than one table it should represent the same data in **every** table. The *data element* NAME, for example, should not refer to **employee** name in one table and **department** name in another table.

Among the major decisions of the application developer is the decision on whether to place all of the data in one table or to distribute different columns of data in multiple tables. The employee *table* may actually be divided into three or more tables depending, in part, upon how the data is used. One table might consist of the columns needed on a daily basis:

Employee Number, Name, Department, Sex, Annual Salary

A second table might contain the data needed biweekly or monthly for salary calculation:

Salary Rate, Regular Hours, Social Security Number, Tax Rate, Dependents

A third table may contain rarely used data:

Address, Children's Names, Spouse, Previous Employer

Some of these columns may be switched around, but the technique is to design the tables in accordance with how the data will be used and not just in accordance with the logical relationships.

There is a need to understand the basic relationships between data in different tables. These relationships play an important role in the determination of *referential relationships* (to be discussed later in this chapter). The basic relationships also help the designer determine whether it is possible or advisable to *normalize* or *denormalize* table contents. The four basic table relationships are:

1. **One to One**—An employee record, for example, to the retirement account record. Each employee has only one retirement account and each account is associated with only one employee (and the data is in two different tables). When the DBA has to determine which of the tables will hold the primary key in a referential relationship, a knowledge of the use of the data will be helpful. Either key in a one-to-one relationship can be the primary key but, in this case, considering normal data usage, the employee number in the employee record should be the primary key.

2. **One to Many**—The manager record, for example, and the employee records. Each employee is associated with only one manager and one manager may have many employees. In a *referential relationship,* the "One" is the primary key.

3. **Many to One**—The employee records, for example, and the department record. There are many employees in each department and each employee is in only one department.

4. **Many to Many**—Employee records, for example, and attendance records at annual conferences. There are many employees who attend each conference and each employee may attend more than one conference.

NORMALIZATION

Relational theory includes the concept of *normalization* of data in tables so that there is a minimum of redundant data. Normatization will also ensure that columns in a table belong there because of their relationship to the primary key. It is also to ensure the existence of most data elements in one and only one table. The absence of redundancy is important for data consistency because when each dependent element of data is stored in only one place, only one copy will have to be modified. This section of the chapter will summarize the theory and review some of the practical implications.

Normalization strives to reduce the complexity of tables and to format each row into a structure consisting of a unique key (set of values) that identifies the entity and a set of independent values (elements) related to the unique key that describes it. A personnel table (PERSONNEL_TBL) example will be used to describe some of the levels of normalization. The primary data or key of the personnel record will be the employee as identified by an employee number (EMPLOYEE_ID).

First Normal Form

The first level of normalization will simplify the structure of the data by removing sets of the same type of data from the row. The personnel record, for example, might contain the name of each child and may allow for up to six "child" data elements in each row:

EMPLOYEE_ID, . . . , CHILD1, CHILD2, CHILD3, CHILD4, CHILD5, CHILD6

This *redundancy of data types* will increase the complexity of working with this data element (What if there are less than six children? What if there are more than six?) and is wasteful. The repeating group will be removed from the row and will be placed in a separate table (CHILDREN_TBL). The unique identifier, EMPLOYEE_ID, must be copied to the new table in order to identify with whom each child record is identified. In this case normalization will decrease complexity but will introduce an element of redundancy. The introduction of *referential integrity* in recent versions of SQL/DS has provided the application designer with a means of tagging this redundant column in the CHILDREN_TBL as a foreign key referentially related to the primary key, EMPLOYEE_ID, in the PERSONNEL_TBL. The system will automatically check, each time a new "children" row is inserted, that a valid EMPLOYEE_ID has been entered.:

EMPLOYEE_ID	CHILD_NAME
1023	David
1023	Daniel
3024	Abraham

When an employee has two children, there will be two rows in the new table with his or her EMPLOYEE_ID and when an employee has seven children, there will be seven rows. There is no need for any pointer in the original record to this table. The CHILDREN_TBL can be accessed via its relationship with the EMPLOYEE_ID. The original table might contain a "number of children" column but some would consider this redundant because of the possibility of querying the table and asking, *How many children does employee 2135 have,* as shown in the following example:

```
SELECT COUNT(*) FROM CHILDREN_TBL
    WHERE EMPLOYEE_ID = 2135
```

Second Normal Form

The elimination of the redundancy of data describing nonprimary key values in the row or redundancy across rows is the second level of normalization. When rows in the personnel table contain:

Department Name,   Department Number

a department name always describes a particular department number and may be repeated many times because there are many employees in each department:

Employee ID	Employee Name	Department Number	Department Name
10001	Anderson	12	Computer Appl
10035	Goldberg	12	Computer Appl
13002	Rothstein	12	Computer Appl

Assuming that the primary key is EMPLOYEE_ID, the employee name and department number are directly related to the key but the department name is actually related to the department number and it is not dependent upon the EMPLOYEE_ID. If Department Name had to be modified, it would have to be changed in every table containing the department name. In addition, if there were no employees in the department, there would be no record of the existence of such a department. To conform with the Second Normal Form, the column, Department Name, will be removed from the main table and placed in a separate table (DEPT_TBL) that might contain:

Department Number, Department Name, etc.

The department number in this new table will be a unique, primary identifier and may be used (as was EMPLOYEE_ID) to ensure that employees are not assigned to work in departments that do not exist. The department number in the PERSONNEL_TBL will now become a foreign key related to the department number in the DEPT_TBL.

Third Normal Form

The Third Normal Form will remove columns that while not related to other columns are also not directly dependant upon the primary key. Each employee in the computer department, for example, may have equipment assigned to him or her but the data is not directly related to the employee. To conform with Third Normal Form, the data about the equipment will be removed from the personnel record and a new table, COMP_EQUIP, will be created. The new table might contain:

Equipment Serial Number, Description, Employee Using It, etc.

Here, too, *equipment serial number* will become a unique primary key and the equipment serial number column in the PERSONNEL_TBL could become a foreign key. Care must be exercised, however, not to involve too many columns in *referential relationships* (as discussed later in this chapter).

Fourth Normal Form

In the Fourth Normal Form, which will be the last level to be discussed here, independent columns with multiple values will also be removed from the table. The personnel table might contain a column with information about the courses attended by an employee and another column listing the responsibilities of each employee. Both of these columns are unrelated multi-valued columns:

Employee_id	Courses	Tasks
10001	Job Control	Supervise Projects
10001	Intro to Sys	
10001	Relational DB	

It is very difficult to justify having these unrelated columns in the PERSONNEL_TBL or in any one table. Some columns may require three or four rows for an employee and other columns may require only one row. To conform with Fourth Normal Form these columns are removed from the table and placed in two separate tables.

DENORMALIZATION

Normalization is an excellent technique in the hands of a professional who understands both relational theory and performance tuning methodology. Normalization generally improves performance but application usage of normalized tables might degrade performance.

Normalization is **not** a requirement of SQL/DS. Minimizing the response time of transactions is often much more important than preventing the need for multiple updates, *referential relationships,* or saving disk space. With a million row table, a large amount of disk space may be saved by normalizing tables to remove Department Name, for example, and the importance of this saving should not be minimized. If, however, the saving comes at the expense of unacceptable response time caused by the need for multiple JOINS then there is no profit in saving disk space. There is also the danger that when data becomes too normalized, the repetition of the primary key on each new table may itself require an excessive amount of disk space.

The database designer must always consider how the data will be used. If every query about an employee, for example, would require the department name, then the redundancy of including the department name in the employee's record to avoid a JOIN for every query would become very acceptable. Department names are not modified very often and the result of the redundancy would be very little harm but greatly increased performance benefit. When the department name is not needed by most personnel transactions it should **not** be included in the personnel record.

When a specific column with the same contents and format is found in more than one table, it should have the **same** name. An automated procedure could be used to update the columns. The DBA should develop, if modifications become necessary, an application program, an EXEC, or a DBSU procedure, to ensure that all of the tables that contained the column would be updated.

With the need to ensure reasonable performance and fast response, once normalization is completed, denormalization should be performed where necessary. Denormalization in no way implies going to the extreme of placing *all* data columns into *one* table. The fact that tax tables have to be used with salary information does **not** justify placing them in the same table. It should be emphasized that excessive redundancy will result in greatly expanded row size which will result in excessive I/O and poor performance. Joins often cannot be avoided and going to any extreme will usually lead to poor performance.

The database designer must also keep in mind the need for easy modification. Changes are a fact of life and need to be planned for.

Spending too much effort on *perfect* table design will not usually result in long-term efficient design. The need for changes will rapidly ruin the efficiency of the design. This does not mean to imply that time should not be spent on effective design or redesign. Careful, thoughtful design of tables is the most important part of database tuning. Once the normalization is complete, the DBA should examine the performance implications of the design. The DBA should consider the usage of the data, the lengths of rows, and the other factors mentioned. The DBA should also be guided by the **rule of thumb** that the creation of a row shorter than 35 bytes may be too wasteful and that the designing of a row containing more than 30 columns may be too difficult to manage. Should denormalization be necessary, it should be carried out with care and constant review.

ROW SIZE

A good rule to follow is that *rows of data should be as small as possible* but as large as needed. It is efficient to place many small rows onto one data page so as to minimize database I/O and maximize buffer efficiency. It is much more efficient, however, to design one large row than to continually perform JOINS on two or more tables. SQL/DS permits JOINS and efficiently handles JOINS, but does not encourage JOINS. Joins require extra resources and should be avoided whenever possible. This type of trade-off must often be made and should continually be monitored using the SQL/DS performance tuning facilities.

JOINS

A join is required when column data from two or more tables is required. SQL/DS makes the joining of two tables a trivial task and the user may join up to 15 tables in one query. In practice, more than four tables are rarely joined. A JOIN is specified by simply placing the names of two or more tables side by side in the FROM list of a query as shown in the following example of a three table join:

```
SELECT columns
    FROM PERSONNEL_TBL, DEPT_TBL, CHILD_VIEW
```

If no WHERE conditional clauses are specified to limit the JOIN, every row of every table will be joined with every row of every other table.

The user should ensure that all tables involved in JOINs will have at least one index. The SELECT command should contain enough local predicates (WHERE conditions involving only **one** of the tables in the JOIN) so that an index can be used selectively on each table. The EXPLAIN facility should be used to verify that the optimizer has enough information to selectively use the indexes. Additional indexes and predicates should be considered when the JOIN requires too many system resources and does not use an existing index. One of the few conditions under which an UPDATE ALL STATISTICS command is justified is when a table is involved in a JOIN and an index cannot be used. In that case, the cardinality of non-indexed JOIN columns play a role in the optimizer's decision as to which table should be the inner and which the outer JOIN table.

There are situations involving complex joins where adding an index will actually slow response. When a new index was added to an insurance application, for example, the optimizer chose a different outer table and response became worse until the new index was dropped. This example re-emphasizes the need to monitor the system's reaction to all modifications.

To Join or Not to Join

In order to join columns from more than one table SQL/DS may be required to perform many actions. They may include comparing data, sorting, scanning many rows, reading one of the tables many times and, in general, performing extra processing. **If the application developer can find a way to avoid a join, it is preferable.** Some alternatives to consider when columns are often joined might be to combine the data from the two tables into one table, to include the same (redundant) data in both tables, or to create a temporary table with all of the necessary data to exist only for the life of the query. Each of these methods involves a trade-off and the application developer may decide to use a join because the cost is still acceptable or because the developer does not search for a more cost-effective approach. Even before response time becomes a problem it might be prudent to re-evaluate those applications with excessive join costs. These applications not only impact their own costs and response but, if run often, they also impact the performance of the entire system.

How Tables Are Joined

To join two tables, SQL/DS may use either the *nested loop method* or the *merge scan loop method.* **SQL/DS can only join two tables**

at a time and if more than two tables are involved in the join, repetitive joins of two tables are used. After the first two tables are joined, the second join is performed on the third table and the answer set of the first join. Each table row is first checked against any *local predicates* that involve only one of the tables. These *local predicates* are very important to improved performance because they help screen out rows from each table before additional scans and tests are needed. As many local predicates as possible should be defined.

Nested Loop Join   In a nested loop join, SQL/DS chooses one of the tables to be the inner table and one to be the outer table. A row of the inner table is scanned to see if it satisfies the *local predicates* of this table. When the predicate matches, the rows of the outer table are retrieved and checked against the local predicates of that table. When those conditions are satisfied, the join predicates are applied. A row that satisfies all of the conditions becomes part of the answer set to be used with the next join or to be returned to the user.

This process is repeated for each qualifying row of the first table. The more local predicates on this inner table, the fewer the number of scans of the second table that are needed. When the outer table does not have an index that can be used selectively, the entire table will be read multiple times which will result in very poor response time and high resource utilization. The optimizer, using available statistics, will try to choose the smaller table with a selective index to be the outer table.

To minimize the number of loops it is important to have local predicates delimiting the selective conditions on each of the tables. Indexes on the local predicate columns are usually more important than on the join predicate columns.

Merge Scan   A *merge scan* involves the reading and often the sorting of (all of) the rows in each of the tables when indexes do not exist in the exact sequence on both tables. If usable indexes exist, only those rows satisfying the join predicates are selected.

A pointer is used on one table to indicate which one of the sorted and selected rows is currently being checked against the *local predicates.* When a row satisfies the *local predicates,* a pointer is used on the second table to indicate which row is currently being tested against the *local predicates* of that table and the join predicates. If the join values of the second table are greater than those of the first table, the pointer of the first table is advanced until predicate conditions are satisfied. In this method, after the sort, each row is read only once.

A Join Example

```
SELECT P.NAME, S.SALARY, P.ZIP, P.PHONE, P.AGE, S.EMPNO
    FROM PERSONNEL P, SALARY S
        WHERE P.AGE > 21 AND            (Local)
              S.SALARY > 10000 AND      (Local)
              P.EMPNO = S.EMPNO         (Join)
```

When a nested loop scan is chosen by the optimizer, an index on Age and an index on Salary may be more important than indexes on P.Empno and on S.Empno. When a merge scan is chosen by the optimizer the indexes on Age and Salary are less important and indexes on the join columns P.Empno and S.Empno become very important. If these indexes exist, the rows are read in the JOIN sequence and a SORT may be avoided. The EXPLAIN function should be used to determine which join method was chosen and which indexes are needed on each table.

SUBQUERIES

Subqueries are another very powerful feature of SQL/DS that should be used very sparingly. Subqueries can be simple or complex. A complex *correlated* subquery requires values from the calling query to be used in the subquery.

The subquery portion of a simple subquery would have to be executed only once and might look like this:

```
SELECT NAME, SALARY, (SALARY * 1.10), LAST_RAISE_DATE
    FROM SALARY_TBL
        WHERE EMPNO IN (SELECT EMPNO
            FROM EMP_TBL
                WHERE DEPT = 24)
```

The subquery portion of a *correlated subquery,* as in the following example, would have to be executed once for each qualifying row in the calling query and may take many hours to execute:

```
SELECT NAME, SALARY, (SALARY * 1.10), LAST_RAISE_DATE
    FROM SALARY_TBL S
        WHERE CODE IN (SELECT CODE
            FROM EMP_TBL E
                WHERE S.EMPNO = E.EMPNO
                AND STATE = 'NYC')
```

Another use of subqueries is to reference the **same** table for different types of information. For example, to find all the salaries lower than the average salary:

```
SELECT NAME, SALARY, (SALARY * 1.10), LAST_RAISE_DATE
    FROM SALARY_TBL
        WHERE SALARY < (SELECT AVG(SALARY)
            FROM SALARY_TBL)
```

Subqueries should always be checked by the EXPLAIN function and should be avoided when possible. It might be more efficient to create a temporary table especially if TABLE1 in the following SELECT is small and TABLE2 is very large:

```
SELECT anyfield
    FROM anytable
        WHERE FIELD2 IN
            (SELECT FIELD2 FROM TABLE2
                WHERE FIELD3 = :VALUE1)
```

The temporary table and index can be created and loaded as follows:

```
CREATE TABLE TEMPT1 (FIELDX CHAR(5))
COMMIT WORK
INSERT INTO TEMPT1
    SELECT DISTINCT FIELD2
        FROM TABLE2 WHERE FIELD3 = :VALUE1
CREATE UNIQUE INDEX UINDX3 ON TEMPT1 (FIELDX)
COMMIT WORK
```

The user would then issue the following:

```
SELECT AFIELD FROM ANYTABLE, TEMPT1
    WHERE FIELD2 = FIELDX
```

When processing is completed, the application would issue:

```
DROP TABLE TEMPT1
COMMIT WORK
```

This process may lock the system tables and cause other problems and it is suggested that the EXPLAIN facility be used to ascertain if it is efficient to use this method.

UNIONS

One method of avoiding JOINs may be to use the UNION operator. UNION will result in a combination of the results of the two SELECTs with all of the duplicates removed via a SORT. As mentioned elsewhere, using UNION may also be much more efficient than writing a query using an OR condition. The following, for example, is a SELECT where SQL/DS may not be able to use an index:

```
SELECT *
      FROM PERSONNEL_TBL
          WHERE NAME = :SAVENAME OR
              NAME = 'HAGBI'
```

If this query, however, were written using a UNION, an index might be usable:

```
SELECT *
      FROM PERSONNEL_TBL
          WHERE NAME = :SAVENAME
UNION
SELECT *
      FROM PERSONNEL_TBL
          WHERE NAME = 'HAGBI'
```

When using UNION on more than two SELECTS it is important to use UNION ALL as indicated in the following procedure (the UNION ALL option is only available in recent versions of SQL/DS):

```
SELECT * FROM ANY_TBL WHERE. . . . . . . .
UNION ALL
SELECT * FROM ANY_TBL WHERE. . . . . . . .
UNION ALL
SELECT * FROM ANY_TBL WHERE. . . . . . . .
UNION ALL
SELECT * FROM ANY_TBL WHERE. . . . . . .
UNION
SELECT * FROM ANY_TBL WHERE. . . . . . . .
```

The UNION with the **ALL** parameter specifies that duplicate rows should **not** be eliminated. In the above example of five SELECT commands connected using the UNION function, SQL/DS will execute the UNION between the first two SELECT commands but, because of the **ALL** parameter, will **not** eliminate duplicate rows from the result. The rows outputted by the third SELECT will then be added to the output of the first two SELECTS and duplicate rows will again **not** be eliminated. The same process will be repeated for the results of the fourth SELECT command. The **ALL** parameter, however, was **not** specified on the fourth UNION logical operator. In this case, all of the rows outputted from the previous SELECT commands will be SORTed and checked against the output of the fifth SELECT command and duplicates **will be** eliminated.

This suggested method will produce the same result as would a series of SELECT commands connected via a UNION logical operator with**out** the **ALL** parameter. With the **ALL** parameter, however, performance will improve because a SORT and search for duplicates after each intermediary step will be avoided.

It should be remembered that all of the columns involved in a UNION must be identical. Special care is needed when using literals in SELECT commands involved in a UNION. The literals are treated as VARCHAR columns and will only be valid when they are exactly the identical lengths. The following UNION will **not** be successful:

```
SELECT '9TH TIME', . . . . . other information
UNION
SELECT '10TH TIME', . . . . . other information
```

THE USE OF SORTS

A sort usually involves the use of both CPU resources and I/O resources. The optimizer will make the determination as to whether or not a sort is required. It will also decide whether to do an in-core internal sort (which will only impact CPU utilization) or to use the internal DBSPACES for an external sort (which will require both I/O and CPU resources).

When an index is available in the sort sequence and the optimizer decides to use the index, no sorting will be required. The optimizer must often determine if it is less costly to use an index that is not in the sort sequence, selectively, (and require a sort of the answer set) or to use an index in the sort sequence non-selectively and avoid the cost of a sort.

A sort or an index in sort sequence is usually required by the following activities:

Joining two or more tables.

Creating an index.

Using ORDER BY, GROUP BY, or DISTINCT.

Using a UNION.

After all the rows retrieved are passed to the RDS component, the rows meeting the criteria of the query are selected and sorted. The RDS component tries to ensure that the minimum number of rows is sorted. In order to reduce the cost of a sort the application developer should:

1. Select only those columns and those rows needed.
2. Remove ORDER BY, GROUP BY, DISTINCT, and UNION clauses that are not needed.
3. Create indexes on columns used in ORDER BY clauses.
4. Create indexes on columns involved in JOINs.

PERFORMANCE AND DOCUMENTATION

More and more business concerns are formalizing and automating their documentation procedures. Many now realize that the lack of accurate and functional documentation may result in long delays and a waste of manpower every time modifications need to be made. Unfortunately, change management has not kept pace with documentation standards and in too many installations the application documentation is hopelessly out of synchronization with what is actually designed into the production application. As the use of databases increases, the need for up-to-date, accurate documentation increases. Laxity in enforcing documentation procedures will eventually seriously impact system performance.

SUMMARY

Table design is a straightforward analysis and design function. A data entity is any subject about which data is gathered. An SQL/DS table is made up of data elements. Data element names used in a particular SQL/DS table must be unique.

The four basic relationships between data in different tables are one-to-one, one-to-many, many-to-one, and many-to-many. Normalization strives to reduce the complexity of tables and to format the row into a structure consisting of a unique key and a set of related elements. Basic normalization involves four normal forms. FIRST NORMAL FORM removes sets of the same type of data from the row. SECOND NORMAL FORM eliminates redundancy across rows or the redundancy of data describing nonprimary key values in the row. THIRD NORMAL FORM removes columns that while not related to other columns are also not directly dependant upon the primary key. FOURTH NORMAL FORM removes independent columns with multiple values from the table. Normalization generally improves performance but it is not a requirement of SQL/DS and there are application needs that must be considered.

DENORMALIZATION may be necessary to improve performance. Careful, thoughtful design of tables is the most important part of database tuning but spending too much effort on *perfect* table design will not always result in long-term efficient design.

A JOIN is required when column data from different tables is needed in the same query. A JOIN is specified by simply placing the names of the tables side by side in the FROM list of a query. Alternatives to a JOIN should be tried. The two methods used to join tables are the nested loop method and the merge scan method. SQL/DS can only join two tables at a time and if more than two are involved in the join, repetitive joins of two tables are used. To minimize the number of loops in a JOIN it is important to have local predicates delimiting the selective conditions on each of the tables in a JOIN.

Subqueries can be simple or complex. A complex "correlated" subquery requires values from the calling query to be used in subquery. Unions might be used to avoid a JOIN. Using UNION may also be much more efficient than writing a query using an OR condition. The UNION with the ALL parameter implies that all values are desired and duplicates should not be eliminated.

The lack of accurate and functional documentation results in long delays and the waste of manpower every time modifications need to be made.

RECOMMENDATIONS

1. Data element names should be meaningful. When a data element name is used in more than one table it should represent the same data in every table.

2. Tables should be designed to match the needs of the users and not just in accordance with normalization rules.

3. Once normalization is complete, denormalization should be carried out with care and constant review.

4. Rows of data should be as small as possible but as large as needed.

5. Joins require extra resources and should be avoided whenever possible.

6. More than four tables should not be joined.

7. The user should ensure that all tables involved in joins have at least one index. The SELECT command should contain enough local predicates so that an index can be used selectively with each table.

8. Use the UPDATE ALL STATISTICS parameter sparingly but use it when an index cannot be used on a table involved in a JOIN.

9. Use the EXPLAIN facility to determine how the optimizer will access the data.

10. Subqueries should be used very sparingly and should always be checked by the EXPLAIN function.

11. When using UNION on more than two SELECTS, it is important to use UNION ALL.

12. Select only those columns and those rows needed.

13. Remove ORDER BY, GROUP BY, DISTINCT, and UNION clauses that are not needed.

14. Create indexes on columns used in ORDER BY clauses.

15. Laxity in enforcing documentation procedures will eventually seriously impact system performance.

REFERENTIAL INTEGRITY

Referential integrity allows the user to define relationships between column values in different tables. If a policy holder is deleted from the customer table, for example, all of this customer's policies should also be deleted. On the other hand, when policies for this customer are still in force, SQL/DS should disallow the deletion of the customer record or should nullify the customer number in the policy record.

In the past, keeping track of these logical connections between values in different tables was a manual task dependent on the skill of the application developer. It was either coded into each application program or manually controlled externally from the computer system.

The *referential integrity* function added to recent versions of SQL/DS will prevent the user from introducing inconsistencies into the data and will relieve the application programmer of the responsibility for coding this function. Less effort will be required to logically debug application systems and fewer lines of code will be needed to implement *referential integrity*.

Every environment using the SQL/DS database including the ad hoc transactions via ISQL and the DBSU and the transaction environment via batch or on-line applications is required to adhere to the referential rules. If the function had not been built into the system, each application designer would have had to design his own facility and it would be much harder to control. The built-in function enforces a consistent and unified approach.

PRIMARY AND FOREIGN KEYS

A primary key is the main component of *referential integrity*. This is a set of unique values in a *parent table* that governs the acceptance or rejection of a value which a user tries to insert into a *dependent table* column (foreign key). If a matching value does not exist in the primary key column of the *parent table,* the user cannot insert the value into the foreign key column. When a company, for example, is divided into departments, a *parent table* of department numbers and other data is set up with the department number as the primary key as shown in the following example:

Personnel_TBL	Employee Name	*(foreign-key)* Dept-Num	Emp_ID
	Hadassa Goldberg	34	1037

DEPT_TBL	*(primary-key)* Department	Dept Name	Manager
	15	Personnel	4062
	23	Shipping	3105
	34	Computer	1048
	39	Warehouse	1099

When a new row containing personnel data for an employee is to be inserted, if the department number is designated as a foreign key of the DEPT_TBL, SQL/DS will automatically issue an internally generated SELECT to read the parent DEPT_TBL to ensure that a primary value matching the department number entered for this new employee row exists. If it does not exist, the row will not be inserted and the user will be notified via a return code.

Referential integrity is not a new concept. It has always been required in many applications but in the past each application program had to handle it with code placed in the program. If a user with authority used ISQL, QMF, or DBSU, however, to modify or delete production rows, *referential constraints* built into applications could be bypassed and there was no way to ensure *referential integrity.*

When a bank teller enters a transaction, for example, *referential integrity* can ensure that the account number exists and that the transaction type exists:

TRANS-TBL	*acct #*	*transaction type*	$ amount
	349123	01	– 400

ACCT_TBL	*acct #*	customer name	acct type
	175622	Ruchie Bartuv	checking
	349123	John Smith	savings
	412301	Sara Blaustein	checking

ACCT_TYPE_TBL	*Trans_type*	Description
	01	Deposit
	02	Withdrawal

Assuming that there is no need for the application program to read the data on the account table, the *referential integrity* function of SQL/DS will verify that an account exists for this customer before inserting the new transaction into the database. This internally generated SELECT of the TRANS_TBL may result in increased programmer productivity by removing the need to code this SELECT into the application. If, however, the application will need other data from the TRANS_TBL row for display or other purposes, SQL/DS's internally generated SELECT will be duplicated and, unless its control functions are important, it will prove wasteful to use *referential integrity.*

Creating a referential structure is not recommended unless it is needed!

REFERENTIAL CONSTRAINTS

Recent versions of SQL/DS trigger the creation of a unique index on the primary key to prevent duplication and introduce limitations known as "referential constraints" to control deletion of primary keys when foreign keys from other tables depend upon these primary keys. A bank account from the account table, for example, should not be deleted as long as transactions on the transaction table refer to this account (this is known as the "RESTRICT" rule). Without referential constraints there is little if anything to prevent an application or an ISQL user from deleting a row in the account table. With *referential constraints,* SQL/DS will prevent deletion or initiate a user-selected procedure when an attempt is made to delete this "primary key" row.

From a performance viewpoint, the use of *referential constraints* should only be used when absolutely necessary. They generate actions (sometimes a great many) when a column protected by referential constraints is inserted, updated, or, for primary keys, deleted.

USING REFERENTIAL INTEGRITY

In order to provide a means of defining *referential integrity,* extensions have been added to the CREATE table and ALTER table commands. The major task in defining the structure for *referential relationship*s is the choosing of a column or group of columns to serve as a primary key.

Choosing a Primary Key

The primary key is a unique key for a table that is composed of one or more columns. **A primary key should be composed of columns that require no updating.** A primary key should contain the minimum number of columns needed to uniquely identify the row. The table designer must decide which column or columns would make the best candidates for the primary key.

The table with a primary key becomes a *parent table* to other *dependent tables* that contain a foreign key composed of the exact same columns as the primary key. The account table mentioned earlier should serve as a good example:

ACCOUNT_NUM   ACCOUNT_NAME   SOC_ SEC_NUM ACCT_TYPE

If each account number in the account table must be unique, it is a candidate to be a primary key. There may be other *keys* which are *candidates* for primary key. For example, if each person may only have one of each type of account, then:

ACCT-TYPE   SOC-SEC #

might be a candidate for a primary key. Only one candidate may be designated as the primary key. A primary key may not include a nullable column.

Defining a Primary Key

The **DataBase** Administrator or application developer may use either the CREATE TABLE or ALTER TABLE commands to designate a primary key, as shown in the following examples:

```
CREATE TABLE. . . .
    (col. . . . . .)
            PRIMARY KEY (ACCOUNT# ASC)PCTFREE = 10

ALTER TABLE ACCT_TAB
    ADD PRIMARY KEY (ACCT# ASC,. . .) PCTFREE = 15
```

When a primary key is defined or reactivated (to be explained later in this chapter) the system automatically creates a unique index on the table and assigns a generated name to the index. This generated name consists of the prefix "PKEY" concatenated to a 12 byte time-stamp. A name for primary keys is not specified by the DBA because there can only be one such key on a table. Foreign keys, however, can be assigned user names because there may be several on each table. To view the names generated for the primary keys, the DBA may issue the following command:

```
SELECT INAME, TNAME, CLUSTER, KEYTYPE
    FROM SYSTEM.SYSINDEXES
        WHERE INAME LIKE 'PKEY%'
```

KEYTYPE will be 'P' if the key is active and 'I' if it is inactive. A sample output might contain:

INAME	TNAME	CLUSTER	KEYTYPE
PKEYBT1Q7EWYBLSW	EMP_PROJ_TBL	C	P
PKEYBT1Q7FBZIX3I	EMPLOYEE_TBL	N	P

In the CREATE and ALTER commands, the DBA may supply index information such as ascending / descending and free space (default 10). If no clustering index exists (F or W) **this index will automatically become the clustering index.** The primary key index is a special index and cannot be dropped by the table creator or by the DBA. Only the system can drop these indexes and they are dropped automatically when any of the following situations occur:

1. The primary key is deactivated (to be discussed later in this chapter).
2. The primary key is dropped via the ALTER TABLE DROP primary key command.
3. The table or DBSPACE is dropped.

The creation of a primary key should usually not be done during peak processing periods. The creation process builds an index and may, on large tables, use many resources and negatively impact the response time of other transactions. For performance reasons it is recommended that a primary key definition **not** be specified on a CREATE TABLE command. The table should be created and loaded with data and then the primary key should be specified using the ALTER TABLE command. Defining a primary key with a CREATE TABLE command is the same as creating an index before placing data in the table. The load is much more time consuming because the index must be updated for every row loaded.

When ALTER TABLE is specified after the data is loaded, the system will ensure that the primary key is unique by checking every key value for duplicates. If any duplicates are found, the ALTER TABLE command will fail with a negative return code.

Foreign Keys

The foreign key is a key in a *dependent table* which depends on the existence of a primary key in a *parent table.* For every UPDATE of the foreign key or INSERT of a new row, SQL/DS will enforce this rule by checking the primary key index for a value matching the new foreign key. If one exists, the update or the insert of the row containing the foreign key will be accepted; if not it will be rejected. A table may be both a *parent table* to other tables and a *dependent table* of a different *parent table.* It is implied that a primary key may also not be updated if a foreign key of that value exists without the referential constraint rule being executed.

A table may have more than one foreign key. If a transaction table, for example, consists of the following columns:

TELLER_NUM, TO_ACCT_NUM, TRANS_TYPE, DOL_AMT, DATE, TIME, FROM_ ACCT_NUM

It would be logical to define several of the columns in this row as foreign keys. If there is a TELLER_TBL with the teller number as a primary key then TELLER_NUM in this table may be designated a foreign key dependent upon the TELLER_TBL. TO_ACCT_NUM and FROM_ACCT_NUM may both be foreign keys referring to the same ACCT_TABLE. Both columns will be checked for each INSERT or UPDATE of a row. TRANS_TYPE might also be associated with a transaction type table. It is strongly recommended that, to avoid excessive INSERT overhead, **as few columns as required actually be designated as foreign keys.**

To use the ALTER TABLE command to designate a foreign key, the application designer might specify:

```
ALTER TABLE TRANS_TBL
    ADD FOREIGN KEY TELLERKEY (TELLER_NUM ASC)
        REFERENCES TELLER_TBL
        ON DELETE SET NULL
```

IF the *parent table* Teller_Table, for example, consisted of a TELLER_NUM primary key and the following columns:

DEPT, TELLER_NUM, TELLER_NAME, DATE_HIRED, MANAGER, etc.

and DEPT and MANAGER were foreign keys respectively of the DEPT_TBL and EMPLOYEE_TBL, this table would be both a *parent table* and a *dependent table* of the Department and Employee tables. Two tables that are *parent table*s to each other are difficult to UPDATE or DELETE and must follow special rules. This complexity should be avoided wherever possible. It is also not yet possible in SQL/DS for a table to be a *parent* to itself.

Foreign keys may be nullable and if any part of the value is NULL, the relationship will not be checked until the data is updated. This implies that a foreign key may not be updated if after update it no longer matches any primary key. It also implies that a *parent table* referenced by a foreign key of a *dependent table* must exist before a foreign key is defined. The foreign key must, of course, have the same attributes and contain the same columns as the primary key.

Delete Rules

When a foreign key is added to a table, the creator or DBA may specify other *delete rules* such as CASCADE and SET NULL:

- **CASCADE**—When the primary key is deleted, the system is directed to delete all rows in all tables where this key value is in a foreign key relationship referencing this primary key:

```
ALTER TABLE TRANSACTION_TBL
    ADD FOREIGN KEY ACCT_NO
        REFERENCES ACCT_TBL
        ON DELETE CASCADE
```

- **SET NULL**—When the primary key is deleted, the system is directed to set the foreign keys referencing this key value to NULLs (at least one field in the key must be nullable):

```
ALTER TABLE TRANSACTION_TBL
    ADD FOREIGN KEY ACCT_NO
        REFERENCES ACCT_TBL
        ON DELETE SET NULL
```

It can readily be seen that when SET NULL or CASCADE are the delete rules, a delete of one row of a *parent table* may result in large numbers of rows being deleted or updated in *dependent tables*. This will negatively impact performance and should be avoided during peak transaction hours. The system should default to the RESTRICT delete rule and planned action should be carried out during off-peak hours to delete unwanted rows before the deletion of the primary key.

There are, however, applications where the SET NULL effect is specifically desired. In a table containing work task projections for the coming year, for example, all rows detailing the work to be performed by a particular employee should have the employee-id column set to NULL when the employee leaves the company. In this case, a delete of the employee row should set to NULL all of the rows of work assigned to the employee in the PLANNED_ASSGNMNT table.

If the DBA or developer wants to see what the delete rules of the foreign keys are, a new catalog table, SYSTEM.SYSKEYS, may be scanned. The table contains one row for each primary or foreign key created. The command might be:

```
SELECT KEYNAME, KEYTYPE, DELETERULE, STATUS
    FROM SYSTEM.SYSKEYS
        WHERE TNAME = 'PERSONNEL_TBL'
```

The output might contain:

KEYNAME	KEYTYPE	DELETERULE	STATUS
PFKEYBT1Q7FEWYBLSW	P		A
DEPTKEY	F	R	A
PROJ_NUM	F	N	A

Should the DBA want a list of the columns in the keys, another new catalog table, SYSTEM.SYSKEYCOLS, may be scanned. The table contains one row for every column in every primary or foreign key:

```
SELECT KEYNAME, KEYTYPE, CNAME, KEYORD
    FROM SYSTEM.SYSKEYCOLS
        WHERE TNAME = 'PERSONNEL_TBL'
```

KEYNAME	KEYTYPE	CNAME	KEYORD
PFKEYBT1Q7FEWYBLSW	P	user_id	1
DEPTKEY	F	dept_num	1
PROJ_NUM	F	proj_col	1
PROJ_NUM	F	proj_type	2

ENFORCEMENT OF REFERENTIAL INTEGRITY

Referential integrity is enforced by SQL/DS in **all** environments:

ISQL—ad hoc modifications
On-line application/transaction environment
Batch
Pre-processed applications
DBSU utility
RXSQL, CSP, QMF, and so on.

The enforcement is consistent and not dependent upon the programming skills of the developer. The enforcement of integrity begins as soon as a referential relationship is defined.

RULES

The use of *referential integrity* requires adherence to some specific rules. Some of these rules as they relate to foreign or primary keys are listed on page 115:

PRIMARY KEYS	FOREIGN KEYS
No NULLS allowed	Nulls allowed. Value is not tested when it is Null
No duplicates (unique)	Duplicates allowed
One per table	More than one per table
May **not** be deleted unless not referenced by foreign keys (unless CASCADE or SET NULL are specified)	May be deleted at any time
May be referenced by many foreign keys	May reference only **one** primary key
No *dependent table*s need exist	*Parent table* **must** exist
A new value may be inserted into the table at any time	A new value may be inserted **only** if a primary key value matches
May be a foreign key of another table	

Two foreign keys may **not** be defined with the same or different constraint rules on the exact same columns of a table but two foreign keys may overlap columns. SQL/DS only allows one level of deletes and a *dependent table* with a foreign key which will be deleted by the CASCADE rule may not be a *parent* to any other table and may not, therefore, have a primary key.

DEACTIVATION

To provide a means of adding quantities of data without the overhead of *referential integrity* checking for each row, the foreign and primary keys may be deactivated. When a key is deactivated, *referential integrity* rules on that key are no longer applied by the system. The tables involved, however, are no longer accessible to anyone but the owner and the DBA. This measure is taken to protect the validity of the data. When the primary key, for example, is deactivated, the system created unique index is dropped and the values inserted are no longer checked. The keys are deactivated by the use of the ALTER TABLE command, as shown in the following examples:

```
ALTER TABLE TRANS_ACT DEACTIVATE PRIMARY KEY
ALTER TABLE TRANS_ACT DEACTIVATE FOREIGN KEY FARKEY
```

When a primary key is deactivated, the foreign keys referencing it are also affected because they are no longer checked for validity. To protect the table from corruption **a foreign key is implicitly deactivated when its referenced primary key is deactivated.**

Deactivating a key does not imply a lack of concern for the constraint represented by that key but it is rather a temporary measure usually used to process mass inserts or deletes in a more efficient manner. The SQL/DS system, therefore, does not allow free access to the table or tables involved in a *referential relationship* when a key is deactivated.

Deactivating a primary or foreign key may have a profound negative impact on the response of those applications trying to access the tables involved. Great care should be taken when deactivating keys. When either type of key is deactivated **both** become inactive and can cause bottlenecks in the system.

When the primary key is reactivated, the foreign keys which only became inactive as a result of the inactivation of the primary key, are automatically reactivated. To reactivate a key the following command may be used:

    ALTER TABLE PRIMTBL ACTIVATE PRIMARY KEY

or

    ALTER TABLE PRIMTBL ACTIVATE ALL

When a foreign key is explicitly deactivated it can only become active again when it is explicitly reactivated. The following commands may be used to reactivate a foreign key:

    ALTER TABLE PRIMTBL ACTIVATE FOREIGN KEY JUSTAKEY
    ALTER TABLE PRIMTBL ACTIVATE ALL

When to Drop and When to Deactivate

All keys may be dropped and re-created at a later time. Keys are dropped and added by specifying:

    ALTER TABLE DEPARTMENT DROP PRIMARY KEY
    ALTER TABLE DEPARTMENT ADD PRIMARY KEY(DEPT_NO)

When a key is dropped, it is a sign that the application developer is no longer interested in the referential constraint represented by that key, and it is removed. If a primary key is dropped, the unique index that was automatically created is dropped and the foreign keys dependent on this primary key are dropped. The values in the foreign key columns, however, are not touched but they are no longer checked. This process should rarely be initiated during peak processing periods.

Dropping a key does not make the table inaccessible to other users; it just removes any constraints. It is used only:

1. When a constraint is no longer required.
2. To avoid performance degradation when mass inserts are needed yet users need to retain access to the table. The users retain their ability to access, but referential constraints no longer exist to be checked. When the table is again altered and the key re-created, the system will check to ensure that any values added to the column are matching values. Foreign keys will have to be re-created.

Instead of dropping a key, the user might decide to deactivate it. Deactivation is more restrictive than dropping a key. It is used when:

1. A constraint is still needed but a mass insert is required. The owner of the constraint, for example, can deactivate the primary key to drop the index so as to improve insert performance. When the insert is completed, the key is reactivated and a new unique index will be automatically created. A foreign key might also be deactivated to prevent the checking of the primary key for each insert.
2. No access should be available to users until the key is reactivated.
3. The tables with foreign keys referencing this primary key should also be unavailable to users.

The impact of deactivation on performance and response times is too great to allow its use during peak processing periods unless absolutely necessary. When a key is deactivated, the system will return the message:

-668 The table ----- is inactive and cannot be accessed

REORGANIZING THE PRIMARY INDEX

When the DBA decides that the unique index created when a primary key was specified requires reorganization, there is no need to deactivate and activate it. Simply specifying:

ALTER TABLE PRIMTBL   **ACTIVATE** PRIMARY KEY

causes the old unique index, if one exists, to be dropped and a new one to be created. Keep in mind that this will also invalidate access modules dependent upon this index or referential constraint.

Added Overhead

If the SET NULL delete rule is in effect when a primary key is deleted, both the table with the primary key and all tables with foreign keys referencing this primary key are updated. The primary key table row is deleted and the column or columns of the foreign key table(s) are updated to NULL. **All** nullable columns in the foreign key are set to NULL. This implies that if this rule is specified, at least one column in the index must be nullable.

Care should be taken to only make those columns nullable where the user wants the rows to be modified to NULL when the primary key is deleted. Otherwise columns in the key that are needed might be modified to NULLs. When many rows, even in many tables, have, for example, a DEPT_NO as a foreign key that is deleted from the *parent table*, they will **all** be updated. Thus the delete of one row in a table may result in the update of hundreds or thousands of rows in *dependent tables*. The impact on performance should be readily apparent.

When CASCADE is specified, all of the rows from *dependent tables* will be deleted when the primary key row is deleted. This may also negatively impact performance when there are many rows with a foreign key referencing the deleted primary key.

INDEXES ON FOREIGN KEYS

Indexes are **not** automatically generated on foreign keys nor are they required when a foreign key is defined but, for performance reasons, **an index should be created on each foreign key.** It should contain the same columns as the foreign key in the same sequence of columns so as to avoid DBSPACE or nonselective table scans when internal SELECTS are generated.

Indexes on foreign keys are also useful to avoid deadlock situations and to minimize lock contention. The index may also include extra columns that are not part of the foreign key.

REFERENTIAL RELATIONSHIP SUPPORT

The **GRANT** command has been modified to include a new parameter, REFERENCE, which allows the grantee to use the ALTER parameter to add, activate, and deactivate primary and foreign keys. To give the user, DOV1, for example, authority to reference this table when adding foreign keys in other tables and to manipulate primary and foreign keys on this table, the following GRANT command may be specified:

GRANT ALTER, **REFERENCE** ON PERSONNEL_TBL TO DOV1

When any table is altered to add, drop, activate, or deactivate a key, any access modules with a dependency on this key will be marked invalid.

During **DBSU** UNLOAD, indexes marked as primary key indexes will not be unloaded, but they will automatically be re-created when the table is reloaded. If the DBSU RELOAD TABLE with the NEW option is run, none of the keys, indexes, or referential constraints will be re-created for the new table. Use the NEW option with extreme care.

When a table is reloaded by the DBSU with the PURGE option as shown in the following example:

RELOAD TABLE PERSONNEL_TBL PURGE . . . . . . **etc.**

All active primary and foreign keys will be deactivated and the foreign key indexes information will be saved.

All indexes, except primary indexes, will be dropped and their definitions saved.

All the rows of the object tables will be deleted.

All the data will be reloaded.

The **FIRST** clustering index will be re-created.

The primary key will be activated and if there is no FIRST index it will become the FIRST index.

The remaining indexes (if any) will be created.

The referential constraints deactivated by the first step, except for primary keys, will remain inactive until the user selectively activates them.

The meaning of some **SQLERRD** fields has been changed. SQLERRD(3) will contain the number of rows changed by INSERT, UPDATE, or DELETE and SQLERRD(5) will contain the number of dependent rows affected by a DELETE or UPDATE. It includes the number of rows SET NULL or deleted due to the CASCADE option.

When the table is not part of a referential structure, SQLERRD(5) will be set to zero.

The **EXPLAIN** command has been expanded to include in its calculations the statements internally generated for *referential integrity* processing. The EXPLAIN tables contain this information, when it is applicable, in rows with the contents of the QUERYNO column incremented by **+1**. It is recommended, therefore, that query numbers be set in increments of 10 or 100 so that the referential constraint information will be readily visible (11, 21, etc.).

Assuming that the ACCT_TBL has a primary key associated with a foreign key in the TRANS_TBL with a constraint of RESTRICT and an account number is to be deleted:

```
EXPLAIN ALL SET QUERYNO = 500 FOR
     DELETE FROM ACCT_TBL
        WHERE ACCTNO = 35247
```

An internal SELECT of the TRANS_TBL will be required to verify that there are no transactions for accntno 35247. Some of the columns in the PLAN_TABLE, for example, might look like this:

QUERYNO	CREATOR	TNAME	ACCESSTYPE	ACCESSNAME
50	GILOR	ACCT_TBL	I	ACCT_INX
51	GILOR	TRANS_TBL	W	TRAN_IX1A

QUERYNO 51 was a generated query against the TRANS_TBL to ensure that no transactions existed for this account. The ACCESSTYPE 'W', which may indicate a performance problem, is discussed in Chapter 6.

SOME ADDITIONAL COMMENTS

When a column of a *dependent table* is shared by two or more foreign keys:

Foreign Key 1 $\Rightarrow$ Columns 5, 8, **13**
Foreign Key 2 $\Rightarrow$ Columns 7, **13**, 15

the shared column(s) should be defined as NOT NULL. This will prevent the primary key referential constraint of one of the foreign keys from setting the column to NULL. If, for example, column 13 is **not** defined as NOT NULL and one or both of the foreign keys is defined with the SET NULL option, when Primary key 1 is deleted SQL/DS will set column 13 to NULL. When one column of a foreign key becomes NULL, the entire key is considered null. As a result of foreign key 1 becoming null, foreign key 2 became null and foreign key 2 is no longer considered a dependent of its primary key.

When a column is both a foreign key and part of a primary key, some primary key restrictions apply to the foreign key. The column, for example, may **not** be nullable.

The performance rule is that **more columns than are absolutely necessary should never be SELECTed or UPDATEed.** This is especially true with columns involved in *referential integrity.* Avoid the unnecessary updating of columns that are part of a primary or foreign key.

Do **not** create indexes on primary keys. This is very wasteful because a unique index is created automatically when the table is created or altered and the referential definition added.

The recommended sequence of specifying primary and foreign keys is as follows:

1. Create tables but do not specify keys.
2. Load all of the data into the tables (it is more efficient to insert rows when no indexes exist on the tables).
3. If the primary index is not to be the clustering index, CREATE the FIRST index.
4. Add the definition of the primary keys by using the ALTER TABLE command. A unique index will automatically be created.
5. Create indexes on the foreign key columns and on any other columns desired.
6. Add the foreign keys by using the ALTER TABLE command.

This procedure reduces load time and index page splits. Once the *referential relationship*s are in place, SQL/DS will check that they are valid. If there are duplicate keys in the primary key column or if a foreign key value does not match a primary key value, the ALTER will fail. Prior to altering the table the DBA can issue the following SELECT to check for duplicates:

```
SELECT ACCTNO, COUNT(*)
    FROM ACCT_TBL
        GROUP BY ACCTNO
            HAVING COUNT(*) > 1
```

To find the foreign keys that do not have valid primary key values, the DBA should specify:

```
SELECT ACCTNO
       FROM TRANS_TBL T
             WHERE ACCTNO IS NOT NULL
             AND NOT EXISTS
                   (SELECT 'A' FROM ACCT_TBL A
                          WHERE A.ACCTNO = T.ACCTNO)
```

COMBINATIONS

Referential constraint implies that a value may only exist in a *dependent table* when a matching value exists in the *parent table*. The *referential constraints* might be used to ensure that combinations of columns are valid. When a specific transaction may only be carried out on a certain type of bond, for example, a *referential constraint* can be used to enforce the restriction:

BOND TYPE	TRANSACTION TYPE	
Government	Buy	
Government	Sell	
Corporation	Swap	
Corporation	Sell	etc.

The primary key may consist of a two column key:

```
BOND_TYPE, TRANSACTION_TYPE
```

and only that combination of security transaction will be allowed.

ADVANTAGES OF REFERENTIAL INTEGRITY

The main advantage of *referential integrity* in a production system is that the end-users may no longer introduce inconsistencies into the tables. All of the checking is done by the system and it does not depend upon code in each application program. In the past, every program had to have a SELECT and the attendant code to ensure that only valid account numbers or part numbers were entered by receiving clerks or tellers. With referential integrity no code is required in any program. The DBA just has to define the connection as referring to a primary and foreign key and SQL/DS will ensure the integrity.

The application developer is freed from coding and debugging the many routines which test these integrity situations. Referential integrity may also be introduced on old tables without having to modify existing applications. The following ALTER TABLE command adds a foreign key and specifies a *delete rule* restricting the deletion of a primary key in the *parent table*s as long as rows in this table exist with matching values:

```
ALTER TABLE TRANSACTION_TBL
    ADD FOREIGN KEY ACCT_NO
    REFERENCES ACCT_TBL
    ON DELETE RESTRICT
```

This will alter the TRANSACTION_TBL and make the Acct_No a foreign key that has to match a value in the ACCT_TBL. If an attempt is made to delete the primary key associated with any row in the TRANSACTION_TBL, a return code will indicate to the user that the row may not be deleted until all foreign keys matching the primary key are deleted. Old programs will not usually be affected if an automatically defined index on a primary key replaces an old, manually created, index. Additional code, however, may be required to check the return codes if the applications DELETE rows from tables involved in *referential relationships*.

PERFORMANCE

When a user plans to include user-enforced *referential integrity* rules similar to those built into SQL/DS in an application, it is usually preferable to use the built-in functions. If the user does not enforce integrity rules and does not need the function, *referential integrity* should **not** be used. A single multi-row DELETE command is more efficient, for example, than the use of the SQL/DS CASCADE function.

When using *referential constraints* some additional overhead will occur during preprocessing and dynamic execution because the new catalog tables will have to be accessed and the *referential constraints* will have to be included in the access module. The fact that *referential constraint* checking is done at precompile time implies that an *independent table* with no primary or foreign keys will be accessed as efficiently by an application program as it was accessed before *referential integrity* was introduced. The new system tables are only referenced when *referential integrity* is active for an application table.

SYSTEM CATALOGS

Recent versions of SQL/DS have added two new system catalogs and several new columns to some existing catalog tables. These catalogs and columns contain information to help plan the definition of primary and foreign keys and to avoid performance degradation. Some of the columns and new tables are:

SYSTEM.SYSKEYS - Contains one row for every primary and foreign key in the system.

KEYTYPE - Indicates primary(P) or foreign key(F).

TNAME/TCREATOR - Standard table name and creator.

REFTNAME/REFTCREATOR - The *parent table* name if this is a foreign key.

STATUS - Indicates active (A) or inactive (I or D) key.

DELETERULE - For a foreign key, what should be done when the primary key is deleted - Restrict, Cascade, or Set NULL.

SYSTEM.SYSKEYCOLS - Contains one row for every column in every primary and foreign key in the system. A column may appear more than once in this table when it is part of more than one key.

KEYTYPE - Primary (P) or foreign (F).

KEYNAME - The name given to a foreign key or the generated key for a primary or foreign key.

KEYORD - The position of this column in the key.

TABLEORD - The position of this column in the table.

SYSTEM.SYSCATALOG - Three columns to describe the *referential relationship*s of each table have been added.

PARENTS - The number of parents that this dependent table has?

DEPENDENTS - The number of dependents that this parent table has?

INACTIVE - The number of inactive keys in this table.

SYSTEM.SYSINDEXES - A column was added to indicate if this index was generated for a primary key.

KEYTYPE - Blank if not a primary key. 'P' if primary and active, 'I' if inactive.

SYSTEM.SYSTABAUTH - Two columns were added to this table to indicate new user privileges

ALTERAUTH - Is the user allowed to alter the table? Can the user GRANT this authority to others?

REFAUTH - Can the user create, drop, or activate foreign keys referencing this table? Can this authority also be granted to others?

It is important to ensure that indexes on the foreign keys are used by the optimizer and that excessive locking of *dependent table*s does not occur.

The command to determine which tables have primary keys and which columns are part of that key is:

```
SELECT K.TNAME, K.TCREATOR, C.KEYORD, C.CNAME, K.KEYNAME,
           K.INAME, K.KEYCOLS
    FROM SYSTEM.SYSKEYS K, SYSTEM.SYSKEYCOLS C
       WHERE K.KEYTYPE = 'P' AND
             K.KEYNAME = C.KEYNAME
    ORDER BY 1,2,4
```

The keyname for a primary key will start with the letters 'PKEY' and will be followed by a 12 position timestamp in base 35 notation. The foreign key will either have the name used to create it or a default name starting with 'FKEY' followed by a timestamp as indicated above. The command to determine which tables have foreign keys and which columns are part of that key is:

```
SELECT K.TNAME, K.TCREATOR, C.KEYORD, C.CNAME, K.KEYNAME,
           K.REFTNAME, K.DELETERULE, K.KEYCOLS
    FROM SYSTEM.SYSKEYS K, SYSTEM.SYSKEYCOLS C
       WHERE K.KEYTYPE = 'F' AND
             K.KEYNAME = C.KEYNAME
    ORDER BY 1,2,4
```

SUMMARY

Referential integrity allows the user to define relationships between column values in different tables. Referential integrity prevents the user from introducing inconsistencies into the data and relieves the application programmer of the responsibility for coding this function. Every environment using the SQL/DS database is required to adhere to the referential rules.

SQL/DS enforces *referential integrity* by utilizing the concepts of primary and foreign keys and creates a unique index on the primary key to prevent duplication. It also introduces *referential constraint*s to control deletion of primary keys. There can only be one primary key on a table. The primary key index is a special index created automatically by the system and cannot be dropped by the table creator or by the DBA. Indexes on foreign keys are useful to avoid deadlock situations and to minimize lock contention.

In order to provide a means of defining *referential relationships,* extensions have been added to the CREATE table and ALTER table commands. The table with a primary key becomes a *parent table* to other "dependent" tables that contain a foreign key. Foreign keys have user-given names because there may be several foreign keys on one table. When a foreign key is added to a table, the delete rule is specified. The delete rule may be: CASCADE, SET NULL, or RESTRICT. When SET NULL or CASCADE is the delete rule, a delete of one row of a *parent table* may result in large numbers of rows being deleted or updated in *dependent tables*. A single multi-row DELETE command is more efficient than the use of the SQL/DS CASCADE function.

A *parent table* referenced by a foreign key of a *dependent table* must exist before a foreign key is defined.

Primary and foreign keys may be deactivated. When a key is deactivated, *referential integrity* rules on that key are no longer applied by the system. When a primary key is deactivated, the foreign keys referencing it are also deactivated. When a foreign key is deactivated, its primary key is deactivated. Deactivating a primary or foreign key may have a profound impact on the response of those applications trying to access the tables involved.

When the primary key is reactivated, the foreign keys which became inactive only because the primary key made them inactive, are automatically reactivated.

The GRANT command has been modified to include a new parameter, REFERENCE, and to expand the function of the ALTER parameter to enable the user to add, activate, and deactivate primary and foreign keys. When any table is altered to add, drop, activate, or deactivate a key, any access modules with a dependency on this key will be marked invalid. The EXPLAIN command has been expanded to include in its calculations the statements internally generated for *referential integrity* processing.

Two new system catalogs have been added to contain information about primary and foreign keys.

RECOMMENDATIONS

1. A referential structure is not recommended unless it is needed.
2. A primary key should be composed of columns that usually are never updated and should contain the minimum number of columns needed to uniquely identify the row.
3. The creation of a primary key should usually be done during nonpeak processing periods.
4. A primary key definition should **not** be specified on a CREATE TABLE command. The table should be created and loaded with data and then the primary key should be defined using the ALTER TABLE command.
5. Two tables that are *parent tables* to each other are difficult to UPDATE or DELETE and this complexity should be avoided.
6. The impact of deactivation on performance and response time is too great to allow its use during peak processing periods. When either type of key is deactivated, both become inactive and can cause bottlenecks in the system.
7. An index should be created on each foreign key. Do **not** create indexes on primary keys. This is very wasteful because a unique index is created automatically.
8. When a primary key requires reorganization, simply ACTIVATE PRIMARY KEY.

CHAPTER 5

Some New and Useful Functions

In recent versions of SQL/DS, several new functions have been introduced that have improved the *user friendliness* of SQL/DS by extending the functions of the SQL language. These include CONCATENATE, SCALAR functions, and KEYWORD PAIRS. Scalar functions permit the translation of a value from one format into another format or the extraction of one element of a value such as the *day* part of a date. There are some limitations to the use of scalar functions. LONG VARCHAR columns, for example, can only be used with the SUBSTR and LENGTH functions, but scalar functions and concatenate may otherwise be used wherever expressions are allowed (except in an IN list). The scalar functions are applied to a **single value** and may be used wherever an expression may be used even as an argument in another scalar function, except where noted. Among the functions are:

CHAR	DATE	DAY(S)	DECIMAL
HEX	HOUR	INTEGER	LENGTH
MICROSECOND	MINUTE	MONTH	SECOND
STRIP	TIMESTAMP	SUBSTR	TRANSLATE
VALUE	VARGRAPHIC	YEAR	TIME
DIGITS	FLOAT		

These functions are included in this book because they are new and very useful. Yet, despite their enhancing the SQL language, **scalar functions should be used sparingly and only when actually needed.** This is especially true when they are used as part of a WHERE clause (predicate). When scalar functions are part of the predicate, the predicate **cannot** be used as a search argument and **cannot** be used with an index.

CONCATENATION

Concatenation is a new SQL/DS operator that is used to combine two columns and is indicated via the || symbol. If the ID_PREFIX is 'R', for example, and the first ID is '0437A', then:

```
SELECT ID_PREFIX || ID, DEPT, etc.
      FROM USER_TBL
             WHERE NAME = 'SI' || :SUFFXFLD
```

will yield 'R0437A'. If SUFFXFLD contains 'LVER' then NAME = 'SILVER' is the predicate.

The operands to be concatenated must all be character compatible (CHAR, VARCHAR, DATE, TIME, TIMESTAMP). If either operand in the concatenation is NULL, the result is NULL. When VARCHAR operands are used, the actual length is used rather than the greatest possible length but when CHAR is used, the full length is used, even if padded with blanks. If two fields are concatenated as follows:

```
VARA || VARB
```

and VARA is defined as VARCHAR(8) and contains 'BAR' and VARB is defined as VARCHAR(6) and contains 'DOV1', the result of the above concatenation is 'BARDOV1'. If VARA is defined as CHAR(8) and VARB is defined as CHAR(6), the result is:

```
'BAR        DOV1 '
```

The maximum defined length of the two variables concatenated to each other may not be greater than 254. This means that if a column is defined as VARCHAR (200) and contains 'ARIEL' its actual length is 5 but its defined length is 200. It could not be concatenated to a column or field defined as VARCHAR(55).

SUBSTRING

The substring function is a scalar function that allows the user to indicate that only part of the string should be used as the value. For example, if the host variable :BEGIN contains a 6 and :LENGTH holds a 3 and the column CITY contains:

```
CITY = '10001NYCBROOKLYN'
```

the conditional clause which states:

SUBSTR(CITY, :BEGIN, :LENGTH)

uses the substring which starts at position six for a length of three bytes and the result is "NYC." LONG VARCHAR columns may be used with the SUBSTR scalar function as long as the result is less than 254. This is a problem when host variables are used to contain the length value. The optimizer has no way of knowing the value of the length in the host variable so it assumes that the host variable contains a value equal to the defined length of the column. The defined length of a LONG VARCHAR column is greater than 254. To be able to use the substring function on LONG VARCHAR columns, the strategy is to first extract the 254 bytes containing the substring and then to extract the actual value desired. The following example which requests a substring of a substring demonstrates how substrings of LONG VARCHAR columns can be extracted:

WHERE ACOL = SUBSTR(**SUBSTR(LONGCOL, :BEGIN,254**), 1, :LENGTH)

The inner substring starts at the starting position value of BEGIN for a length of 254 and thereby limits the length of the result value to 254. The outer substring is then evaluated and it too starts at the value in BEGIN for a length of the value in LENGTH.

DIGITS, DECIMAL, INTEGER, FLOAT, AND HEX

The DIGITS function is very useful because in previous releases of SQL/DS, when no calculations were performed on them, many application tables were designed with numerical values in character format columns. If tables designed at a later time contain numeric data in matching columns, the DIGITS function can be used to convert the numeric columns (SMALLINT, INTEGER, DECI-MAL) into character format for comparison with these character columns.

A new table, for example, has a six-digit identification number in an integer column while the old table has the identification in two columns of character data in the following format:

NEWCOL   ⇒ **INTEGER**   OLDPREFIX ⇒ **CHAR 1**

OLDCOL   ⇒ **CHAR 5**

The comparison of the data in the two tables can be done using the following condition:

WHERE **DIGITS**(NEWCOL) = **OLDPREFIX||OLDCOL**

Similar functions were added to convert a string value to HEX equivalent or to convert any numeric value to decimal, integer, or floating point, as shown in the following examples:

DECIMAL(colname,4,2) ⟹ will convert a numeric value in a column or an expression into a decimal value with the precision and scale indicated. If colname contains 2456, the result of this function is 24.56.

INTEGER(expression) ⟹ will convert a non-integer numeric value (or an integer) into an integer. For example, if the condition clause states:

WHERE INTFLD = INTEGER (DECFLD * 2.3)

and DECfld contains 5.4, the result is:

(5.4 * 2.3) = 22.42   (i.e.   WHERE INTFLD = 22).

If the number needs to be rounded, the following example should be used:

WHERE INTFLD = **INTEGER** ((DECFLD * 2.3) + .5)

FLOAT(expression) ⟹ will convert a numeric expression into a double precision floating-point value.

HEX(string) ⟹ will convert a string of up to 127 characters or numbers into a HEX character string and the result will be twice as long as the original string.

TRANSLATE

TRANSLATE is a very powerful function. It can be used to:

1. Correctly SORT mixed lower and upper case.
2. Reorder characters in a string.

3. Translate a string to upper case.

4. Change some characters into different characters.

The format of TRANSLATE is:

TRANSLATE(STRINGCOL, TOSTRING, FROMSTRING, FILL)

To translate lowercase characters to uppercase only the first stringcol value is required. The *tostring* parameter defaults to upper-case of the characters specified in SYSTEM.SYSCHARSETS. The use of this function will solve the problem of matching names or other data in a table where upper and lower case characters were mixed. For example:

MacDavid Macdavid macdavid MACDAVID

To match these names to a constant value the user would specify:

WHERE **TRANSLATE**(COLUMNNAME) = 'MACDAVID'

In whatever way the name was written in the table it would be translated to upper case and compared to the constant. It should be remembered that while it is convenient to use this function, it may result in poor performance because an index will not be used on this predicate and a DBSPACE scan may be required. This potential for poor performance exists in **every** instance where a scalar function is used on a column value in a predicate.

Translate can also be used to change one character to a different character as, for example, to translate the letter '*' to an 'E', use:

TRANSLATE (:HOSTFLD, 'E', '*')

If the input string was:

*V*RY GOOD BOY DO*S FIN*

the output would be:

EVERY GOOD BOY DOES FINE

STRIP

The STRIP scalar function allows the user to remove leading and/or trailing characters (usually blanks or zeros) from a column value.

If, for example, the total salary, TOTAL_SAL, was stored in the PERSONNEL_TBL in character format, CHAR(7), and the value in the column was '0053000', the user could request the return of the value with the leading zeros removed:

```
SELECT   STRIP(TOTAL_SAL,L,'0'), . . . etc.
     FROM PERSONNEL_TBL
```

The result would be "53000." If by mistake the user specified that both leading and trailing should be stripped 'B':

```
SELECT STRIP(TOTAL_SAL,B,'0'), . . . etc.
     FROM PERSONNEL_TBL
```

the result would be 53. The result of STRIP is always a VARCHAR value. To compare a name in a VARCHAR column, USER_NAME defined as VARCHAR(25), the user might specify:

```
SELECT . . . . . . .    FROM PERSONNEL_TBL
     WHERE STRIP(USER_NAME,B,' ') = 'AMIAD'
```

In general the strip command is not needed when CHAR is compared to a VARCHAR because SQL/DS will pad the CHAR before the comparison. When VARCHAR is compared to a VARCHAR value, they are **not** padded. The only time STRIP would be necessary is if the VARCHAR column value were specified with leading or trailing blanks when inserted into the column. In that case, SQL/DS includes the blanks in the length and returns the value with the blanks, and the VARCHAR values would not match. If a VARCHAR colume containing 'AMIAD' were compared to the USER_NAME column updated as follows:

```
UPDATE PERSONNEL_TBL    SET USER_NAME = '   AMIAD '
```

they would **not** match.

LENGTH

When a user needs to know the length of a column value, the LENGTH scalar value may be used. It returns the length of the value rather than the value itself. As mentioned in the description of the STRIP command, if blanks are included in the VARCHAR column when the value is inserted, they will be included in the length count; otherwise the function will return the actual length of the value found in the column or constant:

LENGTH ('   SHILO') = (5 LETTERS + 3 BLANKS) = **8**

The length of DATE, TIME, or TIMESTAMP column values is the internal length (DATE is 4, TIME is 3, etc.). To receive the actual length of a DATE value, the user might specify:

LENGTH (**CHAR**(DATECOL))

VALUE

The VALUE function examines each of the expressions in the parentheses and returns the first one that is not NULL. Assuming, for example, that the USER_ID is a nullable column, the expression:

VALUE (USER_ID, 'THE USER ID WAS NOT FOUND')

would either return the USER_ID value or, if it were NULL, would return the constant 'THE USER ID WAS NOT FOUND.'

The result of a value scalar depends upon the types of values being tested. When two DATE columns are tested, as in the following example:

VALUE (*DATECOLX, DATECOLY*)

the result is a date. If one of the values in the test was not a date, however, the result would be in character format. The following VALUE will not produce a DATE result:

VALUE (*CHARCOLX, DATECOLY*)

even when the first value is NULL.

DATE, TIME, TIMESTAMP, AND DURATION

The introduction of date, time, and timestamp data types, durations, and functions has made it easier to handle date and time arithmetic calculations and to stamp transactions with a timestamp. Columns can be defined with the attribute DATE, TIME, or TIMESTAMP, for example, and SQL/DS will handle it properly:

CREATE TABLE PERSONNEL_TBL (USER_ID CHAR (8), STRT_DATE
DATE, STRT_TIME **TIME**, LAST_USE **TIMESTAMP**)

These column values can also be used in arithmetical expressions as will be shown later in the chapter. DATE and TIME column values may be used with the MIN and MAX built-in functions even though they are not numeric column types. They cannot be used with AVG or SUM or with the LIKE function.

The DATE, TIME, and TIMESTAMP functions are used to transform an expression or column value into a DATE, TIME, or TIMESTAMP. Valid examples of these functions are:

DATE('1991-03-10')   **DATE**(TIMESTMPCOL)   **DATE**(:HOSTDTE)
TIME('10.15.19')   **TIME**(TIMESTMPCOL)   **TIME**(:HOSTTME)
TIMESTAMP('1991-03-10-10.15.19.000000')
TIMESTAMP(:HOSTDTE, :HOSTTME)

The resulting value from DATE and time arithmetic calculations, however, is sometimes a bit tricky. Care should be taken to ensure that the value expected is the value received. For example, if END_DATE has the DATE equivalent of January 1, 1990 and the SELECT is:

SELECT END_DATE + DECIMAL(00010101,8,0)

the result is February, 2, 1991 (one year, one month, and one day are added, as will be explained later in this section). The above SELECT contains a DATE and a DATE duration.

Date Function and Column Type

There is a DATE function, a DATE column type, and a DATE duration. A DATE value designates a particular day in a calendar year ranging from January 1, 0001 to December 31, 9999. It is a three-part value based on the Gregorian Calendar and designates a point in time. The year part of the DATE is a value from 0001 to 9999, the month is a value from 1 to 12, and the day is a value from 1 to 31 (depending upon the month). The Gregorian Calendar began in **1600** and the results of calculations **before** that year may **not** be accurate. Two DATE values may be subtracted but **not** added. The result of subtracting two dates is a DATE duration and not a DATE value. Date values may be in any of the following formats:

09/30/1991   1991-09-30   30.09.1991

The DATE function extracts a DATE value from a TIMESTAMP, a numeric expression, a seven-digit Julian DATE, a DATE string, or a DATE value in a DATE column type. The format of the function is:

DATE (expression)

When the expression is a TIMESTAMP column type:

"TIMSTMP_COL"

containing the value

'1991-09-30-15.05.30.000000',

the result is:

DATE (*TIMSTMP_COL*) ⇒   '1991-09-30'

When the expression is a numeric expression, the expression represents the number of days since January 1, 0001. The smallest acceptable value would be equivalent to the lowest DATE possible:

DATE (1)   ⇒   '0001-01-01'

and the largest number acceptable would be equivalent to the highest DATE value:

DATE (3652059)   ⇒   '9999-12-31'

When the expression is a valid Julian DATE in character format, the result is a valid DATE value:

DATE ('1991001')   ⇒   '1991-01-01'

When the expression is a DATE character string it yields, of course, a DATE value:

DATE ('1991-11-13') ⇒   '1991-11-13'

When the expression is a DATE column type the result will be a DATE value. It is a waste to use the DATE scalar function on a DATE column type. If STRT_DATE, for example, held '1991-11-23':

DATE (STRT_DATE)   ⇒   '1991-11-23'

Keep in mind that when a DATE function finds a literal numeric constant with**out** quotation marks, it assumes that it is a numeric expression. This implies that:

DATE (1990-01-01)

specifies that the value 01 should be subtracted twice from 1990 to yield 1988 and the function should return the DATE that is equivalent to the 1,988th day since January 1, 0001. The user, therefore, should make sure that the quotation marks are included whenever a DATE constant is specified.

A DATE column type is defined in the CREATE TABLE command:

CREATE TABLE PERSONNEL_TBL (USER_ID CHAR(8), . .
    STRT_DTE **DATE,** END_DTE **DATE**)

When a DATE column is to be used in an application program it should be defined as a ten character field despite the fact that internally it is only 4 bytes. In COBOL, for example, STRT_DTE would be defined:

01   STRT-DTE-COL   PIC **X(10)**.

Time Function and Column Type

There is a TIME function, a TIME column type, and a TIME duration. A TIME column value designates a point in time on a 24 hour clock. It is a three-part value consisting of HOURS (00-24), MINUTES (00-59), and SECONDS (00-59). 24.00.00 and 00.00.00 are equivalent and both are valid. A TIME value of 24.00.00 + 1 SECOND will yield 00.00.01.

The TIME function extracts a TIME value from a TIMESTAMP, a TIME character string, or a TIME value in a TIME column type. The format of the function is:

TIME (expression)

When the expression is a TIMESTAMP column type:
"TIMSTMP_COL"

containing the value
'1991-09-30-15.05.30.000000',

the result is:

TIME (TIMSTMP_COL) ⇒ '15.05.30'

A TIME character string will yield a TIME value:

TIME ('4:15 PM')   ⇒   '04.15.00'

When the expression is a TIME column type, the TIME function will yield the same TIME value. This is a wasted use of the scalar function but it works. If STRT_TIME held '04.15.00':

TIME (STRT_TIME)   ⇒   '04.15.00'

A TIME column type is defined in the CREATE TABLE command:

CREATE TABLE PERSONNEL_TBL (USER_ID CHAR(8), . .
    STRT_TIME **TIME,** END_TIME **TIME)**

When a TIME column is to be used in an application program it should be defined as a eight character field despite the fact that internally it is only 3 bytes. In COBOL, for example, STRT_DTE would be defined:

01   STRT-TIME-COL   **PIC   X(8)**.

TIMESTAMP

There is a TIMESTAMP function and a TIMESTAMP column type but **there is no TIMESTAMP duration.** A TIMESTAMP column data type designates a specific time on a specific day. It is a three-part value consisting of a DATE, a TIME, and a microsecond (000000-999999).

The TIMESTAMP function is used to translate a DATE and a TIME, a TIMESTAMP value or expression, a compressed DATE and TIME, a store clock string, or a TIMESTAMP column value into a TIMESTAMP value. The format of the function is:

TIMESTAMP (DATE expression, TIME expression) or
TIMESTAMP (TIMESTAMP expression)

When the expression includes a DATE and a TIME, the result is a TIMESTAMP value. When STRT_DATE contains '1991-10-12' and STRT_TIME contains '15.05.30':

TIMESTAMP (STRT_DATE, STRT_TIME)
            ⇒   '1991-10-12-15.05.30.000000'

When the expression is a TIMESTAMP column, the TIMESTAMP value is returned. This is a wasteful use of the function but it works:

```
TIMESTAMP (TIMSTMP_COL)
          ⇒    '1991-10-12-15.05.30.000000'
```

When the expression is a TIMESTAMP literal, the result is a TIMESTAMP value:

```
TIMESTAMP ('1991-10-12-15.05.30.000000')
          ⇒    '1991-10-12-15.05.30.000000'
```

When the expression is a compressed DATE, the result is a TIMESTAMP value. A compressed DATE and TIME omits the '-' and the '.' and the microseconds. It is a 14 byte character string:

```
TIMESTAMP ('19911912150530')
          ⇒    '1991-10-12-15.05.30.000000'
```

When the expression is a store clock value, the result is a TIMESTAMP value. A store clock value is an 8 byte Hex value and it assumes a value between 1900 and 2042. The X'0' value, for example, corresponds to '1900-01-01-00.00.00.000000'.

Programming Note

The use of DATE, TIME, and TIMESTAMP in a table has to be planned because neither blanks nor zeros are acceptable values for DATE or TIMESTAMP columns and zeros is a valid TIME. Allowing the column to be NULLable is one alternative. When the DBA wants to use the more efficient NOT NULL format, an installation must decide which default value will be used to designate the absence of a value. As a default DATE a company might use 9999-01-01 and for a default TIME they might use 24.00.00. Each program will have to check for this default value and substitute blanks or a message, when printing reports, that the TIME or DATE is missing.

DURATION

Duration represents an interval of TIME expressed as a decimal number. There are three types of duration: simple duration, DATE duration, and TIME duration. Timestamps **cannot** be subtracted so there is no TIMESTAMP duration. A simple duration is a two-part constant value consisting of a number followed by a keyword:

```
3 YEARS          15 HOURS          700 MINUTES
2 MONTHS         :TDAY DAYS        (MCOL + 2) MICROSECONDS
```

The absence of a DURATION datatype limits the operations that these durations can be used for. Simple durations can**not** be stored in a column. The following UPDATE, for example, is **not** valid:

```
UPDATE .... SET SPECOL = 1 MONTH
```

Simple durations also can**not** be compared because there is no column type that is a duration. A duration also can**not** be used as shown in the following WHERE clause:

```
WHERE WEEKCOL > 2 WEEKS
```

Simple durations can**not** be added or subtracted to each other and the following is also invalid:

```
WHERE DATECOL + (1 MONTH + 3 DAYS) < ......
```

Simple durations can be added to or subtracted from a DATE value in a column so that both of the following are valid:

```
WHERE DATECOL + 1 MONTH < ......
     AND (DATECOL + 1 MONTH) + 2 DAYS > ...
```

An integer can**not** be added to a DATE or TIME because the system cannot know what is meant. Therefore:

```
DATECOL + 2
```

is **invalid** while:

```
DATECOL + (2 + 3) DAYS
```

is valid but:

```
DATECOL + (2 + 3 DAYS)
```

is **invalid.** The keywords are considered before the arithmetical operations so it is important to specify parenthesis to insure accuracy.

Be aware that adding or subtracting durations from dates, times, and TIMESTAMPs may result in overflow conditions. When twelve hours, for example, are added to a TIMESTAMP, the day, month, and year may also change. If TIMESTCOL contains '1991-12-31-18.01.01.000100' :

```
SELECT (TIMESTCOL + 12 HOURS), . . . . . . . . . .
```

The result will be '1992-01-01-06.01.01.000100'. A change to seconds, minutes, hours, day, month, and year will occur with the addition of one microsecond to:

```
'1991-12-31-23.59.59.999999'
```

A DATE duration is a decimal number with a precision of 8 and a scale of 0. It has a structure of *yyyymmdd* where *yyyy* is the number of years, *mm* is the number of months, and *dd* is the number of days. That is why the 00010101 in the example earlier was equivalent to one year, one month, and one day and not 10,101. The DATE duration must be decimal. It is **not** valid to specify:

```
SELECT END_DATE + 00010101
```

because 00010101 is not a decimal number, but if a decimal point were added:

```
SELECT END_DATE + 00010101. FROM PERSONNEL_TBL
```

SQL/DS would assume that it was a decimal value constant and it would be valid.

While there is no DURATION datatype, as explained earlier, the DBA may create a table with a column defined as a DECIMAL(8,0), a DECIMAL(6,0), or as an INTEGER, and use it to store a DATE or TIME durations but not simple durations. If DURDATE is a DECIMAL(8,0) column and DURINT is an INTEGER column then the following are valid:

```
UPDATE  . . . .  SET DURDATE = ENDATE - STARTDATE
UPDATE  . . . .  SET DURINT = ENDTIME - STARTIME
UPDATE  . . . .  SET DURINT = ENDATE - STARTDATE
```

DURDATE can then be used as a DATE duration:

```
SELECT STARTDATE + DURDATE, . . . .
```

but DURINT cannot because it is not a DECIMAL(8,0) datatype. The DATE/TIME arithmetic function does **not** do any datatype conversions.

A TIME duration is a six position decimal number with a precision of 6 and a scale of 0 (DECIMAL (6,0). The structure is *hhmmss* where *hh* is the number of hours, etc. When two TIME values are subtracted the result is a TIME duration.

The TIMESTAMP can only be expressed as:

yy-mm-dd-hh.mm.ss.nnnnnn

Internally, DATE, TIME, and TIMESTAMP are always stored in the same unsigned decimal format but when they are displayed to the user they are always presented in the character format requested by the application developer or in the default format. Internally, DATE is a 4-byte field containing *yyyymmdd,* TIME is a 3-byte field containing *hhmmss,* and TIMESTAMP is a 10-byte field containing *yyyymmddhhmmssnnnnnn.* This is all transparent to the user except when using the LENGTH function.

When a database is first installed, the default for both TIME and DATE is ISO format. The DBA may change the default format in the SYSTEM.SYSOPTIONS table using one of the following:

DEFAULT STANDARD	The default implies the following format DATE	TIME
USA United States	mm/dd/yyyy	hh:mm AM or PM
EUR Europe	dd.mm.yyyy	hh.mm.ss
ISO International	yyy-mm-dd	hh.mm.ss
LOCAL	both - as defined by the installation	

If the DBA neglects to set the format, the default format remains ISO. Specific queries and applications can use a format different from the default format specified in SYSTEM.SYSOPTIONS by adding a parameter in an SQL command or in a precompile job. In an SQL command, the user can change the default by using the CHAR function. The user would specify EUR, ISO, or USA immediately following the column name or the literal:

```
WHERE CHAR (EURDATE) = CHAR(USADATE, EUR)
WHERE CHAR ('05/10/1991',EUR) = CHAR (:USDTE, EUR)
```

The CHAR function will change the USADATE column value into a European format to allow the comparison. This is important for multinational corporations where DATE formats may differ in different countries. It should be remembered, however, that a predicate using scalar functions cannot be used with an index.

The application developer may also use the CHAR command in an application but it is not imperative. To ensure that all dates in the application are presented as USA, for example, and TIME as European, the precompiler parameters can specify, for a Cobol program:

SQLPREP COBOL PREPPARM (PREP = progname . . . . . . , DATE(USA),
TIME(EUR) . . . . .)

When the DATE parameter is specified, it overrides the default set in SYSTEM.SYSOPTIONS and all dates in the application will be presented in a USA format.

ADDITIONAL FUNCTIONS

Additional functions include YEAR, MONTH, DAY, DAYS, HOUR, MINUTE, SECOND, and MICROSECOND. All of these functions, except DAYS, will extract the requested part of a value from an appropriate expression (TIME, DATE, TIMESTAMP, duration). DAYS will result in an INTEGER value which will be derived from the number of days since (January 1, 0001 + 1) in a DATE, TIMESTAMP, or valid DATE expression.

SOME DATE AND TIME IDIOSYNCRASIES

The DATE and TIME columns cannot be used with the AVG and SUM parameters because they are **not** numeric values. The LIKE function cannot be used with DATE and TIME columns because while externally DATE and TIME columns are represented by character strings, internally they are not character strings. They can, however, be used with the MAX and MIN built-in functions.

The user should keep in mind that adding and subtracting months is like flipping the pages of a calendar and does not necessarily involve the passage of the same number of days. The only way to be sure that two intervals represent an equal number of days is to use the DAYS function. This is often necessary because of the following examples:

	DAYS
January 31, 1990 + 1 MONTH = February 28, 1990	28
January 31, 1992 + 1 MONTH = February 29, 1992	29
February 28, 1990 − 1 MONTH = January 28, 1990	31
February 29, 1992 − 1 MONTH = January 29, 1992	31
August 31, 1990 + 1 MONTH = September 30, 1990	30
September 30, 1990 − 1 MONTH = August 30, 1990	31
February 29, 1992 + 1 YEAR = February 28, 1993	365
February 29, 1992 − 1 YEAR = February 28, 1991	366

In all of the above cases, SQL/DS will set warning codes.

The use of the DAYS function is more accurate but also needs to be understood. This function will transform a DATE, TIMESTAMP, or DATE expression into an integer value:

DAYS(DATE('1991-03-10')) - **DAYS**(DATE('1991-02-09')) = **29**
DAYS(DATE('1991-04-10')) - **DAYS**(DATE('1991-03-09')) = **32**

If only DATE were used, the result would be a duration and the two expressions would be equal (one month and one day):

DATE('1991-03-10') - DATE('1991-02-09') = **00000101**
DATE('1991-04-10') - DATE('1991-03-09') = **00000101**

When a DATE duration or a DECIMAL(8,0) field is used, care is necessary to ensure that the correct value is in the field. A DATE duration, for example, has its own unique format and consists of three parts: year ($yyyy$), months (mm), and days (dd). As mentioned earlier, a value in a decimal column or field of 00010101 is equivalent to a duration of one year, one month, and one day and not ten thousand, one hundred, and one **anything**. If the duration field DURFLD contains 00000035 (35 days) and it is used in a calculation:

DURFLD * 4

the result is **not** 140 days but rather one month and 40 days (68 or 71 days depending on the DATE it is added to or subtracted from).

It is important to note as mentioned earlier, that there is a difference between the following two conditions:

WHERE DATECOL > DATE(**1991-01-01**)
WHERE DATECOL > DATE(**'1991-01-01'**)

The first predicate will compare DATECOL to the 1989th day since 01/01/01 and will determine if DATECOL is greater than June 12, 0006. The DATE function treated the expression as a numeric value and subtracted 01 and 01 from 1991 yielding 1989. The DATE that is equal to the 1,989th day since 01/01/01 is June 12, in the year 0006. The DATE function in the second predicate treated the expression as a DATE expression and compared DATECOL to January 1, 1991. **When the results seem unexpected, check the quotation marks.**

SQL/DS accepts the input of a DATE or TIME value in the WHERE condition clause and in the INSERT and UPDATE commands in **any** valid format and converts it into the format needed. The output DATE or TIME, however, is only presented in the default format as specified in the SYSTEM.SYSOPTION table, in the CHAR command, or in the precompile option. An UPDATE command, for example, may contain different dates or times in different formats all mixed together. The following example with three dates, each in a different format, will be executed correctly and all three dates will be stored in the internal format. It does **not** matter in which format they were written in the query:

```
UPDATE PERSONNEL_TBL
    SET STARTDTE = '1991-01-02',
        ENDATE = '01/02/1991', PREMDTE = '02.01.1991'
```

The reader should note that all three dates in the above query are equivalent. If SYSTEM.SYSOPTIONS specifies that the DATE should be displayed in ISO format, then:

```
SELECT STARTDTE, . . . . . .
```

will present the DATE in the *yyyy-mm-dd* format. The following is an example of how the display format can be explicitly stated:

```
SELECT CHAR(STARTDTE, USA), . . . . . .
```

When the application developer wants to ensure that dates and times used in application programs are always presented to the data areas in the correct format, the DATE and TIME parameters of the precompiler should be specified. This is especially important when the same application is run against different databases.

The users of these functions must decide how the data needs to be used. Installations billing or reporting, for example, on a monthly basis can use simple durations while those that bill on a daily basis should use the DAYS function.

KEYWORD PAIRS

There are four very useful keyword pairs which may be used in SQL/DS commands. They are:

CURRENT DATE
CURRENT TIME
CURRENT TIMESTAMP
CURRENT TIMEZONE

These values are taken from the system TOD clock at the **time** of SELECT execution or at OPEN cursor time. This implies that when a keyword pair is used in a predicate, the value will not change for each individual row processed. In an application, for example, despite the time delay between each FETCH, CURRENT TIME will not change:

```
EXEC SQL DECLARE TIMSW CURSOR FOR
    SELECT . . . . WHERE LAST_UPDATE < CURRENT TIME
END-EXEC
EXEC SQL OPEN TIMSW END-EXEC
EXEC SQL FETCH TIMSW INTO : . . . . . . . . END-EXEC
```

If the CURRENT TIME at execution of the OPEN command was 03.02.15, the LAST_UPDATE column of **every** row will be compared to 03.02.15. The same rule applies when a keyword pair is used in a noncursor INSERT or UPDATE command or in a DATALOAD or DATAUNLOAD command in a DBSU run.

The following is an example of noncursor UPDATE and INSERT commands:

```
UPDATE PERSONNEL_TBL
    SET TIMSTMP = CURRENT TIMESTAMP
        WHERE USER_ID > 2354
INSERT INTO PERSONNEL_NEW_TBL
    SELECT USER_ID, . . . . . , CURRENT TIMESTAMP
        FROM PERSONNEL_TBL
        WHERE USER_ID > 2354 AND . . . . .
```

Every id greater than 2354 will have the exact same TIMESTAMP.

The exception to the above rule is when a cursor is used with an

UPDATE or a PUT command. When a cursor is used, the keyword pair will be evaluated at the time each individual row is updated or inserted. When the *timstmp* cursor is used, for example, to SELECT values FOR UPDATE, the subsequent SET TIMESTMP = CURRENT TIMESTAMP will be evaluated at the microsecond that it is executed:

```
EXEC SQL DECLARE TIMSTMP CURSOR FOR
        SELECT USER_ID, TIMESTMP, . . .
            FROM PERSONNEL_TBL
                WHERE USER_ID > 2354
        FOR UPDATE OF TIMESTMP
END-EXEC
EXEC SQL OPEN TIMSTMP  END-EXEC
EXEC SQL FETCH TIMSTMP
        INTO :USER_ID, :TIMESTP, . . . . .
END-EXEC
EXEC SQL UPDATE PERSONNEL_TBL
        SET TIMESTMP = CURRENT TIMESTAMP
            WHERE CURRENT OF TIMSTMP
END-EXEC
```

The TIMESTAMP column in each row that has a user_id with a value greater than 2354 will contain **a different value** from that of the other rows updated.

Unless it is required by the transaction, it is wasteful to use the keyword pairs to retrieve DATE and TIME values:

```
SELECT CURRENT TIME, CURRENT DATE, CURRENT TIMESTAMP
    FROM anytablename
```

It is more efficient to use the functions in the higher level language (COBOL, etc.) to get TIME and DATE values.

CURRENT TIMEZONE is a special value which specifies the amount of hours, minutes, and seconds required to add to Greenwich Mean Time to equal local time. It is a DECIMAL(6,0) signed TIME duration value and can be used to convert local time to GMT:

```
SET GRENTIMESTMP = CURRENT TIMESTAMP – CURRENT TIMEZONE
```

SUMMARY

CONCATENATE, SCALAR functions, and KEYWORD PAIRS have been introduced in SQL/DS to improve usability. With concatenation the user can combine two columns. SUBSTRING allows the user to indicate that only part of the string should be used as the value. DIGITS converts numeric columns into character format. DECIMAL will convert a numeric value in a column or an expression into a decimal value. FLOAT will convert a numeric expression into a double precision floating point value. HEX will convert a string of characters or numbers into a hex character string. TRANSLATE is used to SORT mixed lower and upper case, reorder characters in a string, translate a string to upper case, and change some characters into different characters. STRIP allows the user to remove leading and/or trailing characters from a column value. LENGTH returns the length of the value rather than the value itself. VALUE examines each of the expressions in the parentheses and returns the first one that is not NULL.

DATE, TIME, and TIMESTAMP data types, durations, and functions have made it easier to handle DATE and TIME arithmetic calculations and to stamp transactions with a TIMESTAMP. A DATE value designates a particular day in a calendar year. A DATE duration is a decimal number with a structure of yyyymmdd. A TIME column value designates a point in TIME on a 24 hour clock. Simple durations cannot be stored in a column.

The resulting value from DATE and TIME arithmetic calculations is often a duration and is sometimes a bit tricky. The DATE, TIME, and TIMESTAMP functions are used to transform an expression or column value into a DATE, TIME, or TIMESTAMP. The DATE function extracts a DATE value from a TIMESTAMP, a numeric expression, a seven-digit Julian DATE, a DATE string, or a DATE value in a DATE column type.

There is a TIMESTAMP function and a TIMESTAMP column type but there is no TIMESTAMP duration. A TIMESTAMP column data type designates a specific TIME on a specific day. DATE, TIME, and TIMESTAMP when displayed to the user are represented as fixed length character strings each with a length and format determined by the DBA.

Additional functions include YEAR, MONTH, DAY, DAYS, HOUR, MINUTE, SECOND, and MICROSECOND.

CURRENT DATE, CURRENT TIME, CURRENT TIMESTAMP, and CURRENT TIMEZONE are four very useful keyword pairs which may be used in SQL/DS commands. Their values are taken from the system TOD clock at the time of SELECT execution or at OPEN cursor time. Unless it is required by the transaction, it is wasteful to use the keyword pairs to retrieve DATE and TIME values. CURRENT TIMEZONE is a special value which specifies the amount of hours, minutes, and seconds required to add to Greenwich Mean Time to equal local time.

RECOMMENDATIONS

1. It should be remembered that while it is convenient to use scalar functions, they may cause poor performance because an index will not be used on the predicate and a DBSPACE scan may be required.

2. When a DATE duration or a DECIMAL(8,0) field is used, care is necessary to ensure that the correct value is in the field.

3. Care should be taken to ensure that the DATE or TIME value expected is the value received.

4. Carefully plan the use of DATE, TIME, and TIMESTAMP in a table because neither blanks nor zeros are acceptable values for DATE or TIMESTAMP columns and zeros is a valid TIME value.

5. The user should keep in mind that adding and subtracting months is like flipping the pages of a calendar and does not necessarily involve the passage of the same number of days.

CHAPTER 6

Application Development

Every computer application requires careful analysis and design to fit the needs of its users and exploit the strengths of the database and operating systems utilized to implement it. SQL/DS applications are no different despite the very easy-to-use and very powerful SQL commands. The composition of the user population, for example, is a very important element of application design. Are the users sophisticated and computer literate? Do they frequently make errors and have poor memories for detail? Is there a steady turnover of personnel and do new trainees usually operate the system? The answer to these questions will help the designer select the best interface to support the users and will assist the design of a successful computer application.

After analysis of the needs of the users, the application designer must determine which of the SQL/DS facilities will be used by the application and in which language or languages the application will be programmed. Most VSE/SP installations develop their SQL/DS applications using COBOL or CSP both for batch and for on-line. The on-line CICS/VS screens are developed using either BMS or the CSP Screen Definition Facility.

VM/SP installations often develop their applications under the Interactive System Productivity Tool (ISPF) that has special services for the development and use of on-line applications. COBOL or COBOL II, CSP, and RXSQL are the major development languages. The Query Management Facility (QMF), which has many useful features in a production environment, is often also available. QMF for the VSE/SP system is not a viable alternative because Version One was the last QMF/VSE version developed.

SQL/DS may also be accessed using PL/I, FORTRAN, *C,* APL, AS, ASSEMBLER, and other products. There are many more products available under VM/SP than under VSE/SP and most installations having both operating systems installed on the same CPU will be encouraged to use SQL/DS under VM/SP so that both VSE/SP users and VM/SP users can access the same database.

Each of the application development vehicles utilizes the same set of SQL/DS commands to manipulate the data in the tables. This enables the designers to mix and match application languages without having to re-learn the database manipulation commands.

This section will provide a general overview of application development in SQL/DS with an emphasis on those aspects specifically related to performance tuning. It is important to note that while the logical design of a VSAM application may seem similar to that of an SQL/DS application, the power of the commands to access VSAM is not as great as that of the SQL commands to access SQL/DS tables, and the use of VSAM files is not the same as the use of SQL/DS tables. Application designers should be very wary of using VSAM concepts and techniques when designing SQL/DS tables. The existence of the new SQL/DS application interface for VSAM does not imply that they are similar.

In SQL/DS, for example, the application has easy access to the data and can access data directly, sequentially, or via a specific key range. SQL is a very powerful nonprocedural language and the application developer should learn its strengths and idiosyncrasies before starting to design. Unlike VSAM, there is, for example, a built-in recovery function that does not require the programmer to code any modules in order to use it. Other sections of this book will describe the powerful commands and the many functions available. **Please note that for consistency, the examples in this chapter will be COBOL examples.**

FIRST STEPS IN APPLICATION PROGRAMMING

To enable SQL/DS to work with higher level languages, the application developer must add several special commands to DECLARE to the SQL/DS precompiler those data definitions that will be used by SQL commands in the application. The actual SQL commands are written in a format very similar to those that are used in ISQL or in the database utility (DBSU). A SELECT command is used to read a row from a table or tables and an INSERT command is used to add a row to a table. The UPDATE command will modify one or more rows and the DELETE command will remove one or more rows. In addition, there is a FETCH command to SELECT more than one row and there is a PUT command to INSERT more than one row.

Commands such as CREATE TABLE, CREATE INDEX, and GRANT authority may also be included in application programs but it is recommended that they **not** be used because they lock and hold system resources.

HOST VARIABLES

Data fields to be used in SQL commands to hold user input or output variables, are called *host variables*. The application developer declares these data definitions in a section delineated by DECLARE statements. In COBOL, for example, the programmer might include the following in the WORKING-STORAGE SECTION:

```
EXEC SQL BEGIN DECLARE SECTION END-EXEC.

01   USERNAME      PIC   X(15).
01   SALARY        PIC   S9(7)V9(2) COMP-3 VALUE +0.
01   USERID        PIC   X(8) VALUE 'DOV1'.
01   USERPW        PIC   X(8) VALUE 'A298689'.
01   ADDRFLD       PIC   X(27) VALUE ' '.
01   NAMINDV       PIC   S9(4) COMP.

EXEC SQL END DECLARE SECTION END-EXEC.
```

The fields are defined in the same way as are all of the other data definitions and they may be used in regular COBOL commands as well as in SQL commands. To move a user name into the variable, for example, and use it in an SQL command, the application programmer should code:

```
MOVE 'DONNY' TO USERNAME.
EXEC SQL
SELECT ADDRESS INTO . . . . .
     WHERE NAME = :USERNAME
END-SQL.
```

In the MOVE instruction, the USERNAME field is treated as would be any other COBOL variable. In the WHERE clause of the SELECT command, it is delineated by using the colon (:) prior to the name which will identify it as a host variable to the SQL/DS preprocessor. Without the colon, SQL/DS would assume that it was a column name.

It is very important, for performance reasons, that the *host variables* be correctly defined. Performance is enhanced if the host variable is defined in such a way that it **exactly** matches the column datatype that it will be compared with. This will eliminate the need to expand or translate the value in the column to match the variable data. In the above example, if the NAME column in the table were defined as CHAR(12), the optimizer would not be able to use an index to find a matching NAME value. This is true even though the USERNAME field will never hold a value greater than 12 bytes because the column value has to be padded to be compared to the field value.

When an index is not used, SQL/DS has to do a DBSPACE scan instead of directly reading the row. This can take a long time when a large table is being accessed. It is recommended that each host variable exactly match the column definition so that similar simple errors do not degrade response time and lock out other users. In COBOL, for example, *host variables* should be defined as follows to match the column type:

Column Type	Matching Host Variable
SMALLINT	PIC S9(4) COMP
INTEGER	PIC S9(9) COMP
DECIMAL(7,2)	PIC S9(5)V9(2) COMP-3
CHAR(15)	PIC X(15)

SQL DELIMITER STATEMENTS

In an application, the SQL commands are written with a delimiter informing the precompiler where an SQL statement begins and ends. The delimiters in COBOL, for example, are:

```
EXEC SQL              ⇐ delimiter
     SELECT ADDRESS, . . . .
          INTO :HOSTADDR, . . .
          FROM . . . . . .
END-EXEC              ⇐ delimiter
```

Every SQL command requires these delimiters. The "EXEC SQL" is the standard beginning of an SQL command and the end delimiter depends upon the host language used.

CURSORS

SQL/DS does not require that every key be unique. When the key or conditional clause of the SELECT command matches more than one data row, SQL/DS will return every matching row to the application. Application programming languages have the limitation that they can only handle one row at a time. The application has only one set of *host variables* and can only store the contents of one row. A procedure to enable the application to handle this situation is built into SQL/DS by the use of a placeholder called a CURSOR.

The application developer declares a *cursor* as part of the SQL/DS command in the PROCEDURE DIVISION and can then use the FETCH command to retrieve one row at a time. The application might specify:

```
EXEC SQL DECLARE ADDR1 CURSOR FOR
        SELECT ADDR, ......... FROM .....
             WHERE ........
END-SQL
```

The label ADDR1 does not have to be defined to COBOL because it is used only by SQL/DS processing. The above command is not translated into an executable COBOL CALL command by the preprocessor because it is simply the definition of what is needed. Other commands will be translated and will do the actual processing.

When the application is ready to begin processing the SELECT command, an OPEN *cursor* command is specified to CALL SQL/DS to begin the command. The appropriate SQL/DS routines are called to send the command to SQL/DS which initiates the execution of the requested SQL/DS function. The SELECT and any required SORT are executed and the *results table* or *answer set* is prepared:

```
EXEC SQL OPEN ADDR1 END-EXEC
```

No rows, however, are returned to the application because no fields to hold the column data have as yet been allocated. When the application is ready to receive the data, the FETCH command is issued to designate the fields to be used to hold the data. The column values of the first and subsequent rows will be moved into the *host variable* fields. The format of the command is:

```
EXEC SQL  FETCH ADDR1  INTO :ADDRFLD  END-SQL
```

After the command is executed, ADDRFLD will contain the value taken from the ADDR column that was in the first row that satisfied the conditional clause or predicate. When the application is ready to read the next row, it will return to the loop and issue another FETCH command. The OPEN command is only issued once and should not be in the loop.

The FETCH facility only allows forward scrolling. If backwards scrolling is required, one of the following procedures should be used:

1. Store the data in a temporary storage area.
2. FETCH the data again using a second *cursor*.
3. Use a second *cursor* to SELECT and FETCH the data in reverse sequence. The SELECT might be:

```
EXEC SQL DECLARE REVRS1 CURSOR FOR
        SELECT anyfields FROM anytables
            WHERE anyconditions
        ORDER BY 1 DESC
```

The procedure to process an INSERT command that will insert more than one row into a table is similar to that of a SELECT command. A *cursor* is declared, and the *host variables* are filled with the data to be inserted into the row. The rows are PUT one at a time, in a loop, until all the data rows are inserted. The following example will INSERT rows into the PERSONNEL_TBL until no more rows are available to be inserted:

```
        EXEC SQL DECLARE INSRT1 CURSOR FOR
            INSERT INTO PERSONNEL_TBL
                        VALUES (:NAME, . . . . . )
        END-SQL
        PERFORM prepare first row
OPEN—CURSOR.
        EXEC SQL OPEN INSRT1 END-EXEC
        PERFORM LOOP UNTIL NO-MORE-DATA
        EXEC SQL CLOSE INSRT1 END-EXEC
        EXEC SQL COMMIT WORK END-EXEC
        RETURN
LOOP.
        EXEC SQL PUT INSRT1 END-SQL
        PERFORM prepare next row
ENDLOOP.
```

When **BLOCK**ing is used, the OPEN command acquires 8K of storage for the blocks. Blocking is used both for SELECT and INSERT. The individual rows, however, are not inserted into the database table until the block is filled.

The CLOSE *cursor* command tells SQL/DS to INSERT the last block of rows into the table and to release the *cursor*'s remaining resources. This command should be issued as soon as practical. It is **not,** however, a COMMIT WORK and it does not release the locks held by this command. It is important to **first CLOSE the *cursors* before issuing the COMMIT.**

Cursors and Host Variable Modifications

When modifications are made to the contents of *host variables* used in the conditional clauses (predicates) of SQL/DS commands, they do not take effect immediately. For a SELECT command, for example, when *cursor*s are utilized, host variable values are usually evaluated and used in the predicate at the time that the CURSOR is opened. **Modifying the contents of the host variable after the OPEN has been executed has absolutely no effect upon the FETCH.** To test for a different condition, the application developer must first CLOSE the *cursor,* modify the *host variables,* and then OPEN the *cursor*.

This closing and opening of *cursor*s is a time-consuming process because the SQL/DS command must be re-executed, the database accessed, and the answer set prepared and possibly re-sorted. This is often a major cause of poor performance and response in an application program. When closing and opening a *cursor* becomes necessary, the application developer should search for alternate ways to process the query or should re-structure the query.

INDICATOR VARIABLES

When a row that is to be fetched contains one or more columns that are nullable, an *indicator variable* should be added to the host variable in the FETCH statement. These *indicator variable*s are used to contain the indicator bytes returned by SQL/DS (or passed to SQL/DS on INSERT or UPDATE). These *indicator variable*s are fields that must be defined in the DECLARE SECTION of the application program and are defined in the same way as a SMALLINT column would be defined. The *indicator variable* for a name column might be defined in COBOL as:

```
01   NAMINDV      PIC  S9(4)  COMP.
```

When the value in the selected column contains a NULL, the *indicator variable* is initialized by SQL/DS to **-1.** If an *indicator* *variable* is not specified and a column to be SELECTed is NULL, a negative SQLCODE would be returned to the application. When a column value to be updated or inserted into a row should contain a NULL, the application developer should move a **-1** into the *indicator variable* to indicate to the system that the column being used in the UPDATE or INSERT command should receive a NULL value.

The *indicator variable* must be preceded by a colon (:) when used in the SQL/DS command and both the host variable and the *indicator variable* represent the **same** column. They are **not** separated by a comma as shown in the following example:

```
FETCH ADDR1 INTO :USERNAME :NAMINDV, . . . . . . .
```

If an *indicator variable* is used with a column that is defined as NOT NULL, it causes no harm but is simply ignored. The practice, however, of placing an *indicator variable* next to every column (just to be sure) is confusing and often misleading. The maintainer of the application is never quite sure whether or not the column is really nullable and must continually check the documentation.

The keyword INDICATOR may precede the *indicator variable* to provide better documentation but the *host* and *indicator variables* are still not separated by a comma:

```
FETCH ADDR1 INTO :USERNAME INDICATOR :NAMINDV, . . . . . . .
```

The use of the keyword INDICATOR is optional and may be omitted or included with some or all of the *host variables* in one command as shown in the following example:

```
FETCH ADDR1 INTO :USERNAME INDICATOR :NAMINDV,
                :ADDR :ADDRIND, . . . . . .
```

After the execution of a FETCH, when the *indicator variable* contains a zero, it is an indication that the column value selected is not null. When the *indicator variable* is **-1,** the value is NULL and when it is **-2,** an error occurred and the value is NULL because of a numeric conversion error or an error in evaluating an arithmetic expression in part of the select clause. When the *indicator variable* contains a value greater than zero, it indicates that the value from the column was truncated because the host variable was too small to contain it. **The *indicator variable* should always be checked.**

SQL/DS RETURN CODES

After every executable SQL command, SQL/DS returns a code that indicates whether or not the command was executed successfully. Warning flags and diagnostic information are also returned. Every application program must provide storage for an SQL/DS error handling area by including an SQL Communications Area called SQLCA. The SQLCA contains host language variables for the warning flags, error codes, and diagnostic information. Error handling helps protect the integrity of the database, and tests of these areas should be made an integral part of every application that modifies the database.

The SQL/DS commands for application programs include a WHENEVER command that provides a means of specifying the action that should be taken when SQL warnings, errors, and NOT FOUND conditions are encountered. The application developer may specify CONTINUE processing, STOP processing, or GOTO a subroutine when an error condition occurs. The following WHENEVER statements tell SQL/DS that should a warning be received, control should be given to the TESTWHY routine. When an error occurs, processing should cease, but when the record sought is not found, the condition should be ignored:

```
EXEC SQL WHENEVER SQLWARNING GOTO testwhy END-EXEC
EXEC SQL WHENEVER SQLERROR STOP END-EXEC
EXEC SQL WHENEVER NOT FOUND CONTINUE END-EXEC
```

These statements may be placed anywhere in the application PROCEDURE DIVISION. The scope of each statement is determined by its **physical position in the source code** and not by its position in the logic flow. When the WHENEVER statements are omitted, the default for each is CONTINUE and all warnings and errors are ignored. This, of course, is not the recommended reaction of an application program. These commands should always be coded to explicitly inform the system what action should be taken in each specific case. Even when the desired action is CONTINUE, the WHENEVER statement should be coded for documentation purposes.

PRECOMPILE

Application programs containing SQL/DS statements have to be preprocessed to change the SQL/DS commands into host language commands. The precompiler provided with SQL/DS changes the SQL code into CALLs and comments out the original source code. In this way, the regular high-level language compiler will subsequently prepare the application program successfully for execution.

This preprocessing step also uses the SQL/DS commands to prepare an access module. This *access module* creation saves time during application execution because the command does not have to be evaluated and an access path chosen each time it is executed. The *access module* contains the information needed by the RDS and DBSS components to access the data. All evaluation is done during precompile (or re-preprocess) time and any changes made at a later time which do not force re-creation of an *access module* will have no positive or negative effect on the access path.

The SQLPREP command is used to preprocess an application. In VM/SP, the SQLPREP EXEC is used either in single user mode or in multiple user mode. It can also be used to preprocess an application **to more than one database** at a time. In VSE/SP, the procedure may be used on only one database at a time. A COBOL II VM/SP example of a preprocess might be:

```
SQLPREP COB PREPARM
(PREPNAME=myprog1,USER=DOV1/dov1pswd,ISOL(RR),BLOCK,COB2)
    SYSIN(myfile1 cobsql A) SYSPRINT(myfile1 listprep A)
    DBFILE (dbnmes prepdb A)
```

The DBFILE file, if used, should contain a list of the database names where *access modules* for this application should be created.

PRECOMPILE PARAMETERS

ISOL and BLOCK are the two main performance parameters for the precompile. ISOL has three options and indicates whether the application should access the database using CURSOR STABILITY (CS) or REPEATABLE READ (RR) or whether the method to be used will be indicated at the time of execution. The BLOCK parameter determines whether blocking will or will not be used for all opened *cursors* in the application program.

In general, the application developer should **not** allow the precompile to default to a installation-wide default. These parameters are very sensitive and have a high impact on application performance and should be carefully considered for each individual application.

Isolation Level

The application developer may choose one of three options when deciding upon the isolation level. *Repeatable Read* (RR) may be specified to ensure that no user modifies a row or page being viewed by the user of the application until the *logical unit of work* (LUW) is complete. This isolation level limits the ability of other users to update the tables that are being accessed by those who only SELECT data. *Repeatable read* is the SQLPREP default but it can also be explicitly indicated by coding as shown in the following example:

SQLPREP COB PP (. . . . . , **ISOL(RR)**)

If isolation level *Cursor Stability* is desired, do not allow the precompilor to use its default option.

Cursor Stability (CS) should be specified when a lock is only needed to be held on the last row or page accessed by the application. This isolation level enhances concurrency and allows SQL/DS to release the lock on any page or row as soon as the *cursor* has moved on. The danger of CS is that a row may be updated by a different user after it was viewed by this user. When this user pages backwards, different data may be seen and when he pages forward, the same pages may be displayed twice or not at all. **CS has, however, a very significant positive impact on concurrency and should be used whenever appropriate.**

CS is useful when large numbers of end-users simultaneously SELECT data from the same tables that are being updated by other users. UPDATEs request exclusive locks that keep other users locked out or the exclusive locks may not be acquirable because other users are reading the data. If *Repeatable Read* were used and locks were not released quickly, little updating would be possible and the users would interfere with each other's processing. To choose *cursor* stability, the application developer would specify:

SQLPREP COB PP (. . . . . , **ISOL(CS)**)

The third possible option is to specify that the isolation level will be dynamically modified in the application during execution. This is specified by coding:

SQLPREP COB PP (. . . . . , **ISOL(USER)**)

To use this option, a one-byte character variable must be defined in the application, customarily labeled SQLISL or, in COBOL, SQL-ISL.

ISOL is determined at OPEN *cursor* time and a value of **"R,"** or **"C"** must be placed in the SQLISL field before the *cursor* is opened or before the SELECT is executed (when no *cursor* is used). This lets the system know which method to use with the particular *cursor*. This option is very useful when different SELECTs or INSERTs in an application need to use different isolation methods.

Blocking

The option to block or not to block the rows returned to the application program is also a parameter that can have a very significant impact on performance. Batch applications often transfer large volumes of data to and from the database. In VM/SP, for example, SQL/DS uses the IUCV mechanism to transfer this data. If many rows of data need to be transferred, it is far more efficient to transfer an 8K block than to transfer one row at a time. On the other hand, if only one or two rows need to be transferred, it is very wasteful to transfer an entire 8K block.

Blocking is useful for SELECTing or INSERTing multiple rows. Unlike ISOL, there is no way to modify the BLOCKing option and whichever option is chosen at precompile time is applied to the entire program. Many applications contain more than one SQL command and the application developer's decision whether or not to use blocking must be based on the SQL/DS commands used most intensively in the program. Blocking is usually beneficial in application programs that utilize *cursors* to retrieve or insert multiple rows. Even if only one or two FETCHes or PUTs in an application involve multiple rows, blocking may prove worthwhile.

Blocking does not reduce I/O because SQL/DS must still FETCH or INSERT the same number of rows. It does reduce CPU overhead by greatly reducing (assuming fairly small rows) IUCV or XPCC overhead. This parameter is useful only in multi-user mode. In single-user mode, there is no transference from machine to machine (in VM/SP) or from partition to partition (in VSE/SP) and blocking is suppressed.

Blocking is not appropriate in every case and should be carefully evaluated rather than allowing the precompilor to default to BLOCK or to NOBLOCK. The application developer should be aware that special processing is involved when blocking is used to insert data into tables that have unique indexes created for them. When BLOCKing is used in an application and a *cursor* is opened and a row is PUT, SQL/DS *cannot* test each key to ensure that it is not a duplicate key until the block is filled and the rows are physically inserted into the table. When a non-unique key is inserted, an error occurs and the application will receive an SQLCODE of -803 but the row currently being PUT will not necessarily be the offending row. The SQLERRD.3 field will indicate how many rows were successfully inserted and the application programmer will have to calculate which row contains the duplicate key.

The seeming complexity of inserting with the BLOCK parameter should in no way deter the application developer from using the blocking facility. **Blocking reduces CPU overhead** and is often much more efficient (especially in VM/SP) than unblocked inserts. If the developer decides to modify the BLOCKing, the application program should be re-preprocessed with the NOBLOCK parameter.

There are several restrictions which limit the use of blocking and even when blocking is specified there are instances where it will not be used, such as:

- Rows are so large that two will not fit into a block.
- 8K of virtual storage is not available for blocking.
- UPDATE or DELETE ..... WHERE CURRENT OF CURSOR is specified.
- The *cursor* contains a FOR UPDATE clause.
- The *cursor* retrieves LONG fields.

COBOL II

COB2 is a new parameter that informs the precompiler that a COBOL II application is being precompiled. This parameter is only applicable to VM/SP because COBOL II is not available with VSE/SP.

Application developers using early versions of SQL/DS who plan to use the IF / END-IF commands in the application will have to carefully edit the application to add END-IF statements after certain SQL commands. In many cases, the SQL/DS precompiler will generate IF / ELSE statements to test return codes after SQL commands. When the IF / END-IF structure is used, the COBOL statements following the SQL commands will **not** be executed correctly. The following pseudo-code will demonstrate why. The application developer will have written the following:

```
1.  IF previous-code = 'OK'
2.      EXEC SQL FETCH CURSOR A INTO : .....
3.      END-EXEC
```

4.   ADD SQLTOT TO USERTOT
5.   **END-IF**
6.   **MOVE** INPUT TO OUTPUT.

The SQL/DS precompiler will generate an *IF* and an ELSE statement after it translates the EXEC SQL into a CALL:

```
CALL . . . . . . . . .
IF SQLCODE NOT EQUAL 0
     GO TO LABELERR
ELSE
```

When the generated code is placed in its proper location the application program now reads:

1.   **IF** PREVIOUS-CODE = 'OK'
2.   *   EXEC SQL FETCH *CURSOR* A INTO : . . . . .
3.   *   END-EXEC
(generated code)   CALL . . . .
                         IF SQLCODE NOT EQUAL 0
                              GO TO LABELERR
                         ELSE
4.   ADD SQLTOT TO USERTOT
5.   **END-IF**
6.   MOVE INPUT TO OUTPUT

Note that item 5, which previously was paired with the **first IF** statement, now is paired with the **generated IF** statement and changes the logic of the application. When the program is compiled, the MOVE will now be conditional upon the first IF being 'OK' where previously it was not. A solution might be to add:

```
     CONTINUE
END-IF
```

after each executable SQL instruction to close the IF / ELSE structure generated by the SQL/DS precompilor. This procedure was used successfully in at least one installation but takes a lot of time to implement. It should be noted that the precompilor sometimes adds two *IF* statements (this depends on the number of WHENEVER statements which do not specify CONTINUE). This situation was found in an application and solved by adding two *END-IF* statements which corrected the application logic:

```
        CONTINUE
    END-IF
    END-IF
```

This problem **has been corrected** in recent versions of SQL/DS. The COB2 option informs the precompiler that the IF / END-IF structure is being used in the application and the precompilor will then generate the appropriate statements as shown in the following:

```
    CALL . . . . . . . . .
    IF SQLCODE NOT EQUAL 0
        GO TO LABELERR
    END-IF
```

The default parameter is **not** COB2. The users of COBOL II with older releases of SQL/DS should prepare the programs so that the extra code can be easily removed after a later version of SQL/DS is installed. Adding an identifier before and after the code will enable the code to be removed from all programs via an EXEC. The additions might look like this:

```
    ******************************
    * REMOVE THIS LATER *
    ******************************
        CONTINUE
    END-IF
    ******************************
    *       TILL HERE       *
    ******************************
```

ACCESS MODULE DBSPACES

An *access module* is created whenever an application is preprocessed or a command is dynamically executed. The *access module* is stored in table format in a DBSPACE specially created to hold *access modules*. Access modules are created in public DBSPACES with names beginning with PUBLIC.SYS:

```
    PUBLIC.SYS0002  PUBLIC.SYS0003 . . . . . .
```

Each *access module* is treated like a table and therefore the DB-SPACE is limited to 255 *access modules*. When the number of pages in the DBSPACE is small, the DBSPACE may not be able to hold all 255 *access modules*. When the DBSPACE is very large, most of the potential space will be wasted because the maximum number of *access modules* is still only 255.

These DBSPACES also hold VIEW definitions in table format. When an installation uses a large number of views, many DBSPACES to hold *access modules* and views may need to be defined. To determine if space exists for additional *access modules* in a DBSPACE, check the FREEPCT column in the SYSTEM.SYSDBSPACES table:

```
SELECT DBSPACENO, FREEPCT
    FROM SYSTEM.SYSDBSPACES
        WHERE DBSPACENAME LIKE 'SYS0%'
```

When FREEPCT is zero, the DBSPACE is filled and when FREEPCT contains a 1, space is still available. The acquisition of DBSPACEs should be done during off-peak hours because when the DBSPACE is acquired, the tables are pre-allocated.

ACCESS MODULES

In the newer versions of SQL/DS, *access modules* contain instructions instead of the machine code contained in the *access modules* of previous releases. While the manuals indicate that old *access modules* will be automatically converted and that there is no need to re-preprocess (and there **is** no need to re-preprocess), many installations have decided to re-preprocess to avoid any *unknown* problems. When there are relatively few applications to re-preprocess, the resources wasted by this unnecessary work is minimal. The larger installations, however, should avoid re-preprocessing.

The *access modules* contain header information, SQL statements, and global data. The SQL statements from the application are stored in two formats in the *access module*: internal format and character format. The internal format incorporates the access path for SELECT, UPDATE, INSERT, and DELETE and describes the actions to be performed for other types of instructions (DCL and DDL). The character format is used for dynamic re-preprocessing and for the portable *access module* re-preprocessing when *access modules* are transported to other databases.

There are three types of *access modules*:

Modifiable—created by extended dynamic statements

Nonmodifiable—created by extended dynamic statements

Regular—created by the preprocessor

The *access modules* created by extended dynamic statements have a flag to differentiate them from regular *access modules*. The difference between modifiable and nonmodifiable *access modules* is that the nonmodifiable *access modules* cannot be executed by the *logical unit of work* that created it. It must first be committed which ends the *logical unit of work*.

Modifiable *access modules*, however, can be executed before they are committed and are available to other LUWs after they are committed. An example of the Assembly language extended dynamic SQL language commands to create a nonmodifiable *access module* is shown below:

```
CREATE PROGRAM PERSPROG
    USING OPTION NOMODIFY
PREPARE . . . . . . . . . . . . . .
COMMIT WORK
```

When an *access module* is loaded into the system, it is placed in a PROGS list. This list contains several chains including an in-use list and a free list. Each user may have **up to ten** active *access modules* associated with an application. When an *access module* is needed by the system, the user's in-list is searched. If it is not found there, the free list of *access modules* available to all users will be searched. If the module is found, it will be moved to the user's in-list. If it is not found, it will be loaded from the database.

When a user no longer needs the *access module* and the free list has available space, the module is stored on the free list and made available to other users, otherwise it is discarded. The ten *access module* limit implies that an application should not be divided into too many independent modules.

When large numbers of modules are moved to a new database, the precompile process can be very time consuming. This precompile time is avoided when *access modules* are transported using the UNLOAD/RELOAD PROGRAM commands of the database utility program. It is a very useful technique of moving tested applications to the production environment. When the module arrives at its new database it is automatically re-preprocessed.

INVALID ACCESS MODULES

Whenever a table or an index used by an application is dropped or a *referential relationship* changed, the *access module* must be tagged invalid by the system. The *access module,* however, contains the code necessary to enable the system to automatically re-preprocess the application the next time a user tries to start it. If the table, index, or referential relationships have subsequently been re-created and other conditions have not changed, the access path will be unchanged. If, however, the environment has changed and, for example, a user attempts to start the application before the DBA has finished re-creating an index, the optimizer will be unaware of the existence of the index and will choose a different access path.

After the index is re-created, it still will not be used until the *access module* is again created. There are several ways to force the system to re-create an *access module.* The easiest but most wasteful way is to simply recompile the program. As an alternative, a developer without DBA authority might drop another index used by the same application (and re-create it) to force the *access module* to be re-preprocessed. This, too, is quite wasteful. The preferred way is to request a user with DBA authority to tag the *access module* as invalid by updating the SYSTEM.SYSACCESS catalog table, as shown in the following example:

```
UPDATE SYSTEM.SYSACCESS
    SET VALID = 'N'
        WHERE TNAME = APPLICNAME AND
            CREATOR = USER
```

The DBA should be aware that this process of invalidation does **not usually** take effect immediately because the *access module* is *in use* and stored in the buffers. Experience has shown that with a fairly active system it requires 15 to 30 minutes before an *access module,* artificially tagged as invalid by the DBA, is re-preprocessed. In the meantime, any new end-users will continue to use the old *access module.* This *wait* period does not occur when the system tags the *access module* as invalid. The SQL/DS system also purges it from the buffers and from memory and it is immediately re-created at the time that the next user starts to execute the application.

The first user of an application that requires the re-creation of an *access module* will experience a degradation in response time while the new *access module* is being created. Subsequent users will not experience this degradation.

To avoid inconveniencing the users, the DBA should avoid invalidating great numbers of *access module*s in a production system at any one time. Many installations, for example, reorganize their application tables on a weekly schedule by processing a series of tables each night. The process involves the following steps:

Backup of the DBSPACE.

Drop the DBSPACE—which automatically drops any indexes, views or referential relationships.

Acquire the DBSPACE.

Restore the tables, indexes and relationships.

This process will invalidate many *access modules*. Each morning a different group of end-users will complain about the early morning poor response. The reason for the poor performance that they will experience is the contention caused by *access module* re-creation.

To avoid the *morning after* syndrome, an application or an EXEC can be developed to *exercise* each application and force the re-creation of the *access modules*. A better alternative might be to use the DBSU to UNLOAD and RELOAD PROGRAM. When the RELOAD PROGRAM is run, a new *access module* is automatically created. The DBSU command formats to unload and reload are:

```
UNLOAD PROGRAM(PERSPROG)
    OUTFILE(BACKPROG);

RELOAD PROGRAM(PERSPROG) REPLACE KEEP
    INFILE(BACKPROG);
```

This application, EXEC, or DBSU should be run at night after the reorganization.

Preprocessing can also have a negative impact on overall system performance and response. When all of the *access module* spaces are filled, for example, SQL/DS will initiate a process to check all of the DBSPACES where the value in the FREEPCT column is 1 (which indicates that space is still available to hold additional *access modules*) and will mark all of the unavailable *access module* spaces in all of the *access module* DBSPACEs as AVAILABLE. SQL/DS then will try to find enough space to insert the new *access module*. This process will consume resources, take a long time, and negatively impact the response of other users. Preprocessing in the production environment should usually be done during off-hours.

To determine in which DBSPACE additional *access modules* can be stored, execute the following command:

```
SELECT D.DBSPACENO
      FROM SYSTEM.SYSDBSPACES D, SYSTEM.SYSACCESS A
      WHERE D.FREEPCT = 1     AND
            A.TNAME LIKE '% AVAILABLE' AND
            A.DBSPACENO = D.DBSPACENO
      ORDER BY 1
```

VSE/SP users who only have one database both for production and for test have a serious performance problem and may just have to limit precompiling and testing during peak on-line periods. Running VSE/SP under VM/SP may provide a solution by allowing the systems programmer to define both a test VSE/SP machine and a production VSE/SP machine each with its own SQL/DS database. The latest versions of SQL/DS and VM/SP allow VSE/SP to access an SQL/DS machine running under VM/SP. This, too, may help alleviate the VSE/SP problem because on-line applications and batch applications can access different databases.

SYSUSAGE CATALOG TABLE

SQL/DS records index, view, and other dependencies in the SYSTEM.SYSUSAGE catalog table. When either an index, view, or table is dropped or when a referential relationship is modified, the SYSTEM.SYSUSAGE or SYSTEM.SYSKEYS table is searched for all of those applications dependent on this object and the *access module* in SYSTEM.SYSACCESS is marked invalid.

When performance is slow, knowing which *access module*s are marked invalid can often point to a problem that occurred (or a reorganization that was done without proper notification). To check which *access module*s are marked invalid the DBA should specify:

```
SELECT TNAME, CREATOR
      FROM SYSTEM.SYSACCESS
            WHERE VALID = 'N' AND TABTYPE = 'X'
            ORDER BY 1
```

DROP PROGRAM

When a program is no longer needed, the application developer or the DBA should issue:

```
DROP PROGRAM PERSAPPL
```

to free *access module* space. Only the user who created the *access module* or the DBA may drop the application. This command does not have to be issued before preprocessing because when an application is preprocessed again, the old *access module* is automatically deleted. In fact, the system tries to place the new *access module* in the same table used to store the old one. If the new *access module* is significantly larger, there may not be sufficient space in the DBSPACE and the developer will receive a return code indicating "*no more space available for access modules.*" This is not accurate because there may be available space in another DBSPACE. It simply means that the original DBSPACE has no more data pages available. If the developer simply recompiles, the system will search for available space in other DBSPACEs. The old *access module* was already deleted so the system will not try to place the new *access module* in any particular DBSPACE but will place it in a DBSPACE which has enough room.

LOGICAL UNIT OF WORK (LUW)

In SQL/DS a *logical unit of work* begins with the first SQL/DS statement and ends with the COMMIT WORK or ROLLBACK WORK statement. When these commands are not explicitly coded in an application, they are executed automatically when the program ends. The application developer should **never** allow this default COMMIT/ROLLBACK to execute but should explicitly end the transaction one way or the other.

GRANTING AUTHORITY

When the application is precompiled, a user identification and a password are specified. This identification should usually be that of the application developer. If user DOV1 is the developer, for example, the SQLPREP command should specify:

```
SQLPREP COB PP(PREP=PERSPROG,USERID=DOV1/DOV1PSWD, . . )
```

If the USER identification used to compile the application has the authority to access **all** of the tables in the application, then authority is automatically granted to that user to run the application. To GRANT authority to others to run the application the application developer must be authorized to perform all of the SQL/DS actions specified in the application. Other users receiving authorization to

RUN the application do not need authority to use the individual tables accessed by the program. DOV1 can issue the following command to grant run authority on the PERSPROG to other users:

GRANT RUN ON PERSPROG TO SHIRA, DAVID **WITH GRANT OPTION**

If at precompile time, one or more of the tables or views does not exist, the *access module* will still be created but the authorization checking will be executed dynamically at **every** run time. This implies that the user executing the application not only has to have authority to run the application but also needs to have the authority to use the tables or views that were missing at the time of precompilation. This authority check at run time, if unnecessary, may negatively affect performance and should be removed. This can be accomplished by creating the tables or views and re-creating the *access module*.

Granting authority adds a row to the SYSTEM.SYSPROGAUTH table. No check is made to determine if this authority already exists. If authority has already been granted, a second row will be inserted. When authority is granted automatically as part of a procedure or an EXEC, the table may become very full of duplicate grants. Steps should be taken to remove unnecessary authority from the table.

The creator of an application may not only grant others authority to use the application as shown in the following example:

GRANT RUN ON PERSAPPL TO DOV2, NORMAN1

but may also grant users the authority to grant authority to others. This is done by adding the WITH GRANT OPTION clause as shown in the following example:

GRANT RUN ON PERSAPPL TO DOV2 **WITH GRANT OPTION**

After this command is executed, DOV2 not only receives authority to run PERSAPPL but may also grant authority to other users to execute the application.

Authority may be revoked from a user by issuing a REVOKE command. To remove DOV2's authority to run the PERSAPPL program, the user can specify:

REVOKE RUN ON PERSAPPL FROM DOV2

When RUN authority is revoked from a user who had the authority to GRANT RUN to others, the authorization to run the application is **also** revoked from any other users who received their authorization from this user. This implies that if DOV2 issued a GRANT RUN to user MARTHA, MARTHA's authority is automatically revoked when DOV2's authority is revoked.

To check that the application creator has the authority to use the tables accessed the DBA could execute:

```
SELECT BNAME, BCREATOR, SELECTAUTH, INSERTAUTH, UPDATEAUTH,
                DELETEAUTH
    FROM SYSTEM.SYSTABAUTH, SYSTEM.SYSUSAGE
    WHERE BNAME = TTNAME AND BCREATOR = TCREATOR AND
        DCREATOR = :CREATORNAME AND GRANTEE IN
                (:CREATORNAME, GRANTOR) AND DTYPE = 'X'
    ORDER BY BCREATOR, BTNAME
```

The AUTH columns in this query should contain the letter **'Y'** if the user has authorization. The columns and tables accessed contain the following information:

TCREATOR $\Rightarrow$ userid of the person who created the table (or view).

BNAME $\Rightarrow$ the table or view name.

BCREATOR = TCREATOR $\Rightarrow$ implies that the row being queried is one where the creator of the table accessed in the application (BCREATOR) is the same one who created the table being checked (TCREATOR).

BNAME = **TTNAME** $\Rightarrow$ the table accessed in the application (BNAME) whose authorization is being checked, is the same one that is in SYSTEM.SYSTABAUTH (TTNAME).

DCREATOR $\Rightarrow$ the person who defined the *access module.*

SYSTABAUTH $\Rightarrow$ a catalog table listing the users who have privileges to access tables or views.

SYSUSAGE $\Rightarrow$ a catalog table which lists the dependencies of *access modules* on tables, views, indexes, or dbspaces.

DTYPE $\Rightarrow$ 'X' means *access module,* 'Y' means view.

Grant to Public

The GRANT command, in the past, allowed the specification of WITH GRANT OPTION to PUBLIC:

GRANT ... TO PUBLIC **WITH GRANT OPTION**

This allowed the application programmer who did not have the explicit GRANT authorization to GRANT RUN to others on a program so that they would not have to be concerned with authority. In order to comply with the ANS SQL standard which requires that the WITH GRANT OPTION part of the GRANT TO PUBLIC statement have no effect, recent versions of SQL/DS no longer give the WITH GRANT OPTION authority to those who receive their own authority via GRANT . . . to PUBLIC.

This change can create a problem because the user no longer has the authority to GRANT the authority to use the table or view to other users and it is immaterial that they have authority themselves from the GRANT TO PUBLIC command. If this user installs an application or a program product, for example, he or she must have the authority to GRANT access to the tables to other users before the authority to run this application can be granted to them. This authority to GRANT authority to others is no longer given to the public and explicit GRANTs are now required for application developers and DBAs installing packages that use SQL/DS.

DYNAMIC SQL

It is better to execute one command than to execute many similar commands. This is especially true when internal DBSPACEs are used for sorting. An application recently examined because it was running out of internal DBSPACE was found to have multiple copies of the same command each with a slightly modified predicate. Each command used its own internal DBSPACE and exhausted the supply. One command would have reused the same internal DBSPACEs each time it was executed.

Use of dynamic SQL should be considered if an additional predicate will be added, if an additional column will be retrieved, if the table or view name is changed in the query, or if the form of an SQL statement changes in any other way during processing. Dynamic SQL can be efficient because it is possible to prepare an SQL/DS statement for execution once and then use it many times. Users executing the application programs need the proper authority on any tables or views accessed in the program. For additional information, please refer to Chapter 3.

CREATING TEST DATA

In order to properly test any application system, "good" test data must be prepared. There is a number of points to take into consideration when test data for SQL/DS is prepared. Some of the following should be used:

1. The test tables should be large enough to enable a reasonable test to be run.
2. A realistic range of key values should be used.
3. Data that tests as many program paths as possible should be used.
4. If the data changes significantly after the index was created, UPDATE STATISTICS should be run.
5. The EXPLAIN facility should be used when testing.
6. The catalog table, SYSCOLSTATS, and LOW2KEY, HIGH2KEY, and COLCOUNT columns should be checked to ensure that the values match the data.
7. Modify the test database system catalog values with care to reflect the values in the production system.

In VSE/SP, the use of SYNONYMs to point to the correct table may be very helpful in testing applications that will use test tables that also exist in production in the same database. One table may be labeled **TEST.PERSONNEL_TBL** and the other **PROD.PERSONNEL_TBL**. SYNONYMS can be used during precompile, for example, to indicate which table should be accessed.

SUMMARY

The quality of the user population is a very important element of application design. After analysis of the needs of the users, the application designer must determine which of the SQL/DS facilities will be used by the application and in which language the application will be programmed. COBOL or COBOL II, CSP, and RXSQL are the major development languages. SQL/DS may also be accessed using QMF, PL/I, FORTRAN, 'C', APL, AS, ASSEMBLER, and other products. SQL is a very powerful nonprocedural language and the application developer should learn its strengths and idiosyncrasies before starting to design.

Host variables are defined in a DECLARE section. They may be used in regular COBOL commands as well as in SQL commands. Each host variable should exactly match the column definition. The

SQL commands are written with delimiters indicating the beginning and end of the command.

Indicator variables are used to contain the indicator bytes to be used by SQL/DS. The keyword INDICATOR may precede the *indicator variable* to provide better documentation.

The application can only store the contents of one row at a time. A *cursor* is used to control the next row to be read or inserted. When the application is ready to receive the data, the FETCH command is issued to specify the *host variables* to be used to hold the data. The PUT command is used to INSERT multiple rows into a table. Once a *cursor* is opened, any modifications made to the contents of *host variables* used in the conditional clauses of SQL/DS commands have no effect unless the *cursor* is closed and reopened. A major cause of poor performance is excessive opening and closing of *cursor*s.

After every executable SQL command, SQL/DS will return a code. Error handling helps protect the integrity of the database and every program should test these error codes. The WHENEVER command indicates the action that should be taken when SQL warnings, errors, and NOT FOUND conditions are encountered. The scope of each statement is determined by its physical position in the source code and not by its position in the logic flow.

Applications are preprocessed using the SQLPREP command. An *access module* is created with the access path to the data. ISOL and BLOCK are the two main performance parameters for the precompile. Isolation level *Repeatable Read* ensures that no one will be able to modify a row or page being viewed by the user until the *logical unit of work* is complete. *Cursor Stability* should be specified to enhance concurrency and when a lock is only needed to be held on the last row or page accessed by the application. Blocking can have a very significant impact on performance.

Access modules are created in public DBSPACES. These DBSPACES also hold VIEW definitions in table format. Whenever a table or an index is dropped or a referential relationship changed, the *access module* is marked invalid. The first user of an application requiring the re-creation of an *access module* will experience a degradation in response time while the new *access module* is being created.

A *logical unit of work* begins with the first SQL/DS statement and ends with the COMMIT WORK or ROLLBACK WORK statement. The USER who precompiled an application can GRANT authority to others or REVOKE authority from others to run the application.

RECOMMENDATIONS

1. Commands such as CREATE TABLE, CREATE INDEX, and GRANT authority should not be used in application programs.

2. The host variable should exactly match the column datatype with which it will be compared.

3. Do not close and open a *cursor* too many times in an application.

4. An *indicator variable* should be added to the host variable when a column is nullable.

5. The *indicator variable* should always be checked.

6. WHENEVER commands should always be coded explicitly to inform the system what action should be taken in each specific case.

7. To avoid the "morning after" syndrome when tables and indexes are reorganized, the DataBase Services Utility should be used to UNLOAD and RELOAD PROGRAMS to automatically create a new access module.

8. When a program is no longer needed it should be dropped.

9. A transaction should always be explicitly terminated.

ISQL AND DBSU

ISQL

ISQL is a very powerful tool that can be used to test queries, produce one-time *"quick-and-dirty"* reports, handle one-time updates and deletes, check catalog statistics, and extract many other types of information. A user who learns how to use ISQL will find it very helpful.

The DBA, however, should severely limit the use of ISQL in the production environment. Not only is there no *audit trail* when using ISQL, and little control over the commands entered by the users, but there is also a very excessive use of system resources especially when inefficient queries are made. VSE/SP system programmers can limit the number of simultaneous users of ISQL by assigning the CICS task (ISQL) to a specific CICS class and by limiting this class to one user at a time. The VM/SP systems programmer cannot practically control the number of ISQL users but should administratively ensure that its use is limited in the production environment.

When ISQL initiates a query, the optimizer dynamically prepro-cesses the query and creates a temporary *access module.* This entails locking and system resource usage that may impact the performance of other transactions.

One of the default values of ISQL is **Repeatable Read.** In many installations, the DBA neglects to create an SQLDBA default profile to modify the isolation level to *cursor stability.* When the inexperi-enced user queries the database via ISQL, many tables may be locked without the user remembering to free them quickly. If the ISQL user then becomes involved in a telephone conversation or takes a coffee break, the tables will be locked for long periods of time. The DBA should use ISQL to create the following profile:

```
ISQL
CONNECT SQLDBA IDENTIFIED BY SQLDBAPW
INPUT ROUTINE
'PROFILE', 10, 'SET ISOL CS', NULL
END
EXIT
```

While the above will not prevent ISQL problems, it will establish *cursor stability* as the default, rather than *repeatable read,* for all users who have not created their own profiles.

ISQL users should follow a few basic rules to avoid negatively impacting the performance of the entire system:

1. Use very selective queries by specifying the column names desired. Do **not** use SELECT * when it is not necessary.
2. The user should **always** respond promptly after an update or a delete that modified a number of rows.
3. PF3 should be used as quickly as possible to end a query. The user should **not** leave displayed data on the screen and become involved in other business.
4. When stored queries and routines are used often, the user should consider writing a preprocessed program that would eliminate the continual dynamic preprocessing of the queries.

ISQL Routines

ISQL routines can be used to simplify and standardize work with ISQL. The user can INSERT commands into the ROUTINE table and RUN them. The following is an example of a routine that will SELECT, format, and display data from the table. The developer could also build a routine to accept parameters so as to make the routine more flexible by inserting the following commands into the ROUTINE table:

```
PRNTPERS   010   SET ISOL CS
PRNTPERS   020   SELECT NAME, STRTDTE, ENDDTE, DEPT -
PRNTPERS   030   FROM PERSONNEL_TBL -
PRNTPERS   040   WHERE USER_ID = &1
PRNTPERS   050   FORMAT COL 2 NAME 'START DATE'
PRNTPERS   060   FORMAT COL 3 NAME 'END DATE'
PRNTPERS   070   FORMAT TTITLE 'PERSONNEL INFO FOR &1'
PRNTPERS   080   DISPLAY
PRNTPERS   090   PRINT
PRNTPERS   100   END
PRNTPERS   110   COMMIT WORK
```

To see the information about user 2143, the following RUN command would be issued:

RUN PRNTPERS (2143)

The 2143 would be substituted for &1 in both places.

In VM/SP, an EXEC could be used to run ISQL without the user having access to ISQL directly as shown in this example of a partial EXEC:

```
/*    To run ISQL within an EXEC      */
/*    The name of this is PERS EXEC    */
      say " enter user_id "
      pull userid .
      QUEUE    'SET ISOL CS'
      QUEUE    'SELECT NAME, STRTDTE, ENDDTE, DEPT -'
      QUEUE    'FROM PERSONNEL_TBL -'
      QUEUE    "WHERE USER_ID =" USERID
      QUEUE    "FORMAT COL 2 NAME 'START DATE'"
      QUEUE    "FORMAT COL 3 NAME 'END DATE'"
      QUEUE    "FORMAT TTITLE 'PERSONNEL INFO FOR"USERID""
      QUEUE    'DISPLAY'
      QUEUE    'PRINT'
      QUEUE    'END'
      QUEUE    'COMMIT WORK'
      QUEUE    'EXIT'

EXEC ISQL  /*  this executes the stacked commands  */
```

DATABASE SERVICES UTILITY (DBSU)

There is a distinct advantage to using the SQL/DS DBSU instead of ISQL for the creation of VIEWS and tables and for other tasks of the DBA. Using the DBSU provides a copy of the jobs run both for documentation and for re-use when necessary.

As with ISQL, the DBSU creates an *access module* dynamically every time it runs and its use for creating tables, indexes, and views can involve many system resources and locks. The data or table LOADs and UNLOADs, which should also be performed via the DBSU, use large amounts of resources and locks. Most DBSU activity should be done after peak on-line periods and should be carefully tuned to ensure minimum usage of resources.

SET AUTOCOMMIT ON should be specified when possible or explicit COMMIT WORK commands should be included in the DBSU job stream. When unloading data, it is usually necessary to specify REPEATABLE READ but when *cursor stability* can be specified, it should be used by including *SET ISOL CS* in the commands.

The DBSU also runs with the default SET STATISTICS ON which implies that an UPDATE STATISTICS command will be automatically executed **every** time a table is loaded. When several tables are being loaded in the same DBSPACE the DBA should first specify:

SET STATISTICS OFF

and COMMIT WORK after each table is loaded. When all of the tables have been loaded, UPDATE STATISTICS on the DBSPACE should be specified. This will also reduce the locking on system tables and will allow other users to continue their transactions.

Very long-running DBSU jobs should be run in single-user mode with no logging so as to reduce the LOG I/O and to avoid exhausting the log space. DBSU jobs should be as selective as possible and if queries are required frequently they should be made part of a preprocessed program. The COMMITCOUNT parameter should be used for large DATALOAD jobs so that the entire job does not have to be rerun when a problem forces an ABEND toward the end of the job. When unloading a large table, use TABLE or DBSPACE locking to reduce locking overhead.

Using EXEC in VM/SP

As with ISQL, EXECs can be used to run DBSU jobs. DATALOAD and DATAUNLD and any other DBSU command can be prepared in a CMS file and executed using the following example:

```
/*  DBSU EXEC to run DBSU jobs  */
pull flenme fletyp flemode .
"EXEC SQLDBSU IN(" flenme fletyp flemode ") PR(PRNT)"
```

The user must prepare a CMS file with the DBSU commands and issue the following command:

```
DBSU fn ft fm
```

EXPLAIN TABLES

One of the more powerful tools accessible to the SQL/DS professional is the EXPLAIN facility. This facility is available to inform the user how the SQL/DS optimizer will access the data when a specific SQL command is executed. EXPLAIN will indicate whether or not an index will be used and whether or not a SORT will be required. If an index will be used, EXPLAIN will record the name of the index and how it will be used. It will also estimate the number of rows that must be accessed and how often subqueries, if present, will be executed. When a JOIN is specified, EXPLAIN will record which JOIN method was used and which columns could use indexes.

The EXPLAIN command, in effect, describes how the optimizer will access the tables to satisfy each (part of the) query. As does the optimizer, EXPLAIN depends upon the accuracy of the statistics in the system catalogs and upon the indexes, buffers, volume of data, and other resources that exist at the time the command is executed. If new indexes are created or old ones dropped or the statistics are updated after a massive insert or delete of data, the results of earlier EXPLAINs will not necessarily reflect the methods that will now be used by the optimizer to precompile the query.

When EXPLAIN is executed, the estimates and decisions of the optimizer are recorded in one or more of four EXPLAIN tables. These tables must be created for each user prior to the execution of the EXPLAIN command. The information is then available to the application developer or DBA.

The EXPLAIN facility uses the following four SQL/DS tables:

1. **PLAN_TABLE.** This is usually the most useful table because it indicates whether or not an index was used. When an index was used, it specifies which index was used and how it was used (selectively or non-selectively). It also specifies the JOIN

method used, if applicable, and if SORTs are needed. One quick glance and the index usage is known. In many cases, between 50 percent and 75 percent of performance tuning improvements are achieved through the proper use of the best index.

2. **REFERENCE_TABLE**. For the only column in a predicate (WHERE clause) or for every column referenced in a predicate connected by an AND connector, this table has one row which describes how the column is used. It also indicates which columns might make useful index columns.

3. **STRUCTURE_TABLE**. This table contains data concerning the estimated number of rows returned by a query and its subqueries. It contains one row for each query block (section of code) in the statement that has been EXPLAINED. It also contains the estimated number of times a *child* query of this *parent* will be executed each time the *parent* is executed. This information enables the user to differentiate between the costs of each individual part of the query.

4. **COST_TABLE**. Contains the internally calculated cost of the I/O and CPU to execute the query. The optimizer examines all or many of the possible paths to satisfy the command and estimates the "cost" of each. The "cost" of the most efficient path is returned in the COST_TABLE. This value is **not** very useful because it cannot accurately be used to compare queries. If every path examined, for example, had a fixed cost of 3.0, then 3.0 would not be included in the cost value. The only use of this value may be when comparing the exact same query after adding or dropping an index, after deleting or inserting massive amounts of data, and after updating statistics. Even in the above case the value may not be dependable for comparison.

How to Get Started

To use the EXPLAIN facility a user must create EXPLAIN tables. It is recommended that the DBS Utility commands be used to create the tables, as shown in the example that follows. The tables could also be created using ISQL, QMF, or an application program. If the DBA will be creating the tables for a user, each table name should have the user's ID as a prefix:

MIKE1.REFERENCE_TABLE

Creating EXPLAIN Tables

The following example uses DBSU commands to create the EX-PLAIN tables:

COMMENT ' Create Explain Tables If the tables already exist and need to be re-created, remove the DROP TABLE commands from the COMMENTs.

DROP TABLE REFERENCE_TABLE; '

CREATE TABLE **REFERENCE_TABLE**

```
(QUERYNO         SMALLINT,
QBLOCKNO         SMALLINT      NOT NULL,
CREATOR          CHAR (8)      NOT NULL,
TNAME            VARCHAR (18)  NOT NULL,
TABNO            SMALLINT      NOT NULL,
COLNO            SMALLINT      NOT NULL,
FILTER           FLOAT         NOT NULL,
DETAIL           VARCHAR (28)  NOT NULL)
IN PRIVDBSP;
```

COMMENT 'DROP TABLE PLAN_TABLE; '

CREATE TABLE **PLAN_TABLE**

```
(QUERYNO          SMALLINT,
QBLOCKNO          SMALLINT      NOT NULL,
PLANNO            SMALLINT      NOT NULL,
METHOD            SMALLINT      NOT NULL,
CREATOR           CHAR (8)      NOT NULL,
TNAME             VARCHAR (18)  NOT NULL,
TABNO             SMALLINT      NOT NULL,
ACCESSTYPE        CHAR (1)      NOT NULL,
ACCESSCREATOR     CHAR (8)      NOT NULL,
ACCESSNAME        VARCHAR (18)  NOT NULL,
SORTNEW           CHAR (1)      NOT NULL,
SORTCOMP          CHAR (1)      NOT NULL)
IN PRIVDBSP;
```

COMMENT ' DROP TABLE COST_TABLE; '

CREATE TABLE **COST_TABLE**

```
(QUERYNO          SMALLINT,
QBLOCKNO          SMALLINT      NOT NULL,
COST              FLOAT         NOT NULL)
IN PRIVDBSP;
```

COMMENT 'DROP TABLE STRUCTURE_TABLE;'

CREATE TABLE **STRUCTURE_TABLE**

(QUERYNO	SMALLINT,	
QBLOCKNO	SMALLINT	NOT NULL,
ROWCOUNT	INTEGER	NOT NULL,
TIMES	FLOAT	NOT NULL,
PARENT	SMALLINT	NOT NULL,
ATOPEN	CHAR (1)	NOT NULL)
IN PRIVDBSP;		

COMMENT 'THIS IS THE END OF THE CREATE EXPLAIN TABLES DBSU '

Using the EXPLAIN Command

The EXPLAIN command can be issued from an application program, via the database utility (DBSU), or interactively from ISQL. The user can key in the command as it would normally be written, preceded by the EXPLAIN keyword. Each EXPLAIN command should be given a query number to facilitate the retrieval of the output from the EX-PLAIN tables. As mentioned earlier, the QUERYNO should be set in multiples of 10 because when internally generated statements are required by referential integrity, a **+1** is added to the QUERYNO to indicate that it is an internally generated statement.

The user might key in the following command from an ISQL terminal:

EXPLAIN SET QUERYNO = 10 FOR -
    SELECT * FROM PERSONNEL_TBL -
      WHERE USER_ID > 3324

An example of a query and a sample output in each table will be found at the end of this section.

Not every SQL command needs to or can be EXPLAINed. The commands that are eligible are SELECT, INSERT, UPDATE, and DELETE. The SELECT commands are the major candidates for the EXPLAIN command. They are usually the most heavily used and abused. These commands are found in application programs and utility procedures and are heavily used in ISQL, RXSQL, and QMF. It is especially important to test SELECT and UPDATE commands in long-running batch applications and highly used on-line applications. One-time statements and rarely used DBS utility commands are not usually worth testing unless they have a great impact upon performance.

In an application, the SELECT and other commands usually utilize *host variables.* To receive accurate test results, it is important to

use the EXPLAIN facility from within the application rather than via ISQL because *host variables* used with certain clauses can**not** be used with an index. Host variables can**not** be specified when ISQL or the DBSU are used. When a test is run from ISQL, a constant must be substituted that may result in the EXPLAIN facility placing inaccurate information in the EXPLAIN tables for this query.

Running EXPLAIN in a test environment is only partially accurate but it is usually the best that can be done. Most installations do not allow the application developers to run EXPLAIN in the production environment. The optimizer not only uses indexes to determine access paths but also considers table size, data distribution, buffers available, and many other resources which are **not** the same in the TEST environment as in the production environment. In an enlightened and experienced environment, the DBA might be allowed to modify the TEST database catalogs so that they duplicate the production catalogs and in that way give the EXPLAIN facility the same statistics available to the optimizer in production. Any changes to the system catalogs should be done with extreme care and **only** in a test database. These changes should usually be made via a DBSU both for documentation purposes and in order to facilitate backout and re-modification when needed. VSE/SP users who only have one database should **not** modify the catalog.

The EXPLAIN facility should be used to ensure proper index usage and acceptable performance levels before commands are included in application programs, DBSUs, or EXECs. Where EXPLAIN was not executed before a command was used, it may also be tested after the command has been placed into production. Its use may suggest ways of improving or determining the cause of poor performance.

Testing EXPLAIN in an Application

Prior to modifying an application the user should ensure that a backup copy exists. The application does **not** have to be compiled or executed to be tested with EXPLAIN. The precompile of a program will not only prepare an *access module* based upon the decisions of the optimizer but will use those same decisions to update the EXPLAIN tables. To execute the EXPLAIN of a set of commands, modify the source program as described below and precompile.

The DECLARE CURSOR statements should be removed and all statements to be tested should be modified to contain the EXPLAIN keyword and its parameters:

EXEC SQL **EXPLAIN ALL SET QUERYNO = 10** FOR

```
        SELECT NAME, ADDRESS, BIRTHDTE, SALARY * 1.1
            FROM PERSONNEL_TBL
            WHERE START_DATE > '01-01-1990' AND
                DEPT = :HOSTDEPT AND
                SALARY < :HOSTSAL AND
                (STATUS = 'M' OR EMPTME = 'F') AND
                CHILDNUM > 2
            ORDER BY 4
    END-EXEC
```

When all of the commands are written in a standard way in programs it would be easy, especially under VM/SP, to write an EXEC (or a procedure) to add the EXPLAIN commands automatically. If, for example, the EXEC SQL portion of the command is always placed on a separate line as shown in the following example:

EXEC SQL
```
        SELECT NAME, ADDRESS, BIRTHDTE, SALARY * 1.1
            FROM PERSONNEL_TBL
            WHERE START_DATE > '01-01-1990' AND
                etc.
```

the following EXEC might be used. It will add the "EXPLAIN ALL SET QUERYNO = 000" to the line with the EXEC SQL and will modify the QUERYNO = 000 to a usable number:

```
/* THIS EXEC IS ONLY USEFUL IF EXEC SQL IS ON A SEPARATE LINE.
    filetype should be EXPLAIN ** */
'MAKEBUF'
/*THE EXEC MODIFIES EXEC SQL AND ADDS EXPLAIN . . .*/
clrscrn
say 'ENTER the filename and the approximate number of SQL'
say ' statements in the application program. Please'
say '    overestimate the number. '
say ' EXAMPLE:   APLPR001, 25 '
say ' '
say ' When the EXEC enters the XEDIT portion, check the '
say '    file, remove DECLARE, OPEN, CLOSE cursor statement'
say '    and insure that all statements were '
say '    converted correctly. After the application is'
say '    correct, enter FILE on the command line. '
ARG FN NUM .
```

```
QUEUE  'CHANGE /EXEC SQL /EXEC SQL EXPLAIN / * * '
QUEUE  'TOP'
QUEUE  'CHANGE /EXPLAIN /EXPLAIN ALL SET QUERYNO=000 FOR/* *'
QUEUE  'TOP'
/*  EDIT FILE, REMOVE DECLARE CURSOR AND EXTRA EXPLAINS  */
'XEDIT' FN 'EXPLAIN A (NOPROFILE'
/*  THIS PART OF THE EXEC WILL NUMBER THE QUERYNO FOR EACH
       EXPLAIN STATEMENT AFTER THE USER FILES THE APPLICATION  * */
'MAKEBUF'
NEWNUM = 10 /* to be used to identify query */
cntnum = 0
DO UNTIL CNTNUM > NUM
QUEUE  'LOCATE /QUERYNO=000/'
QUEUE  'CHANGE /QUERYNO=000/QUERYNO=' NEWNUM '/ '
NEWNUM = NEWNUM + 10
cntnum = cntnum + 1
END
clrscrn
say ' The file will now be displayed on the screen '
say ' CHECK the output to insure that the numbering '
say ' of the QUERYNO has been done correctly '
say ' Enter FILE on the command line after the application '
say ' has been checked '
say ' '
say ' HIT the ENTER KEY to continue '
ARG GARBAGE
'XEDIT' FN 'EXPLAIN A (NOPROFILE'

/*  end of the EXEC  */
```

After using this EXEC, review the output as per the instructions displayed on the terminal.

Prior to precompiling the application program, the user might want to delete all of the rows placed in the EXPLAIN tables by previous runs. The following DBS Utility commands might be useful:

```
COMMENT ' THIS DBSU WILL DELETE THE EXPLAIN TABLE CONTENTS '

CONNECT DOV1 IDENTIFIED BY DOV1PSWD;
SET AUTOCOMMIT ON;
DELETE FROM PLAN_TABLE;
DELETE FROM COST_TABLE;
DELETE FROM REFERENCE_TABLE;
DELETE FROM STRUCTURE_TABLE;

COMMENT ' END OF THIS DBSU '
```

COMMIT WORK does not have to be placed at the end of the DBSU commands because it will automatically be executed when the default SET AUTOCOMMIT ON is used. If a COMMIT WORK is added, it will be executed twice. At this point the application program may be precompiled. The following EXEC might be used to precompile a COBOL application program:

```
/* exec to precompile for EXPLAIN facility */
say ' ENTER filename, filetype, filemode of the '
say '    application to be precompiled'
say '    EXAMPLE: TST001, EXPLAIN, A '
say ' To avoid overlaying the access modules of existing'
say '    applications the SQL program name will always'
say '       be DOV001 '
ARG FN FT FM GARBAGE

USERID='DOV1'
PW='DOV1PSWD'

'EXEC SQLPREP COB PP
(PREP=DOV001,USER='USERID'/'PW',BLOCK,KEEP,ISOL(CS)) IN ('FN
FT FM')'

        SAVCODE=RC
        EXIT SAVCODE
/* END of the EXEC */
```

What to Look For

Note that the most useful tables are the PLAN_TABLE and the REFERENCE_TABLE that give the user an immediate picture of the efficiency of the query. The PLAN_TABLE answers the questions, "Are indexes used?," "Which indexes?," "How are they used?," "What is the JOIN method?," "Are SORTs required?," etc. The REFERENCE_TABLE contains the *filter factor* (the *filter factor* is a probability factor and is the estimate of the percentage of all of the rows in the table that need to be accessed) and a listing of the columns that are referenced, how they are used, and whether or not the query might benefit from an index on that column.

The following is a list of some of the columns in each of the tables and a description of the data they contain:

PLAN TABLE

> **PLANNO** $\Rightarrow$ indicates the order in which SQL/DS processes the steps.

METHOD ⟹ indicates how the joins are processed.

Method 1 indicates a nested loop join.
Method 2 indicates a merge scan join.
Method 3 indicates that additional sorts are needed.

ACCESSTYPE ⟹ The most important column.

Type R indicates that **no** index is used. SQL scans the entire DBSPACE each time (not just the table pages).

Type I indicates that an index is used with key values. **The best performance requires a Type I** usage.

Type W indicates that SQL/DS will use an index but **only** to find out on which data pages rows from this table are found. It scans the entire table **every** time. Type W is used to avoid reading data pages which do not have any data belonging to the table being accessed. This situation is only possible when there is more than one table in the DBSPACE.

ACCESSNAME ⟹ The name of the index used. This enables the user to check if SQL/DS is using the index that the user thinks would give the best results.

REFERENCE TABLE

COLNO ⟹ indicates the column in the table referred to by this row.

FILTER ⟹ the fraction of the estimated (number of rows that SQL/DS has to read to satisfy the *predicate* using this column) as compared to the total number of rows in the table
answer set / total rows in table.
If the retrieving of one row, for example, will satisfy the condition and there are 1500 rows in the table, the filter factor is
$$1/1500 \Rightarrow .0006666 \Rightarrow 6.6666E\text{-}04$$
(expressed as a floating point value.) The closer this value comes to $1.0E + 00$, the less the column is useful as an index column. 1.0 means that a scan of the entire table is needed to satisfy the condition.

DETAIL ⟹ indicates some of the uses of the column in the query. More than one of the following values, in any order, can appear in this column.

W ⟹ The column appears in the WHERE clause and the query would benefit if there were an index on this column. This does NOT mean that SQL/DS will definitely use the index on this column. If there are a number of indexes, the optimizer will choose the **"BEST"**.

J ⇒ The column is used in a JOIN.

P ⇒ It might pay to use this column in an index for system dependent reasons.

STRUCTURE_TABLE

ROWCOUNT ⇒ The estimated number of accessed rows. For a DELETE or UPDATE it is an estimate of the rows affected. For a SELECT it is the estimated number of rows returned.

PARENT ⇒ The number of the query block which is the *parent table* of this query block.

ATOPEN ⇒ This specifies whether a query block is executed several times (Y) or only once (N) for each execution of the *parent* query block.

TIMES ⇒ When this query block has a child, this column contains an estimate of the number of times the *child table* of this query block is executed.

COST_TABLE

COST ⇒ This is the total estimated cost including the cost of internally generated statements caused by *referential relationships* for the first QBLOCKNO. If there are other QBLOCKNOs, the cost is a total estimated cost of this block including all *child table* costs.

EXPLAIN Table Example

The following example of one of a series of complex queries in an application will show the query, each EXPLAIN table, and an indication of the what the PLAN table will contain after the indexes were improved. The response on the transaction was reduced from 30 minutes to less than 1 minute. The query was part of what might be called an on-line batch transaction because the report was triggered on-line:

```
EXEC SQL EXPLAIN ALL SET QUERYNO = 20 FOR
SELECT DISTINCT CUSTOMER_NAME, A.CUSTOMER_CODE
     FROM CUSTOMER1 A, AML_REPORT B, ACCT_TO_ACCT C, ACCT D
WHERE (B.ACCT_CODE = C.BEN_COMPANY AND
     (C.ABBA_COMPANY = :SQL_ACCT_CODE OR
     C.ABBA_COMPANY IN (SELECT BEN_COMPANY
          FROM ACCT_TO_ACCT WHERE ABBA_COMPANY =
                         :SQL_ACCT_CODE))) AND
     (B.SALE_DATE BETWEEN :SQL_SEL_STRT AND :SQL_SEL_END)
     AND (B.ACCT_CODE = D.ACCT_CODE AND
     D.INDEX_DEP_FLAG IS NULL OR D.INDEX_DEP_FLAG = ' ')
     AND (B.CUSTOMER_CODE = A.CUSTOMER_CODE) AND
          B.CUSTOMER_CODE IN ('0201', '0409', '6300',
                         '4662', '3990', 'DEAL')
     AND B.CUSTOMER_ = 'Y'     AND
     B.ACCESS_TYPE IN ('G', 'C', 'M', 'N', 'R')   AND
     B.IMA ^ = 'Y' AND ((B.ABG_SALES_ID ^ = '2') OR
               (B.ABG_SALES_ID = '3' AND SAVE_IT = 0))
UNION
SELECT DISTINCT CUSTOMER_NAME, A.CUSTOMER_CODE
     FROM CUSTOMER1 A, AML_HIST B, ACCT_TO_ACCT C, ACCT D
WHERE (B.SALE_DATE BETWEEN :SQL_SEL_STRT AND :SQL_SEL_END)
     AND (B.ACCT_CODE = C.BEN_COMPANY AND
     (C.ABBA_COMPANY = :SQL_ACCT_CODE OR
     C.ABBA_COMPANY IN (SELECT BEN_COMPANY
          FROM ACCT_TO_ACCT WHERE ABBA_COMPANY =
                         :SQL_ACCT_CODE))) AND
     (B.ACCT_CODE = D.ACCT_CODE     AND
     D.INDEX_DEP_FLAG IS NULL OR D.INDEX_DEP_FLAG = ' ')
     AND (B.CUSTOMER_CODE = A.CUSTOMER_CODE) AND
          B.CUSTOMER_CODE IN ('0201', '0409', '6300', '4662',
                         '3990', 'DEAL')
     AND B.CUSTOMER_ = 'Y'    AND
     B.ACCESS_TYPE IN ('G', 'C', 'M', 'N', 'R') AND
     B.IMA ^ = 'Y' AND ((B.ABG_SALES_ID ^ = '2')   OR
               (B.ABG_SALES_ID = '3' AND SAVE_IT = 0))
ORDER BY 1
END-EXEC
```

The query basically is a UNION listing the names of customers from a current table AML_REPORT and a history table AML_HIST where certain conditions exist. The following is the output of the EXPLAIN tables for the above query:

PLAN_TABLE Example

QUERYNO	QBLOCKNO	PLANNO	METHOD	TNAME	ACCESS TYPE
20	2	1	0	ACCT_TO_ACCT	I
20	1	1	0	AML_REPORT	I
20	1	2	2	ACCT_TO_ACCT	W
20	1	3	1	CUSTOMER1	W
20	1	4	1	ACCT	W
20	1	5	3		
20	4	1	0	ACCT_TO_ACCT	I
20	3	1	0	AML_HIST	W
20	3	2	1	ACCT_TO_ACCT	I
20	3	3	1	CUSTOMER1	W
20	3	4	1	ACCT	R
20	3	5	3		

This table describes how the optimizer divided the query into four query blocks and chose an access method for each table each time the table was accessed. The same table was accessed more than once because of the nature of the query and the optimizer did not always access the same table in the same way. This output does not include the ACCESSNAME column which would have also shown the name of the index chosen.

When the DBA or application developer notes an entry other than 'I' in the ACCESSTYPE column, it signifies that an index was **not** used selectively and something usually can be done to improve performance. A 'W' indicates that while an index was used, it was not used selectively and every row in the table had to be accessed at least once. When ACCESSTYPE is 'R', **no index** was used and every page in the DBSPACE was accessed at least once.

Using the PLAN_TABLE, the DBA has a starting point to improve the performance of the query. The query should be examined along with the indexes to determine why the predicates were not *index matching*. The columns in each index for the PERSONNEL_TBL and the DEPT_TBL, for example, may be viewed by executing the following command:

```
SELECT TNAME, INAME, COLNAMES
    FROM SYSTEM.SYSINDEXES
        WHERE TNAME IN ('PERSONNEL_TBL', 'DEPT_TBL')
        ORDER BY 1
```

The output might contain the following information:

TNAME	INAME	COLNAMES
DEPT_TBL	DEPT_IDX1	+DEPT_NO,
DEPT_TBL	DEPT_IX2A	+MAN_EMP_NO, −EMP_NUMS, <
PERSONNEL_TBL	PERS_EMP_IX	+EMPLOYEE_NUM,
PERSONNEL_TBL	PERS_SAL_IX	+SALARY, +DEPENDENTS, <
PERSONNEL_TBL	PERS_SSNO_IX	+SSNO,

The '<' character in COLNAMES indicates that there are **more** names in the column but the maximum display size has been reached. The user can issue a SET VARCHAR command to change the display size to 100 and reissue the SELECT:

SET VARCHAR 100

When additional information is needed, a command to see if the indexes are clustered might be issued:

```
SELECT TNAME, INAME, INDEXTYPE, CLUSTER, CLUSTERRATIO
    FROM SYSTEM.SYSINDEXES
        WHERE TNAME IN ('PERSONNEL_TBL', 'DEPT_TBL')
            ORDER BY TNAME
```

The output might contain:

TNAME	INAME	INDEXTYPE	CLUSTER	CLUSTERRATIO
DEPT_TBL	DEPT_IDX1	U	F	10000
DEPT_TBL	DEPT_IX2A	D	N	3665
PERSONNEL_TBL	PERS_EMP_IX	U	W	9879
PERSONNEL_TBL	PERS_SAL_IX	D	N	411
PERSONNEL_TBL	PERS_SSNO_IX	U	N	1755

It might be noted that the index DEPT_IX2A is actually a unique index but the creator did **not** specify UNIQUE when it was created and SQL/DS does not have any way of knowing that it is unique. A unique index should be created as UNIQUE because the optimizer **prefers** to use unique indexes.

Reference Table Example

The REFERENCE_TABLE contents for the original complex command are as follows:

QUERY NO	QBLOCK NO	TNAME	TABNO	COLNO	FILTER	DETAIL
20	2	ACCT_TO_ACCT	5	**0**	0.0E0	
20	2	ACCT_TO_ACCT	5	2	1.25E−01	WP
20	0		0	0	0.0E0	**00**
20	1	CUSTOMER1	1	0	0.0E0	
20	1	AMI_REPORT	2	0	0.0E0	
20	1	ACCT_TO_ACCT	3	0	0.0E0	
20	1	ACCT	4	0	0.0E0	
20	1	AMI_REPORT	2	20	9.000357E−1	**W**
20	1	AMI_REPORT	2	12	2.5E−01	W
20	1	CUSTOMER1	1	5	9.99423E−02	W
20	1	AMI_REPORT	2	11	5.0E−01	
20	1	AMI_REPORT	2	1	2.5E−01	W
20	1	AMI_REPORT	2	17	6.45161E−03	WJ
20	1	ACCT_TO_ACCT	3	1	6.45161E−03	WJ
20	1	ACCT	4	3	5.0E−01	WP
20	1	CUSTOMER1	1	3	**1.0E+00**	P
20	1	AMI_REPORT	2	13	1.0E+00	P
20	1	ACCT_TO_ACCT	3	2	1.0E+00	P
20	1	ACCT	4	5	1.0E+00	P
20	1	ACCT	4	7	1.0E+00	P
20	4	ACCT_TO_ACCT	5	0	0.0E0	
20	4	ACCT_TO_ACCT	5	2	1.25E−01	WP
20	3	CUSTOMER1	1	0	0.0E0	
20	3	AMI_HIST	2	0	0.0E0	
20	3	ACCT_TO_ACCT	3	0	0.0E0	
20	3	ACCT	4	0	0.0E0	
20	3	CUSTOMER1	1	4	1.0E0+00	0+01
20	3	AMI_HIST	2	44	3.40270E−21	WP
20	3	AMI_HIST	2	18	5.0E−01	W
20	3	CUSTOMER1	1	5	9.99423E−02	W
20	3	AMI_HIST	2	13	7.69239E−01	
20	3	AMI_HIST	2	7	2.5E−01	W
20	3	AMI_HIST	2	14	6.45161E−03	WJ
20	3	ACCT_TO_ACCT	3	1	6.45161E−03	WJ
20	3	AMI_HIST	2	5	5.0E+00	W
20	3	ACCT	4	3	5.0E−01	WP
20	3	CUSTOMER1	1	3	1.0E+00	P
20	3	AMI_REPORT	2	13	1.0E+00	P
20	3	ACCT_TO_ACCT	3	2	1.0E+00	P
20	3	ACCT	4	5	1.0E+00	P
20	3	ACCT	4	7	1.0E+00	P

The DETAIL '00' of the QBLOCKNO 1 indicates that the command was a SELECT. A row entry for each table referenced in the command is artificially generated where COLNO is '0'. The table number and the column number are specified for each referenced column and the *filter factor* value is the estimate of the fraction of the table that will need to be accessed to satisfy the command. The 'W' in DETAIL indicates that an index could be used, if one existed. *Filter factor* 1.0E + 00 indicates that the entire table would have to be read. The DETAIL column only contains data when the column appears in a predicate that might be used with an index, a JOIN, an ORDER BY, and so on.

STRUCTURE_TABLE and COST_TABLE Example

The STRUCTURE_TABLE and the COST_TABLE contained the following data:

STRUCTURE_TABLE

QUERYNO	QBLOCKNO	ROWCOUNT	Times	PARENT	ATOPEN
20	2	19	1.9375E+01	1	Y
20	1	156	1.9978016E−01	0	N
20	4	19	1.9375E+01	3	Y
20	3	0	1.9978016E−01	0	N

COST_TABLE

QUERYNO	QBLOCKNO	COST
20	2	1.145833110E+01
20	1	5.172202148E+02
20	4	1.145833110E+01
20	3	9.045832824E+01

After the indexes were modified and an index added (the application was not touched), the PLAN_TABLE told a different story and the transaction finished in under 1 minute instead of more than 30 minutes:

PLAN_TABLE

QUERYNO	QBLOCKNO	PLANNO	METHOD	TNAME	TYPE
20	2	1	0	ACCT_TO_ACCT	I
20	1	1	0	AML_REPORT	I
20	1	2	2	ACCT_TO_ACCT	I
20	1	3	1	CUSTOMER1	I
20	1	4	1	ACCT	I
20	1	5	3		
20	4	1	0	ACCT_TO_ACCT	I
20	3	1	0	AML_HIST	I
20	3	2	1	ACCT_TO_ACCT	I
20	3	3	1	CUSTOMER1	I
20	3	4	1	ACCT	I
20	3	5	3		

Note that all of the indexes were now used selectively and that the resulting reduction in response time was dramatic.

An Example of How EXPLAIN Might Help

There are times when the user knows how the optimizer **should** access the data and needs to know how it was actually done. The following is an example of a JOIN of two tables and an explanation of what the difference will be when the optimizer accesses each of the tables as the first or inner JOIN. The two tables that participate in the JOIN are:

DEPT_TBL	containing 100 rows
PERSONNEL_TBL	containing 1,000 rows

There are ten employees in each department. The JOIN query is:

```
SELECT * FROM PERSONNEL_TBL P, DEPT_TBL D
    WHERE P.DEPT = D.DEPT AND P.DEPT = 23
```

This analysis will explain the problem without considering the automatic addition of D.DEPT = 23 in recent versions of SQL/DS or which path the optimizer will in effect choose. The existence of the necessary indexes to achieve the stated results will also be assumed in each case.

If the PERSONNEL_TBL is accessed first, for each of the ten qualifying rows in the PERSONNEL_TBL, one row in the DEPT_TBL will be accessed to find the matching row. This will require 10 accesses despite the fact that they will all be to the exact same row in the DEPT_TBL. The total accesses will be 20.

If DEPT_TBL is accessed first, for the one qualifying row in the DEPT_TBL, ten rows in the PERSONNEL_TBL will be accessed to find the matching rows. The total number of accesses will be 11. This is obviously a more efficient way to JOIN the tables.

If the EXPLAIN estimate shows that 20 or more rows are estimated to have to be accessed, the user should check to determine why. Are the predicates of the query written correctly? Are the indexes correct? Were statistics updated? Are the column definitions exactly the same? The EXPLAIN function is the best tool available to help the application developer and the DBA ensure that SQL/DS will perform efficiently.

SUMMARY

The EXPLAIN facility informs the user how the SQL/DS optimizer will access the data for a specific instruction. EXPLAIN will indicate whether or not an index will be used, which index, and how it will be used. It will estimate the number of rows that must be accessed and how often subqueries will be executed. EXPLAIN will record which JOIN method was used and which columns could use indexes.

The EXPLAIN facility uses the
PLAN_TABLE, REFERENCE_TABLE,
STRUCTURE_TABLE, and COST_TABLE
that must be created for the user. The EXPLAIN command can be issued from an application program, via the DBSU, or interactively from ISQL. When internally generated statements are required by referential integrity, a + 1 is added to the QUERYNO and it is used to specify the internally generated statements. The SQL commands that can be EXPLAINed are SELECT, INSERT, UPDATE, and DELETE.

EXPLAIN depends upon the accuracy of the statistics in the system catalogs that exist at the time the command is executed. Running EXPLAIN in a test environment is only partially accurate because the optimizer not only uses indexes to determine access paths but also considers table size, data distribution, buffers available, and many other factors which are not the same in the TEST environment as in the production environment.

The application does **not** have to be compiled or executed to be tested with EXPLAIN; it is enough to precompile. The most useful tables are the PLAN_TABLE and the REFERENCE_TABLE which give the user an immediate picture of the efficiency of the query.

RECOMMENDATIONS

1. Each EXPLAIN command should be given a query number to facilitate the retrieval of the output from the EXPLAIN tables. The query number should be a multiple of 10 or 100.

2. Use the EXPLAIN facility from within the application rather than via ISQL.

3. The DBA should be allowed to carefully modify the TEST database catalogs to duplicate the production catalogs and provide the EXPLAIN facility with the same statistics available to the optimizer in production.

4. A unique index should be created as UNIQUE.

Resource Contention

When evaluating a production system, the Database Administrator (DBA) and the systems programmer must take into consideration the competing elements that are contending for the use of available system resources (CPU, I/O, and real storage). SQL/DS transactions must contend **both** with other system tasks for system resources and with other SQL/DS tasks for agents and locks. The actual response time of a transaction will include all of the contention and wait time as well as the actual time it takes the system to execute the transaction.

An understanding of the SQL/DS locking mechanism is very important to the tuning process. When the user can identify which lock requests are generated by the various SQL/DS commands and knows how conflicts and lock incompatibilities arise, then the lock or isolation levels, the scope of the LUW, or the sequence of the requests for data can be modified.

CPU CONTENTION

CPU contention prevents a dispatchable agent from beginning its processing. The contention may be caused by another agent or by another subsystem. The CPU utilization should be checked using VMMAP or VSE/PT. When the CPU is the bottleneck, and enlarging the CPU is not possible, the CPU utilization of all of the major transactions should be reduced through tuning or by transferring several of the applications to non-peak processing periods. When SQL/DS is the only major production system, the systems programmer should increase its share of the CPU by increasing the priority of the SQL/DS users and database machine or partition at the expense of other applications. In a VSE/SP machine, SQL/DS should usually have the priority immediately below the CICS production partition.

I/O AND BUFFER CONTENTION

In a discussion of I/O contention, there are two operations that need to be considered: the physical I/O to or from the DASD device and the inserting or retrieving of data into or from the buffers. Buffers are used by SQL/DS to store all of the data read from the DASD and to store all of the data to be written to DASD. When a transaction is in process and there are no more available buffers, SQL/DS removes the oldest unused data from its buffer, writes it to disk, if necessary, and assigns the buffer to the current transaction.

When data that has been removed from a buffer is again required, SQL/DS must issue a physical I/O to reread it from the database. This buffer contention occurs when there is an insufficient number of buffers and when the data does not remain in the buffer for the life of its use.

USING THE COUNTER COMMAND

Contention indications can often be found in the output of the COUNTER command. If **all** transactions, for example, have long response times, it is usually a sign that there is an insufficient number of buffers. A high ratio of total reads to reads from DASD (the *Hit Ratio*) is a significant indicator of this problem and the COUNTER command can be used to display the appropriate data. The *Hit Ratio* is determined by calculating the number of times a DBSPACE page of table data had to be read from the disk (PAGEREAD) as compared to the number of times a request to read a page was satisfied by the contents of a buffer (LPAGBUFF):

HIT RATIO = LPAGBUFF/PAGEREAD

The ratio should be 10 or 20 to 1 or greater. In VSE/SP, for example, the operator console may be used to display the COUNTER command. If SQL/DS is running in partition F5, the following would be the input and output of the command. This output, taken from a production system, shows a *Hit Ratio* of 50 to 1, which is excellent (assuming no paging):

```
5    COUNTER    *

F5   005   Counter values at  DATE='11-29-90'  TIME= '19:36:11'
F5   005   CALLS TO RDS                 RDSCALL :  204043
F5   005   CALLS TO DBSS                DBSSCALL: 1613845
```

F5	005	LUWS STARTED	BEGINLUW: 9308
F5	005	LUWS ROLLED BACK	ROLLBACK: 210
F5	005	SYSTEM CHECKPOINTS	CHKPOINT: 4
F5	005	MAXIMUM LOCKS EXCEEDED	LOCKLMT : 0
F5	005	LOCK ESCALATIONS	ESCALATE: 2
F5	005	WAITS FOR LOCK	WAITLOCK: 1
F5	005	DEADLOCKS DETECTED	DEADLCK : 0
F5	005	LOOKS IN PAGE BUFFER	**LPAGBUFF**: 4329866
F5	005	DBSPACE PAGE READS	**PAGEREAD**: 86984
F5	005	DBSPACE PAGE WRITES	PAGWRITE: 10152
F5	005	LOOKS IN DIRECTORY BUF	LDIRBUFF: 108251
F5	005	DIRECTORY BLOCK READS	DIRREAD : 945
F5	005	DIRECTORY BLOCK WRITES	DIRWRITE: 6813
F5	005	LOG PAGE READS	LOGREAD : 16
F5	005	LOG PAGE WRITES	LOGWRITE: 1403
F5	005	TOTAL DASD READS	DASDREAD: 87945
F5	005	TOTAL DASD WRITES	DASDWRIT: 18368
F5	005	TOTAL DASD I/O	DASDIO : 106313
F5	005	ARI0065I SQL/DS OPERATOR COMMAND PROCESSING COMPLETE	

it is especially useful to note the difference in the *Hit Ratio* after the number of buffers has been increased or decreased.

The directory *Hit Ratio* should also be checked: LDIRBUFF/ DIRREAD. Directory buffers are smaller than data buffers and the DBA should usually allocate two or three times as many directory buffers as data buffers. The ratio of 114.5 to 1 shown in the above example is good. It implies that a sufficient number of directory buffers has been assigned.

Not every system can achieve these ratios without increasing system paging. When real storage constraints exist, fewer buffers should be allocated even though the ratios worsen. When real storage is not a problem, the ratios might even be better if more buffers were allocated. The page *Hit Ratio* should normally be high but when the transactions access data in a very random fashion, it may be very low.

When the DBA only wants to see the specific counters needed, the following should be entered:

    5 COUNTER LPAGBUFF PAGEREAD

The output might read:

F5	005	Counter values at DATE='11-29-90' TIME= '19:50:10'	
F5	005	LOOKS IN PAGE BUFFER	LPAGBUFF: 4329866
F5	005	DBSPACE PAGE READS	PAGEREAD: 86984
F5	005	ARI0065I SQL/DS OPERATOR COMMAND PROCESSING COMPLETE	

When buffer contention is severe, the DBA should reduce buffer contention by reducing the number of agents and/or increasing the number of buffers. The results of any changes should be monitored to ensure that excessive paging and/or long waits for agent times do not occur.

Other Counter Data

Several other counters contain a summary of resource usage and resource contention. The resource usage can be seen in the following counters:

DASDIO ⟹ The total I/O to the database. It is the total of DASDWRIT and DASDREAD.

LOGREAD ⟹ The number of log pages read.

LOGWRITE ⟹ The number of log pages written.

RDSCALL ⟹ The number of times an application or an ad-hoc query accessed the database.

DBSSCALL ⟹ The number of times RDS called DBSS.

BEGINLUW ⟹ The number of *logical units of work* started.

The following counters can be used to verify if there was any resource contention:

WAITLOCK ⟹ indicates the number of times that any user had to wait for a lock. This value divided by the number of *logical units of work* (BEGINLUW) is a ratio of lock contention. The value should be very low.

ROLLBACK ⟹ indicates the number of times a *logical unit of work* was rolled back. If this value is not zero, the DEADLOCK counter should be checked to see if the roll backs were caused by deadlocks. When the problem is not deadlock, the LOCKLMT counter should be checked. It denotes the number of times that an LUW was rolled back because an escalation try failed when it would have caused a deadlock.

ESCALATE ⟹ this value plus the LOCKLMT value is the number of times that the maximum number of locks has been exceeded. This value should be zero or very small. If it is not zero, the number of locks may not be sufficient or the applications may be holding too many locks.

To determine if there is hardware contention the system programmer should utilize the VMMAP, VSE/PT, or any other performance monitoring tool. Hardware contention is not specifically an SQL/DS problem and should be handled in the standard way of reducing I/O load, adding DASD to the configuration, and balancing the distribution of data among available channels and DASD.

AGENTS

To access the SQL/DS database, the user must be attached to a real AGENT that requires approximately 200K of storage. This agent serves as the interface between the user and the database. The number of agents is assigned by the DBA in the NCUSERS startup parameter of SQL/DS. To allocate five real agents the DBA would specify:

SQLSTART (PRODDB) PARM(STARTUP=W,**NCUSERS=5**)

Real agents are freed when the *logical unit of work* (LUW) terminates. When an agent is unavailable, the user is placed in a wait queue until another user releases the agent. The greater the number of agents, the greater the number of users that can simultaneously be requesting SQL/DS services.

VM/SP and VSE/SP have slightly different methods of handling a request for an agent from a user. In VM/SP there is a pseudo-agent structure as well as a real agent structure while in VSE/SP there are only real agents. The pseudo-agent is assigned to a user when the IUCV CONNECT command is issued and is freed when the connection is released via a COMMIT WORK RELEASE or when the user logs off. The number of pseudo-agents is equal to the value specified in the VM/SP directory for this user's MAXCONN parameter minus the number of minidisks. Each pseudo-agent only requires approximately 300 bytes of storage and when a pseudo-agent is not available, the user receives an error message. VSE/SP does not have pseudo-agents and the users often experience a wait when they try to sign on. This occurs when there are no agents (links) available and the XPCC service places the user in a wait queue. In this case, the user just waits, but does not receive an error message.

The resources required by real agents have to be balanced against the available resources of the SQL/DS database. When the value in the NCSUSERS parameter is too low, the end-users will wait more often and response time will be erratic. If the value is set too high, SQL/DS will require excessive real storage which may result in additional paging. As the number of users increases, the number of buffers needed will increase, the locking contention will increase, and the CPU and I/O usage will increase. Care should be taken in specifying the number of agents.

THE SHOW COMMAND

The SHOW ACTIVE command issued from the console or from the ISQL terminal can be used to display a list of the users that are connected to real agents and to display the number of free agents. The following command was issued from a VSE/SP operator console:

```
5    SHOW  ACTIVE
F5   005   STATUS OF SQL/DS AGENTS:
F5   005    CHECKPOINT AGENT IS NOT ACTIVE
F5   005    USER AGENT 1: USER ID: CICSUSER IS NIW SUBS
F5   005     AGENT IS NOT PROCESSING AND IS IN COMMUNICATION WAIT
F5   005    USER AGENT 2: USER ID: DOV100A IS NIW SUBS
F5   005     AGENT IS NOT PROCESSING AND IS IN COMMUNICATION WAIT
F5   005    USER AGENT 3: USER ID: DOV200A IS NIW SUBS
F5   005     AGENT IS NOT PROCESSING AND IS IN COMMUNICATION WAIT
F5   005    USER AGENT 4: USER ID: DBDCCICS IS NIW SUBS
F5   005     AGENT IS NOT PROCESSING AND IS IN COMMUNICATION WAIT
F5   005    USER AGENT 5: USER ID: DBDOV4 IS R/W APPL 142EB4
F5   005     AGENT IS     PROCESSING AND IS IN I/O WAIT
F5   005   1 AGENT(S) NOT CONNECT TO AN APPL OR SUBSYS
```

Under VM/SP, the SHOW USERS (as well as the SHOW ACTIVE) command can be used to show the number of users connected to pseudo-agents that are active (connected to a real agent), waiting (for a real agent), or inactive. It also shows the number of free pseudo-agents:

```
                    SHOW USERS
     STATUS OF CONNECTED SQL/DS USERS:
         3    USER(S) ARE CONNECTED TO SQL/DS
         1    SQL/DS USER(S) ARE ACTIVE
                  VM-ID = DOV1 SQL-ID = DOV1
         2    SQL/DS USER(S) ARE WAITING
                  VM-ID = TEST SQL-ID = SQLDBA
                  VM-ID = MIKE1 SQL-ID = MIKE1
         2    SQL/DS USER(S) AR INACTIVE
                  VM-ID = BARB1 SQL-ID = TESTUSE
                  VM-ID = DONNY SQL-ID = DONNY
         2    SQL/DS AGENTS ARE AVAILABLE
         9    SQL/DS USER CONNECTIONS ARE AVAILABLE
```

These commands are useful at the end of the day when the operator needs to determine which users are still processing and which are not but are still connected. SQL/DS will not shut down normally when users are still connected.

In VSE/SP agent links are assigned to CICS when the CIRB command is issued:

CIRB ,5

and they are held until released by the CIRT command prior to CICS shutdown. The agents held by CICS are not available to batch partitions or to other CICS partitions. In CICS, all users including ISQL users and the application program users, compete for the links. Under CICS, the CIRD command can be used to show a display of those CICS users (only) that are waiting for links, holding links and are active, holding links and are inactive, and that previously held links. It also lists elapsed time for users that are waiting for a link and the time since the last access. An example of the CIRD output can be found in Chapter 8.

When the response time for a specific transaction varies greatly each time it is run, it may be a sign that there is an insufficient number of agents allocated. The DBA should monitor the system, ensure that the response problem is not caused by other contention problems, and add agents, where possible. In general, agents do not have to be allocated for batch when on-line applications are running because the two types of applications should usually **not** run during the same periods.

LOCKS AND LOCKING

Why Locks Are Needed

Locks are necessary to protect the integrity of the data in the tables but lock contention is one of the more significant causes of poor response and performance. SQL/DS is a multi-user system and more than one user may conceivably need to update or delete a particular row of data at the same time. The internal locking mechanism is employed to protect the data from being modified by two different transactions at the same time. Locks not only bar other users from freely accessing data but they also use system resources and contribute significantly to SQL/DS overhead. This locking mechanism affects both the reading and the modifying of data rows. The following examples will serve as an introduction to the topic before going into greater detail.

The receipt by a warehouse of two shipments of ribbons, each of which is being handled by a different clerk, is graphically represented by the chart that follows. User *FIRST* and user *SECOND* each want to update the row in the inventory table which contains the record of how many ribbons are currently in stock. The series of events might look like this:

User FIRST	TIME	User SECOND

SELECT INVAMT
    FROM WAREHS1
WHERE ITEM = 'RIBBON'
(check to ensure that
  the item exists)
	Time1	

	Time2	SELECT INVAMT FROM WAREHS1 WHERE ITEM = 'RIBBON' (check to ensure that the item exists)

UPDATE WAREHS1
SET INVAMT =
    :SAVEAMT1 + 5
WHERE ITEM = 'RIBBON'
(add five ribbons to the
  inventory)
	Time3	

	Time4	UPDATE WAREHS1 SET INVAMT = SAVEAMT2 + 8 WHERE ITEM= 'RIBBON' (add eight ribbons to the inventory)

If there were no locking mechanism and INVAMT = 25, the FIRST user would update the inventory by five ribbons and INVANT would then equal 30. User SECOND, however, read the inventory table while INVAMT was still 25 and saved the value in :SAVEAMT2. Adding eight to SAVEAMT2 (25) would result in 33. **The first update would simply be lost.** To prevent this and other similar problems from occurring, SQL/DS uses a locking mechanism that will require an *exclusive* lock on the row to be updated and will not allow the above sequence to occur. (In fact, this might result in a deadlock and the second transaction would be rolled back.)

The number of locks to be available is allocated during SQL/DS start-up. The NLRBU parameter will specify the maximum number of locks that any one user may use and the NLRBS parameter will specify the maximum number of locks available at any one time to the entire system:

SQLSTART DBNAME(DBPROD1) PARM(. . . , **NLRBU=1000, NLRBS=10000**)

Lock Types

The most common locks used by the SQL/DS system for applications are exclusive locks, share locks, update locks, and the intent locks associated with them. These six main types of locks, three of which state, on a high level, an intent to lock a page or a row on a lower level and three of which actually lock the level, are described below. SQL/DS uses a hierarchy of locking levels from DBSPACE to row and index key. The hierarchy is needed to ensure data integrity when different users lock data at different levels. There is also a lock request protocol which specifies that higher level locks must be issued before lower level locks (which is, of course, logical as will be seen). The hierarchy is:

```
                  ========> PAGE ========> ROW
DBSPACE ==> TABLE ==>
                  ========> Index Page ==> Index Key
HIGH----------------------------------------------> LOW
```

These lock levels will be discussed later in the chapter.

Intent locks are similar to **warning signs** that state that a user is holding a low level lock and they are designed to limit the system's ability to lock a higher level. Assuming row level locking, for example, when a user wants to lock a row for updating, SQL/DS may exclusively lock the DBSPACE, the table, and the page with locks that implies that "there is an **intent** to exclusively lock a row of the table on the lower level." The intent lock on the DBSPACE does not mean that another user cannot also issue an **intent** exclusive lock on the same DBSPACE, as will be seen by the compatibility chart that follows, but it does prevent a user from issuing an exclusive lock on the higher level (DBSPACE or table or page) when another user is locking at a lower level. It should be noted, however, that with low-level locking, when a page is actually updated an exclusive lock (**not** an intent lock) is issued on the page because a full page is involved in every SQL/DS I/O. The lock types include:

> **S-Share**. Indicates that the DBSPACE, table, page, or row is being read. It is used to prevent another user from acquiring an exclusive lock on the same level. Other users may acquire share locks on the same row, page, table, or DBSPACE. If a user is waiting to exclusively lock this level, however, other users arriving later and wishing to issue share locks on this same level will have to wait their turn. This prevents exclusive lock issuers from having to wait an excessively long time.

X-Exclusive. Indicates that a change (update, delete, or insert) is to be made to a level. No other user may acquire an exclusive or a share lock on this level. If another user has a lock on this level, the user requesting the exclusive lock is placed in a *lock wait* state and must wait until the lock that has already been acquired is released.

U-Update. A new feature in recent versions of SQL/DS similar to a share lock. It is used to prevent deadlocks when many users are trying to update the same row or page. It allows only one user at a time to scan with intention to update. When the user finishes with the row or page without actually updating it, the lock is changed to a share lock and, if the isolation level is *cursor stability,* the lock is released.

IS-Intent Share. This lock is used to indicate on a higher level that share locks are being used on a lower level. For example, if a row is share locked when an index is used, the page, table, and DBSPACE are locked using IS locks. This will prevent the system from allowing an exclusive lock on a higher level until the LUW holding the share lock on the page or row is completed and the locks released. If an Intent IS indicator were not locking the DB-SPACE and SQL/DS wanted to exclusively lock the DBSPACE, the system would be unaware of the lower level locking and might issue the exclusive lock on the higher level, thereby violating its own rules. Intent locking is designed to prevent this violation.

IX-Intent Exclusive. A lock that indicates that an exclusive lock has been acquired on a lower level. This does not prevent another user from also acquiring an intent share or intent exclusive on the same level but it does prevent other users from acquiring any other types of locks against this level.

SIX-Share with Intent Exclusive. This type of lock is the result of a lock conversion. When the user is holding a share or an update lock, for example, and then requests an intent exclusive (IX) lock on the same level or the user is holding an IX lock and requests a share lock on the same level, a share with intent exclusive (SIX) lock is actually granted.

There are several other locks such as the lock acquired in exclusive mode by the checkpoint agent at the start of a log archive and checkpoint and the rollback lock that is used during rollbacks.

Compatible Locks

To ensure the ability of many users to simultaneously work with the same dbspace (*concurrency*), a user should be able to access a row even when other users lock the DBSPACE or table with intent locks. This is made possible by the designating of certain types of locks to be compatible with other types of locks. Table 7.1 indicates which locks can be acquired on the same item on the same level (*are compatible*) and which can not. **OK** indicates that more than one user may acquire the lock on the horizontal column when another user is holding the lock in the vertical row. **No** indicates that the locks are **not** compatible:

Table 7.1   Lock Compatibility

Type of Lock Requested	Type of Lock Already Held					
	Intent Share	IX	S	U	SIX	X
IS	OK	OK	OK	OK	OK	No
IX	OK	OK	No	No	No	No
S	OK	No	OK	OK	No	No
U	OK	No	OK	No	No	No
SIX	OK	No	No	No	No	No
X	No	No	No	No	No	No

This table shows, for example, that if one user is holding a share lock (column 4) on a page another user will not receive an IX (row 2) lock on the same page but could acquire a share lock (row 3), an update lock (row 4), or an intent share lock (row 1) on the same page. The user should also be aware that while the transaction may be locking only one row, it is also intent locking higher levels.

The following is an example of the locks that are issued when a DELETE of one row is executed:

Locked	Type of Lock
DBSPACE	LONG IX
TABLE	LONG IX
PAGE	SHORT X
ROW	LONG X

To INSERT, UPDATE, or DELETE a row, for example, SQL/DS acquires an intent exclusive (IX) lock on the DBSPACE and on the table. Another user who wants to just read the entire table using a share lock, will not be allowed to acquire the lock until the exclusive intent lock is removed because IX and S locks are **not** compatible on the same level. The page is also locked exclusively while the row is being modified, for a short while, to prevent the compaction of free space or expansion of other rows while this modification is being carried out. This implies that for a short while the page is exclusively locked and no one may even read it. The poorly planned use of exclusive locks by applications is a major cause of performance degradation. Exclusive locks are held till the end of the *logical unit of work.* This implies that on-line UPDATE, DELETE, and INSERT, while trivial from a programming perspective, require thought, planning, and careful use. It is very crucial that LUWs be terminated as quickly as possible.

Table 7.1 makes it easier to understand the output of the SHOW LOCK command. When a SHOW LOCK displays the following information, for example, it shows that even though row level locking is in effect, intent locks are issued on higher levels. (Please note that the "What is Held" column does **not** appear with the SHOW LOCK display but is added by the author as an explanation for the reader):

SHOW LOCK DBSPACE 55

DBSPACE Number	Lock Type	SIX	IS	IX	S	U	X	Number WAITERS	What Is Held
55	DBSP	0	2	1	0	0	0	0	entire DBSPACE
55	IKEY	0	0	0	15	3	0	0	index key
55	PAGE	0	0	1	0	0	0	0	data page
55	ROW	0	0	0	15	0	1	1	one row
55	TABL	0	1	1	0	0	0	0	a table
55	IPAG	0	0	0	1	0	0	0	an index page

The above display incidentally shows that row level locking is in effect and that one user is in a lock wait, waiting to exclusively lock one of the rows currently locked by other share locks. Since an exclusive lock is incompatible with a share lock, the user requesting the exclusive lock must wait until the share locks are released. The IX lock, however, is compatible with the IS lock and an IX lock has already been granted on the DBSPACE, on the table, and on the page, even though the request for an exclusive lock is still pending.

Additional Lock Terminology

Additional terms are used when discussing locking. The definitions provide additional information about locking and how it is used:

Concurrency. The ability of several users to access a database simultaneously.

Adjacent key locking. To prevent duplicate keys on INSERT or DELETE, SQL/DS locks the key and the key following it in the index. This is used to prevent *repeatable read* violations and to prevent the insertion of a duplicate key in a unique index. This situation may occur when the key is deleted by one application and another application tries to insert the same key in the index before the first application has finished its LUW. If the first application were to decide to perform a ROLLBACK, the key would be duplicated in the unique index. The only way the second application can be prevented from inserting the deleted key is if the adjacent key with the next higher key value, which has remained in the index, were locked.

Locking Duration. The longer a lock is held the greater the chance that it will effect concurrency. The shorter a lock is held the greater the concurrency. The types of lock durations are:

Long. Held until the end of an LUW, usually for data modification or for *repeatable read*.

Medium. Held usually on a page when a DBSCAN is required. The lock is explicitly released when no longer needed.

Short. This lock is held for the duration of the DBSS operation only and is usually for Isolation Level *cursor stability* operations.

Instant. The lock is acquired just to be sure that it is available and is immediately released. It is used with *cursor stability* for SELECT or UPDATE and row locking on the key itself.

Lock Escalation. SQL/DS uses lock request blocks to manage the locking mechanism. Each time a lock is requested, one or more request blocks is used. The number of request blocks that are available is controlled by two startup parameters. When applications require more locks than the DBA has allocated, SQL/DS determines which DBSPACE being used by the LUW is holding the most locks and the system automatically will escalate and lock that entire DBSPACE, no matter what the original level of locking for that DBSPACE was. All of its lower level locks will be released. When other users are accessing the same DBSPACE this process can sometimes result in lockwaits or a deadlock.

Lock Wait. The state a user is in while waiting for a lock request to be satisfied. An exclusive lock will prevent others from reading or modifying and shared locks will prevent others from exclusively locking. Update locks prevent other users from reading for update or from receiving exclusive locks. The users in Lock Wait must wait until the resource they are waiting for is unlocked.

Specifying Lock Levels

The DBA selects the locking level when the DBSPACE is acquired:

ACQUIRE PUBLIC **DBSPACE** NAMED PERSONNEL_DBS (**LOCK = ROW**)

This level of locking can later be modified by the ALTER DBSPACE command:

ALTER DBSPACE PERSONNEL_DBS (**LOCK = PAGE**)

An application or an interactive user with DBA authority or DB-SPACE ownership can also, for the life of the LUW, change the locking level to TABLE or DBSPACE locking in exclusive or share mode by issuing the command:

LOCK DBSPACE PERSONNEL_DBS IN **SHARE MODE**
LOCK TABLE SALARY_TBL IN **EXCLUSIVE MODE**

Which Lock Level to Use

If a table is rarely modified and usually just read, table or DBSPACE locking should be used and the application program should be written to complete the LUW quickly. Read-only data should be placed in nonrecoverable storage pools with DBSPACE locking specified to avoid the overhead of acquiring and releasing locks.

Page and row locking should only be used on those tables that are accessed by many users and on which long or frequent on-line modifications are performed. Each user will, most probably, not want to read the same data that is currently being modified by another user. Row level locking will allow many users to concurrently read or modify different rows in the same table. The cost of row level locking is high and should only be used when this concurrency is actually needed. It definitely should be used when needed, otherwise a greater degradation in response time will be incurred due to lock outs than would be caused by the locking overhead.

Each table in a production system should be individually evaluated and the default (of PAGE locking) should **not** be used. The overall system and most applications will be negatively impacted by a generalization of page or row locking. This is especially true because row level locking implies key-level locking which incurs additional overhead cost.

Lock Usage

SQL/DS uses many more locks than the user may imagine. With row level locking, the locking of one row may require intent locks (mentioned earlier) on the DBSPACE, the table, the page, the index pages, the index key, the data row, and several adjacent index keys. Since DBSS does the locking, many rows **not** in the answer set may also be locked. This happens because even though DBSS may apply as many selection criteria as possible before adding the row to the answer set, if not all of the predicates are *sargable,* rows will have to be locked and passed to the RDS component for further selection. RDS will apply the additional criteria, initiate any sorts required, and then send the final answer set to the user. DBSS will have locked all of the rows or pages that were sent to RDS because, to DBSS, they were all part of the answer set (even though they were discarded later by RDS).

SQL/DS uses a concept of GATENAME which is the component that actually gets locked. This GATENAME consists of a DBSPACE number and an identifying value. The value for GATENAME, when index keys are locked, is special. The index keys are hashed to 4 byte values. Keys can be 256 bytes long so that there may be many keys in a table that will hash to the same value. It is this hash value and the DBSPACE number that make up the GATENAME. When two or more keys hash to the same value, **all** are locked when any one is locked. This is one good reason **not to have an index with many non-unique or very similar values** which may all hash to the same value. It also explains why some keys in a table may be locked even though no user is currently accessing them. **Make sure that the keys are unique.**

In general, almost all locking problems could be alleviated if the application design would specify short LUWs and the application programs would COMMIT or ROLLBACK WORK frequently. It is also helpful to do all of the SQL/DS operations in one process or routine so as to complete all accesses to the database in one operation rather than accessing a little data at a time and processing it slowly. This would definitely reduce the probability of interfering with other users.

Keeping queries and processing simple when possible is always good advice. It is, of course, helpful to reduce the number of locks the application will require by using proper indexes and by making predicates *sargable* and *index matching.* The new scalar functions, for example, should **not** be used just because they are available. They should be used **only** when they are really needed. Only the columns needed should be selected. A typical **very wasteful** query is:

```
SELECT CUSIP_NUMBER, NAME, LOCATION
    FROM STOCK_TBL
        WHERE CUSIP_NUMBER = :SQL-CUSIP-VARIABLE
```

If the **cusip number** is already known, it should not be selected from the table.

SHOW LOCK

Every user with access to ISQL, RXSQL, or the console can view what is being locked, who is responsible for the locking, and which users are waiting for locks. The user may issue the SHOW LOCK command as per the following examples and the sample output might show the entries listed below. To display the number of locks held by each user, use SHOW LOCK **ACTIVE**:

AGENT	USER	WAIT STATE	TOTAL LOCKS	LONG LOCKS	WANTLOCK TYPE	WANTLOCK DBSPACE
c	CHECKPT	NIW	0	0		
1	CICSUSER	NIW	0	0		
2	SQL030A	NIW	0	0		
3	SQL021A	NIW	0	0		
4	SQL070B	I/O	24	19		

To display a list of users holding locks showing the type of lock and the DBSPACE number, use SHOW LOCK **USER**:

AGENT	USER	DBSPACE NUMBER	LOCK TYPE	SIX	IS	IX	S	U	X	NUMBER WAITERS
4	SQL070B		DB	0	0	1	0	0	0	0
4	SQL070B	1	DBSP	0	1	0	0	0	0	0
4	SQL070B	1	IKEY	0	0	0	3	0	0	0
4	SQL070B	1	ROW	0	0	0	2	0	0	0
4	SQL070B	1	TABL	0	3	0	0	0	0	0
4	SQL070B	10	DBSP	0	0	1	0	0	0	0
4	SQL070B	10	IPAG	0	0	0	1	0	0	0
4	SQL070B	10	PAGE	0	0	0	1	0	0	0
4	SQL070B	10	TABL	0	1	0	0	0	0	0
4	SQL070B	11	DBSP	0	1	0	0	0	0	0
4	SQL070B	11	IPAG	0	0	0	1	0	0	0
4	SQL070B	11	ROW	0	0	0	1	0	0	0
4	SQL070B	11	TABL	0	1	0	0	0	0	0
4	SQL070B	20	DBSP	0	1	0	0	0	0	0
4	SQL070B	20	ROW	0	0	0	1	0	1	0
4	SQL070B	20	TABL	0	1	1	0	0	0	0
4	SQL070B	9851	INT	0	0	0	0	0	1	0

To display lock allocation and contention information, use SHOW LOCK **MATRIX**:

LOCK REQUEST BLOCK (LRB) AND LOCK STATUS:

NLRBS	IN USE	FREE	NLRBU	MAX USED BY LUW
6778	48	6730	1500	488

*** THE LOCKWAIT TABLE ***

ENTRY = DBSPACE NUMBER ON WHICH THERE IS LOCK CONTENTION
THE PRESENCE OF AN ENTRY SHOWS
THE AGENT REQUESTING THE LOCK AND
THE AGENT HOLDING OR CONTENDING FOR THE LOCK
AGENT   AGENT **HOLDING** OR CONTENDING FOR THE LOCK
REQUESTING
LOCK

	1	2	3	4
1	. . . . SQL070B
2	. . . .
3	. . . .
4 SQL070B	. . . .

Isolation Levels

The isolation level (ISOL) is chosen either when the application program is preprocessed or during program or command execution. The ISOL will determine whether or not one user can modify a row or a page as soon as another user has finished reading it. With *repeatable read* (the default), the user stipulates that every row or page touched during the SELECT should remain unchanged, even after the user has moved on to a new row. The previous row or page will remain locked and it may not be modified until the user releases it. This is to ensure that it will be available for rereading in its original form for the life of the LUW. The first user may want to update the row and *repeatable read* will ensure that the data has not been modified by any user since it was last viewed.

It should be realized that with *repeatable read* (RR), every row touched in any way by the application, even when a nonselective scan or a DBSPACE scan is used and the answer set contains only one row, will remain locked(in this case the table is locked) until the end of the LUW, and other users will be prevented from updating or deleting any rows in the table. In those installations where massive on-line updating is part of the system design, this situation will be unacceptable.

The alternative is to use *cursor stability.* When *cursor stability* is specified, the user is not concerned about what happens to a row or a page of data once it has been read, even if it hasn't as yet been presented to the user but has only been stored. Only the page or row actually being held at the moment is locked and all other rows are freed. The held row is in reality the last row that the DBSS has reached and is not necessarily the row currently being displayed. The application designer should be sure that locks are really not needed before suggesting the use of this option.

Note that when SORTing is required, the entire answer set is stored internally and sorted (using the internal DBSPACES or memory) before any row is returned. With *cursor stability* this implies that all of the locks, except for the last, are released before the first row is even presented to the user.

The **dis**advantages of *cursor stability* are:

- **Rows may be found twice**. This can occur when another transaction updates a row with a key that was already processed by a transaction working with *cursor stability.* If, for example, the user has checked record key 1, 3, 5, 6, 8, and record key 3 is subsequently modified by another user to 11, the first user will now see record 11 which is the same row already viewed as record 3.

- **Paging back and forth may yield varied results if the data is being modified by other users.** Harold Meyer, for example, may be in Department 40. After scrolling forward the user may scroll back again and not find Harold Meyer in Department 40 or he may find that other data in the record has been changed. Most applications cannot tolerate this type of instability.

- **When the table is scanned via an index to read records BE-TWEEN 1 AND 30, for example, some rows may not be seen at all.** If record 1, 3, 4, 7, 9, and 11 were read and subsequently record 18 were modified to record 5, it will never be seen by the user (unless the user scrolls backward).

- **Modifications based on data previously read may be incorrect and may overlay modifications made by other users.**

Candidates for CS or RR

Cursor stability, therefore, should only be used under certain very specific circumstances. It should usually be used by all ISQL and QMF users and it should be used for **all** access to system catalogs. If it is obvious that the design of an application will result in concurrency problems or if it has already caused concurrency problems and the application cannot be modified to remove these problems, CS should be considered. Conversational applications using, for example, CSP in a conversational mode, and those doing selects of massive amounts of data for reports may also be candidates for *cursor stability.* Conversational applications, however, should usually not be used and reports should be run after peak on-line hours, where possible.

All other applications should use *repeatable read* especially when it is necessary to ensure that viewed data has not been changed. RR should be used for pseudo and nonconversational transactions and for applications which include updates. The choice involves the trade-off of reduced *concurrency* vs increased lock overhead.

When both isolation levels are needed in an application program, the developer should compile the application with the **ISOL = USER** parameter. The following procedure to update data demonstrates one application of the ISOL = USER parameter:

- **Read** a row using *cursor stability.*
- **Store** the input in memory and COMMIT WORK.
- **Display** the data to end-user.
- **Receive** the request to update from the end-user.
- Dynamically **modify** the isolation level to RR.
- **Reread** the row and compare it to original row stored in memory.
- If it is an exact copy of the stored row, update and COMMIT WORK (if possible), and restore the ISOL to CS.
- If it is not an exact copy, notify the user after releasing the data.

Deadlocks

When two users prevent **each other** from acquiring a requested lock, there is a deadlock. One type of deadlock occurs when user A is selecting a resource page and user B wants to issue an update to a row on that page. If user A then decides to update a row on that page, a deadlock occurs because user A has a share lock that he wants to change to an exclusive lock while user B has an exclusive lock pending. Neither user can complete the transaction until the other is finished. This deadlock results in the *newest* transaction, as determined from the timestamp, being ABENDed with a **-911** error code. Deadlocks may also be caused when locks on the index are deadlocked because of hashing keys.

The abending of a transaction impacts response and performance and should be avoided. The COUNTER command discussed earlier in this chapter will provide an indication to the DBA that a problem exists. If excessive deadlocking occurs, the DBA should find the causes and recommend that the applications be modified.

Lock Escalation Clarification

Some user applications may receive a message indicating LOCKS EXCEEDED. If locks are escalated when too many locks are used, how is it possible to receive this LOCKS EXCEEDED message? The reason is that SQL/DS will use a **savepoint** whenever more than one row is modified. The message often means that these savepoint locks, which are not released, caused the application to reach the upper lock limit allowed.

Lock Recommendations

All applications should be designed to minimize the duration during which locks are held. The holding of exclusive locks on specific levels of data for long periods of time will interfere with other users wanting to read or modify the data. The holding of share locks for long periods of time will prevent other users from acquiring exclusive locks on that data.

The best compromise for most applications is to use page locking even for data that needs to be modified. A DBSPACE should usually be acquired with the default LOCK = PAGE unless:

- Many users access a small number of rows, usually via indexes, and need to update the rows. (use LOCK = ROW)
- Inconsistencies will not occur in an application or are not important and only one person updates but many users read the data. (use LOCK = ROW and *cursor stability*)
- Tables are used by on-line applications in read only mode. Large tables with few requests but with many rows are scanned. (use LOCK = DBSPACE)
- Most of the rows usually have to be read. To avoid excessive overhead, issue the LOCK DBSPACE command from the application.

This is accurate unless modification to individual rows is a major critical operation carried out by multiple users on the same data. In that case, use row level locking but try to ensure that indexes exist that can be used selectively so as to avoid a DBSPACE scan and reduce the overhead.

Read only data should be placed in nonrecoverable DBSPACES which should be defined with DBSPACE locking.

Most applications do not need to explicitly request locks. An application program, however, which requires that no other user access any of the data while, for example, reports are being printed (to avoid updates which would invalidate the totals already calculated) should use the LOCK command.

Always use *cursor stability* when accessing the system catalogs especially from ISQL and the DBSU. To modify a user's ISQL profile, enter the following ISQL commands while connected via the user's id:

```
INPUT ROUTINE
'PROFILE',10,'SET ISOL CS',NULL
END
```

After the above has been executed, the isolation level will always be *cursor stability* whenever the user signs on, unless the ISOL parameter is modified manually using the command:

```
SET ISOL RR
```

CATALOG CONTENTION

A major contention problem is caused by the simultaneous update of the system catalogs by different transactions. Creating or altering tables, indexes, views or referential relationships, dropping DBSPACEs, tables, programs, views and indexes, and updating statistics result in the update of several catalog tables. One of the major culprits in tying up system catalogs is the application pre-processor program which can potentially update every catalog table. Pre-processing should be carefully controlled by the DBA and should be limited to off-peak hours in a production database. A sample of some of the catalog tables updated by several SQL/DS commands should emphasize the significance of using these commands during peak processing periods. Each command updates other catalog tables as well:

SYSCOLUMNS	SYSCATALOG	SYSINDEXES	SYSACCESS
CREATE TABLE	CREATE TABLE	CREATE TABLE	CREATE TABLE
DROP TABLE	DROP TABLE	DROP TABLE	DROP TABLE
ALTER TABLE	ALTER TABLE	ALTER TABLE	ALTER TABLE
DROP INDEX	DROP INDEX	DROP INDEX	DROP INDEX
CREATE INDEX	CREATE INDEX	CREATE INDEX	
CREATE VIEW	CREATE VIEW		CREATE VIEW
UPDATE STATS	UPDATE STATS	UPDATE STATS	

Some installations have reduced but not eliminated the problem of catalog contention by distributing the system DBSPACEs across several storage pools. It doesn't solve the locking problem but it does reduce I/O contention. One suggestion might be to assign the DBSPACES as follows:

SYS0001	IN STORAGE POOL 1
SYS0002	IN STORAGE POOL 2
ISQL	IN STORAGE POOL 2
HELPTEXT	IN STORAGE POOL 2
SAMPLE	IN STORAGE POOL 2
INTERNAL DBSPACES	IN STORAGE POOL 3

LOGICAL UNIT OF WORK (LUW)

To further control the use of an SQL/DS table by more than one user, the system uses a *logical unit of work* scheme which holds all non-implicitly released locks requested by the user until all of the processing in the user-defined work unit is complete. An LUW can be any series of commands that the user declares should be considered as one entity and in which either **all** of the changes are committed **or none** of the changes are committed. An LUW begins when the first SQL/DS command is executed and ends with an implicit or explicit COMMIT or ROLLBACK WORK. These two commands indicate to SQL/DS that the series of commands has been completed and that any changes made to the database may either be committed, because the user wants them written to the database, or rolled back, because the user does not want to actually modify the database or because an error has occurred. When a rollback is requested, the original data is restored and all of the modifications that were made since the beginning of this LUW must be backed out.

A classic example of an LUW is the transference of funds between two bank accounts. When the value of a check is deposited into one of the accounts, the value must be debited from the other account. The pseudo-code to accomplish this might be:

```
1. UPDATE CHECKING

SET BALANCE = (BALANCE - :CHKAMT)
      WHERE ACCNTNO = :ACCTNODB AND
          BALANCE > :CHKAMT

2. IF SQLCODE = 0

UPDATE CHECKING
SET BALANCE = BALANCE + :CHKAMT
      WHERE ACCNTNO = :ACCTNOCD
```

```
3. IF SQLCODE = 0

     COMMIT WORK
   ELSE
     ROLLBACK WORK.
```

The work is not committed and the LUW is not ended until Step 3 to ensure that the entire transaction has been completed. If each step were committed independently and the system were to ABEND after Step 1, the money would be debited from the first account but would not be credited to anyone. By making both steps part of the same *logical unit of work,* the application designer ensured that both parts of the transaction were completed before either was committed.

COMMITTING WORK

Logical units of work may be explicitly or implicitly committed. While various components of SQL/DS have standard defaults the user should explicitly COMMIT WORK and **not** allow the system to use its default. Implicit commits and rollbacks are hard to control and should not be depended upon. When a default is used, either COMMIT WORK or ROLLBACK WORK is executed, depending on whether an error has occurred or not. The following are examples of the default at the end of different types of LUWs:

- A pre-compiled application reaching EOJ (implicit)
- At the end of a DBSU job (implicit)
- The detection of a serious SQL/DS error (implicit)
- At the end of each ISQL command (implicit)
- Execution of the command COMMIT WORK (explicit)
- Execution of the command ROLLBACK WORK (explicit)

INVALID INDEXES

Invalid indexes are caused by a problem during a ROLLBACK operation. An index can become invalid when a system ABEND occurs during a ROLLBACK or when the space for available index pages is exhausted during an INSERT or a DROP INDEX ROLLBACK. The DBSPACE can run out of available pages when there is more than one table in the DBSPACE and another user is inserting keys into an index during the DELETE and ROLLBACK processing of the first table.

When the index becomes invalid, the index will no longer reflect the data in the table. The latest versions of SQL/DS mark the index INVALID and make it unavailable until it is dropped and re-created.

If any indexes have been marked invalid, the operator will receive a message during system start-up. The DBA can also check if any indexes have been marked invalid by issuing the following command:

SHOW **INVALID**

A sample display might contain the following entries:

ENTITY TYPE	DBSPACE NUMBER	ENTITY ID
INDEX	5	–32567
INDEX	73	–32943

The DBA must obtain the index name from the SYS-TEM.SYSINDEXES and SYSTEM.SYSCATALOG tables by using the DBSPACE number and the Entity ID. The following command, for example, might be used:

SELECT C.TNAME, I.INAME, I.CREATOR
    FROM SYSTEM.SYSINDEXES I, **SYSTEM.SYSCATALOG** C
        WHERE I.TNAME = C.TNAME AND
           C.DBSPACENO = 5 AND
           I.IID = -32567
        ORDER BY 1 , 2

SUMMARY

SQL/DS transactions contend both with other system tasks for system resources and with other SQL/DS tasks for agents and locks. Locking protects data from multiple modification and ensures *repeatable readability.*

Buffers are used to store all data read from the DASD. Buffer contention occurs when there is an insufficient number of buffers and when the data does not remain in the buffer for the life of its use. If transactions have long response times it is usually a sign that there is an insufficient number of buffers. The *Hit Ratio* is a significant indicator of this problem. It is especially useful to note the difference in the *Hit Ratio* after the number of buffers has been increased or decreased. Counters contain a summary of resource usage and indicate resource contention.

To access the SQL/DS database, the user must be attached to a real AGENT. In VM/SP there is a pseudo-agent structure as well as a real agent structure while in VSE/SP there are only real agents. The SHOW ACTIVE command from the console or the ISQL terminal can be used to display a list of the users that are connected to real agents. Under VM/SP, the SHOW USERS (as well as the SHOW ACTIVE) command can be used to show the number of users connected to pseudo-agents. In VSE/SP agent links are assigned to CICS when the CIRB command is issued.

A major contention problem is caused by the simultaneous update of the system catalogs by different transactions. Creating or altering tables, indexes, views or referential relationships, dropping DBSPACEs, tables, programs, views and indexes, and updating statistics result in the update of several catalog tables.

Locks are necessary to protect the integrity of the data in the tables but lock contention is one of the more significant causes of poor response and performance. Locks not only bar other users from freely accessing data but they also use system resources and contribute significantly to SQL/DS overhead. Locks are held until they are released which is often at the end of the LUW. Locking is a function of the DBSS component. Lock waits are caused by locks held by other users. A modification to a row must wait until all SELECTS are completed. A SELECT must wait until all exclusive locks are released.

The number of locks to be available is allocated during SQL/DS start-up. The NLRBU parameter will specify the maximum number of locks for one user and the NLRBS parameter will specify the maximum number of locks for all users.

The most common locks used by the SQL/DS system for applications are exclusive locks, share locks, update locks, and the intent locks associated with them. Intent locks are similar to **warning signs** that state that a user is holding a low level lock. To allow concurrency, certain types of locks are designated as compatible with other types of locks.

Adjacent key locking is used to prevent duplicate keys on INSERT or DELETE. The longer a lock is held the greater the chance that it will affect the work that others can do. Locks can be held for a long period of time or for a short period of time depending upon the action required. SQL/DS uses many more locks than the user may imagine. SQL/DS uses a concept of GATENAME which is the component that actually gets locked. In general, almost all locking problems can be alleviated if the application design would specify short LUWs. When applications require more locks than the DBA has allocated, escalation occurs. SHOW LOCK can be used to display the locks held by the users.

The DBA specifies the locking level when the DBSPACE is acquired. Row level locking will allow many users to concurrently modify different rows in the same table. The isolation level determines whether or not one user can modify a row or a page when another user has finished reading it. With *repeatable read* every row or page touched during the SELECT remains locked even after the user has moved on to a new row. With *cursor stability* only the page or row actually being held at the moment is locked and all other rows are freed. Cursor stability has several disadvantages: rows may be found twice, paging back and forth may yield varied results, some rows may never be seen, and modifications based on a previous read may overlay modifications made by other users.

When two users prevent each other from acquiring the lock requested, it is a deadlock. Deadlocks may also be caused when locks on the index are deadlocked because of hashing keys.

To further control the use of an SQL/DS table by more than one user, the system uses a *logical unit of work* scheme. A *logical unit of work* begins when the first SQL/DS command is executed and ends with an implicit or explicit COMMIT or ROLLBACK WORK.

Creating or altering tables, indexes, views or referential relationships, dropping DBSPACEs, tables, programs, views and indexes, and updating statistics result in the update of several catalog tables.

An index can become invalid during ROLLBACK processing. SQL/DS will mark the index invalid and it will not be available until it is dropped and re-created.

RECOMMENDATIONS

1. System utilization should be checked using VMMAP or VSE/PT.

2. When SQL/DS is the only major production system, the systems programmer should increase its share of the CPU by increasing the priority of the SQL/DS users and database machine or partition at the expense of other applications.

3. In a VSE/SP machine, SQL/DS should usually have the priority immediately below the CICS production partition.

4. The DBA should usually allocate two or three times as many directory buffers as data buffers.

5. When real storage constraints exist, fewer data buffers should be allocated.

6. Reduce buffer contention by reducing the number of agents.

7. The results of any changes should be monitored.

8. Batch and on-line should not usually run at the same time.

9. Pre-processing should be limited to off-peak hours in a production database.

10. Distribute the system DBSPACEs across several storage pools.

11. The user should explicitly COMMIT WORK and not allow the system to use its default.

12. *Logical units of work* should be terminated as quickly as possible.

13. Reduce the number of locks the application will require by using proper indexes and by making predicates *sargable* and index matching.

14. Row locking increases overhead and should not be used unless necessary.

15. Cursor stability should be used, if possible.

16. Cursor stability should only be used when there are concurrency problems.

17. Read-only data should be placed in non-recoverable storage pools with DBSPACE locking specified.

18. Each table in a production system should be individually evaluated rather than allowed to default to PAGE locking.

CHAPTER 8

SQL/DS Data Management

One of the major purposes of a database is to make the storage of data independent of the hardware used so as to provide a high degree of portability and flexibility and to free the users of these concerns. SQL/DS has three logical levels of storage management and one physical level. DASD storage, both in VSE/SP and VM/SP, is divided into physical extents before they are assigned to SQL/DS. Each extent is made up of one or more DASD cylinders of space on a hardware DASD device. An entire DASD device may be defined as one extent or the device may be divided into minidisks (or VSE/SP extents) and assigned to one or more logical SQL/DS storage pools.

MANAGING SQL/DS STORAGE

SQL/DS manages its data in a logical hierarchy which extends from the lowest level of physical extents to the highest level of data rows and columns (Figure 8.1). Physical DBEXTENTS are assigned to logical storage pools. One or more physical DBEXTENTS can be assigned to each storage pool and when all of the available space in a storage pool is exhausted, an additional DBEXTENT may be added. The space in a storage pool is divided into 4K blocks known as *pages*.

ADDING DBEXTENTS

The SQL/DS users generally have no idea on which physical device the tables are stored. The task of assigning physical storage is handled by the systems programmer who allocates disk space to the database when requested to do so by the database administrator (DBA). The VSE/SP systems programmer, for example, must define a VSAM file when adding an extent and will store the job control definitions in the standard or partition standard label area. The DLBL for the added

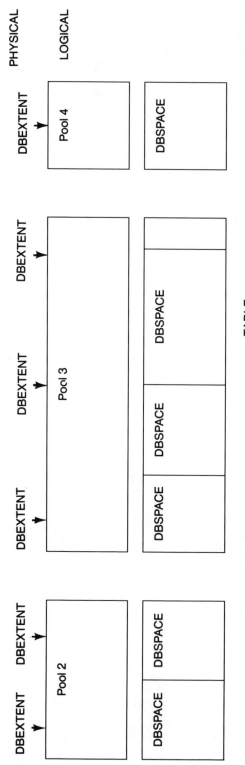

Figure 8.1 Hierachy of Storage

DBEXTENT is similar to any other VSAM disk label definition and might look like this example:

/ / DLBL SQLDSK5,'SQL.EXTENT5',0,,VSAM

To add an extent in VM/SP the systems programmer must define an additional minidisk for the SQL/DS virtual machine in the DIRECTORY similar to the one shown in the following example:

MDISK 23B 3380 101 030 DBDSK5 R RSQLPW WSQLPW

The systems programmer, in cooperation with the DBA, should calculate the number of cylinders to be added. On a 3380, for example, there are 150 4K pages per cylinder. The 30 cylinders that were assigned in the above example would provide 4,500 4K pages. Adding DBEXTENTS should be planned with care because **once DBEXTENTS are added they cannot be removed** without regenerating the database. The DBA should not try to remove a DBEXTENT because if a DBEXTENT is *deleted,* the database will no longer be accessible. Adding an extent is a relatively trivial process; removing an extent is impossible.

After the physical extent has been assigned to the database machine or partition, the DBA must execute a procedure to inform SQL/DS that a DBEXTENT has been added. This procedure is one of the very few procedures that must be run in stand-alone mode. In VM/SP, for example, the DBA would run the SQLADBEX EXEC to update the database directory and add the control information for the new extent:

SQLADBEX DBNAME(PRODDB)

The EXEC will prompt the DBA for the pool assignment and the minidisk id. Each pool can have many DBEXTENTs assigned to it and one or more DBSPACES may be defined in each storage pool. The systems programmer should usually increase the MAXCONN setting on the VM OPTION statement for each DBEXTENT added.

To display a listing of the extents in the system, the DBA could execute the SHOW DBEXTENT command. The output might show:

POOL NO.	TOTAL PAGES	NO. OF INUSE PAGES	NO. OF FREE PAGES	% USED	NO. OF EXTENTS	SHORT ON STORAGE
1	9504	7559	2245	77	2	
2	29754	18645	11109	62	5	
-3	14877	6305	8572	42	2	
4	32832	22580	10252	68	5	

The *–3* indicates that it is a nonrecoverable storage pool. These storage pools are usually transparent to the application developers.

SQL/DS DIRECTORY

It is the size of the database directory that limits the number of data pages that can be defined in the database. Once generated this limit **cannot** be modified without generating a new database. It is very important, therefore, that enough directory space be allocated at generation time. In the sample database, the directory size is determined during database generation of the 201 minidisk, as shown in the following example:

MDISK 201 3380 200 100 sqldsk R RSQLPW WSQLPW

Adding DBSPACES to Storage Pools

When a new storage pool is added, at least one DBSPACE must be added to make it usable. In VM/SP, the SQLADBSP EXEC is available to add the first DBSPACE. It reserves the directory blocks and fixes the DBSPACE size and type (public or private). The SQLADBSP EXEC or procedure should also be used to define additional DBSPACEs in the pool.

DBSPACES

The storage pools are divided into logical DBSPACEs. Many DBSPACEs can be defined in each storage pool. Each DBSPACE has its own characteristics and may contain one or more logical tables. There are three types of DBSPACES:

> **PUBLIC.** Data may be modified by more than one user at a time.
> **PRIVATE.** Data may be modified by only one user at a time.
> **INTERNAL.** Used by the system, mainly for SORT operations.

A DBSPACE consists of HEADER pages and of DATA PAGES. The HEADER pages describe the tables and indexes in the DBSPACE. When a DBSPACE requires a page, the system will search for an unallocated page in its storage pool and will assign it to the DBSPACE. The system will use a bit map to determine if a page is already allocated to a DBSPACE. When a different DBSPACE in the same storage pool requires a page, the system will again examine the bit map and will assign the next available page to the DBSPACE.

Data Page

The data pages in a DBSPACE can be used as data pages, header pages, or index pages. The quantity of each type of page will be determined when the DBSPACE is defined. The following description of the data page format will provide a better understanding of how SQL/DS manages these pages (Figure 8.2).

Each page contains 16 bytes of control information in the page header. The page will also contain a page slot, located at the end of the page, for each row on the page. The slot is a two byte pointer containing the displacement of the row from the beginning of the

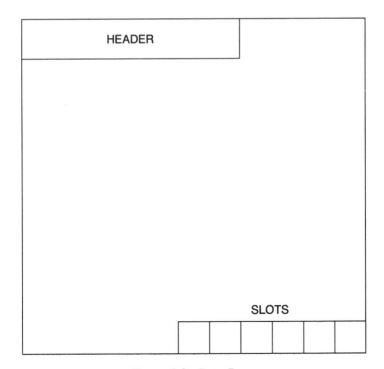

Figure 8.2   Data Page

page. The remainder of the space in the page will be used for rows of data and for free space.

The method of *page assignment on demand* makes it impossible to determine on which page a particular row in a particular table in a particular DBSPACE will be physically placed. This is especially true when a DBSPACE contains more than one table because each data page may contain rows from more than one table. Figure 8.3 is an example of a datapage containing rows from two tables.

Acquiring DBSPACES

After DBSPACEs are added they must be *acquired* to be used. The DBSPACE and its characteristics are defined as part of a particular storage pool using the ACQUIRE DBSPACE command. The parameters to ACQUIRE a public DBSPACE with the minimum number of 4K pages (128), for example, are:

ACQUIRE PUBLIC **DBSPACE** NAMED STOCKDBSPC
    (NHEADER =8, **PAGES=128,** PCTINDEX = 33, PCTFREE = 15,
        LOCK = PAGE, **STORAGE POOL = 2**)

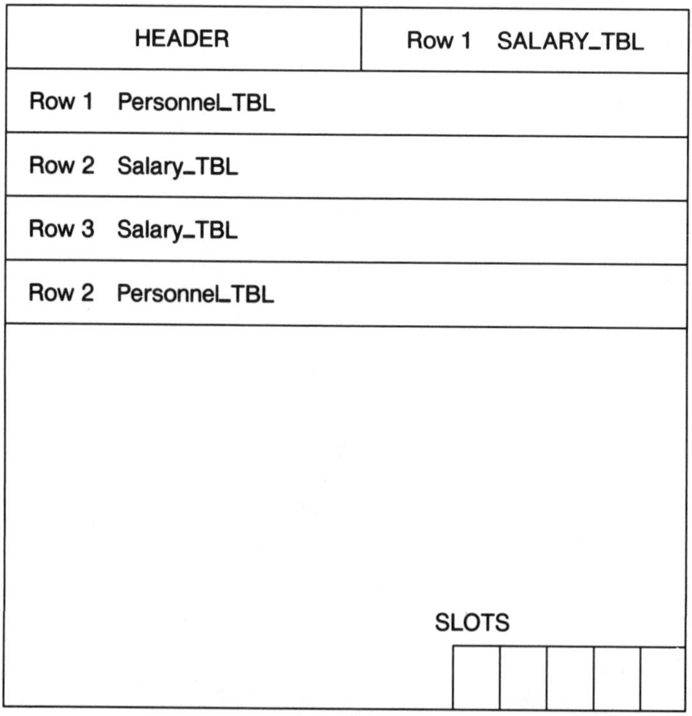

HEADER	Row 1 SALARY_TBL
Row 1 PersonneLTBL	
Row 2 Salary_TBL	
Row 3 Salary_TBL	
Row 2 PersonneLTBL	

SLOTS

Figure 8.3   DBSPACE with Two Tables

The values listed in the above command, except for the DBSPACE name and the storage pool number, are the default values, but, as has been mentioned several times, defaults should rarely be used. The DBA should calculate the sizes that are actually needed. PAGES is the parameter specifying the **minimum** size of the DBSPACE needed. The actual size acquired will depend upon the sizes of the available DBSPACES. If the smallest one available, for example, is 1024 pages, the size of the STOCKDBSP DBSPACE will be 1024 pages. The DBA must also specify whether the DBSPACE will be a public or a private DBSPACE. Private DBSPACES should **only** be used when the data will be updated by only one user at a time. Data belonging to one user and not usually accessed by other users is a good candidate for a private DBSPACE.

Storage Pool 1 is the default storage pool when no pool is specified. The storage pool assignment should **not** be allowed to default because storage pool 1 should be reserved for (several of) the system tables.

DBSPACE Size

To ACQUIRE a DBSPACE to be named SAMPLED in storage pool two, for example, with 20,000 4K pages of storage, the DBA could specify:

ACQUIRE PUBLIC DBSPACE NAMED SAMPLED (**PAGES=20000**, STORAGE=2)

The PAGES parameter in this example indicates that the DBSPACE should be able to hold 82 million bytes of data (20,000 4K pages). The PAGES value indicated, however, is not the actual size allocated when the DBSPACE is assigned.

It would be unacceptable to require the regeneration of the database each time additional space were needed. SQL/DS, therefore, allows the DBA to greatly exaggerate the space requirements during database generation and DBSPACE acquisition without having to provide the actual physical space. The only cost of exaggerating space requirements is eight bytes of directory space for each logical page. Additional physical extents do not have to be allocated until they are actually needed. The DBSPACE acquired above, for example, may be defined as containing 20,000 4K pages even though only 100 4K pages are physically available. Only when they are needed will the additional DBEXTENTS be added to the storage pool.

This is advantageous because when a database is first defined, only a small amount of data is actually loaded. As time passes, more and more data is added and the database grows. With this capability, the installation can save the expense of ordering more disk spindles than are initially required until they are actually needed. The rule is: When first acquired, the DBSPACE should be defined large enough to satisfy all future expansion needs so as to ensure that there will be sufficient space for growth.

SHADOW PAGES

When calculating storage requirements, the *shadow page* mechanism must be taken into consideration because it will use resources for which provision will have to be made. A *shadow page* is the original copy of a page that was modified and it is saved for recovery and performance reasons until a checkpoint is taken. It will be used to restore the page to its original contents in case an error occurs or the user issues a ROLLBACK WORK. SQL/DS will assign an additional page from the storage pool on which to write the modifications but, in order not to deplete the DBSPACE, it will not count it as one of the DBSPACE pages. Thus, when a page is modified, the original page is not touched. The new page acquired from the storage pool is designated the *current page.* At checkpoint time, SQL/DS will synchronize the data stored on the disk and all of the *logical units of work* (LUW) will be committed to the database regardless of the condition of the LUW. The current page will become the *shadow page* and the old *shadow page* will be released. Should a soft failure occur, the system will have enough information on the LOG and on the *shadow pages* to recover.

Each DBSPACE requires two page map tables, one for the shadow page and one for the current page. The first time a page is updated (after a checkpoint), a new physical page slot will be allocated from the storage pool. This is why the size of a storage pool should usually contain many more pages than will be needed for the data alone.

The modified pages will be stored in buffers and written only if the buffer is needed for other transactions or when a checkpoint is taken. The buffer replacement algorithm is based on the assumption that a given page may be needed in the near future. If all of the buffers are filled, the least recently used buffer will be the one to be rewritten when a new buffer is needed. When all of the buffers have been written to disk at checkpoint time, the *shadow pages* will be released.

The system is aware that a *shadow page* exists by checking the *shadow page* directory block. If the pointer in the *shadow page* directory is to the same address as the current page directory pointer, no modification was made.

TABLES AND THE TUPLE-ID

Each DBSPACE may hold one or more tables. A table consists of a collection of rows containing data in a defined format. Each row in the table is uniquely identified by a four-byte row identifier known as a tuple-id (TID) (Figure 8.4). This TID is made up of the DBSPACE page number and the address slot number located at the end of the data page that contains the displacement of the row from the beginning of the DBSPACE. Addressing a row via its tuple-id is the fastest way to access the data:

Figure 8.4   Tuple-ID (TID)

NOVERFLOW

Once an address (TID) is assigned to a data row, the TID address will never change until the row is deleted. When a variable or NULL column of a row is enlarged by an UPDATE command and the row will no longer fit into the data page assigned, SQL/DS will move the data to a new page but will **not** change the address of the data. The row header will remain in the original page with a pointer to the new TID address and an additional I/O will be required to access the *overflow* row. To avoid overflow, free space should be defined, but **only** when many updates are expected to be made and **only** when they will be made on rows randomly distributed throughout the table.

There will only be one *overflow* for any row because when the row again becomes too large for its new page, the data will be moved to a different page and the original pointer will be updated. When this row is again updated, SQL/DS will try to restore this row to its original page and this could result in additional I/O each time the row is updated. The number of overflow rows will be stored in the NOVER-FLOW column in the SYSTEM.SYSCATALOG table. If this number becomes excessively large, the table should be reorganized using UN-LOAD / RELOAD. To check the catalog for tables with excessive overflow, the following command should be used:

```
SELECT TNAME, ROWCOUNT,NPAGES, NOVERFLOW
    FROM SYSTEM.SYSCATALOG
        WHERE NOVERFLOW > 10
```

The result of this query might be:

TNAME	ROWCOUNT	NPAGES	NOVERFLOW
STRUCT_TBL	8442	2816	16
CUST_TBL	436706	33024	143
CONTROL_TBL	2309	291	279

The value in the condition *WHERE NOVERFLOW > 10* can be any value depending upon the experience of the DBA with the particular database. If a very active table containing 100 rows has 5 overflow rows, it is much **too many** and the table should be reorganized. If a relatively inactive 100,000 row table has 50 overflow rows it may not be a problem. The reason the query includes the ROWCOUNT and the number of pages is so that the DBA can review the ratio of pages and rows to overflow rows and, knowing the activity on the particular table, be able to determine if a reorganization is justified. Reorganization may take considerable amounts of time with large tables and should **not** done unless required. Overflow is only one factor to be considered when the need to reorganize a table is being evaluated.

INFLUENCING TABLE PLACEMENT

It is often useful to be able to distribute known *high volume of data* tables among available disk packs in order to apportion I/O activity among controllers and paths and to reduce I/O contention. In general, SQL/DS does **not** provide the DBA with the means to control the placement of data, indexes, and tables in the SQL/DS database, but a knowledge of the data management structure can provide some small measure of control and the systems programmer or DBA can attempt to distribute I/O activity.

This physical location of the tables becomes blurred as the extents are assigned to logical pools that are further logically subdivided into DBSPACES, pages, tables, and rows. There is no practical method of ensuring that a particular row of data resides on a particular hardware track. This is not a deficiency of SQL/DS but rather a basic tenet of database theory to free the systems programmer and application developer from being concerned about physical placement of data as he or she was in the past. When there are five DBEXTENTS, for example, the next available page may come from any one of them. In general, this data independence should **not** be interfered with. In special situations, however, where a very high volume of accesses to data on a particular table makes it imperative that the table be separated from other high volume tables, one of the following procedures may be used:

1. Assign a new storage pool with one extent on a disk with a low volume of activity. Assign one DBSPACE with one table to this storage pool.
2. An alternative might be to assign many very small DBEXTENTS on different disk volumes to one storage pool. Define one large DBSPACE with one table to the pool. This will ensure that the table will be distributed over multiple packs but it will **not** ensure which range of keys will be on each pack.

These manipulations should be avoided where possible. In any case, all of the DBEXTENTS should be distributed among as many nonactive DASD devices as possible so as to minimize the I/O generated to any one disk. The entire database should **NOT** be placed on one disk drive.

DELETED DATA PAGES

When a data row is to be added to a table and there are no data pages in the DBSPACE available with unused space, a new page will be taken from the storage pool and assigned to this DBSPACE. Data is removed from a page by deleting the row or by dropping the table. When all of the rows on a data page are deleted, however, the data page is **not** returned to the storage pool. It remains assigned to this DBSPACE and can **only** be used by new inserts or overflow rows for tables in this DBSPACE. Only when the DBSPACE is dropped are the pages returned to the storage pool. This demonstrates why deleting a large number of rows from a table will **not** free data pages for other DBSPACES in the same storage pool. Dropping the table will **not** free the pages because the data pages containing the rows from the dropped table may also contain rows from other tables in the same DBSPACE. It should be noted that the deleting of rows and the dropping of tables all impact performance and should be avoided during peak on-line hours because *shadow pages* are generated, access modules are invalidated, and log records are written.

DELETED INDEX PAGES

The use of index pages is even more restrictive and should be thoroughly understood. SQL/DS assumes that deleted keys will be replaced at some future time and does **not** release empty index pages for new keys, even for the same table. This means that the now empty pages are only available for **keys in the same key range** as the deleted keys. Index pages with the following key ranges will be used to further explain the concept:

01 → 99	100 → 150	170 → 543	600 →

INDEX PAGES

If keys 170–543 are deleted, for example, the now empty page will remain unused until keys in the range 151–599 (the high key value of page two through the low key value of page four) are added to the table. The pages will not be available to other tables or even to other key ranges in the same table. This is particularly important in installations where *ever-increasing key values* are used (i.e., dates, sequence numbers). The reserve of index pages will rapidly be exhausted even though old values are deleted on a regular basis.

When the index is dropped, however, the index pages are released and may be reused by other tables in the DBSPACE or by the same table for index entries. The way, therefore, to release the pages that were deleted but contained ever-increasing or decreasing keys, is to drop the index and to re-create it. Date values and sequential values are considered poor candidates for indexes but when they must be used the indexes should be periodically dropped and re-created.

There are several reasons why, despite the simplicity of the commands, dropping and re-creating an index are **not** trivial actions. Creating or dropping an index on a large table will require significant amounts of computer time and resources. These functions may impact the performance of other transactions when the process locks the system tables to update them. All of the access modules that had used the dropped index will be tagged invalid and additional performance impact will occur when the first user causes the automatic re-creation of the access modules. Care should also be taken that the access modules will not be automatically re-created after the index is dropped **but** before it is re-created because the new access module will **not** use the index. It is recommended, therefore, that all reorganization be done after peak on-line hours and, where possible, in single-user mode.

When an index is dropped the index pages are not returned to the storage pool but are available only to other indexes within the same DBSPACE.

CONFIGURATION DATA

The SHOW DBCONFIG command provides information that reflects the parameters used at database generation time. The values used at database generation time define the maximum potential size of the database and sufficient resources to satisfy this definition do not have to be allocated until they are actually needed. The following example displays the result of the SHOW DBCONFIG command:

SHOW DBCONFIG

Specified by the DBA at DB Definition

Maximum Pools =	32
Maximum DBEXTENTS =	200
Maximum DBSPACES =	10000

Computed

Total Number of DBSPACE Blocks =	16709
Total Amount of DBSPACE =	4277504 K
Total Number of Physical Pages =	1081344
Total Amount of Physical Space =	4325376 K
Total Number of Directory Blocks =	17856
Number of DBSPACE Blocks Left =	**9135**

The values specified at the time that the database is generated need to be carefully considered because if the values are too low, they may limit the ability of the DBA to tune the database. A low value in maximum pools, for example, will limit the distribution of DBEX-TENTS to many different storage pools. A low maximum value of DBEXTENTs will limit the addition of many small extents to control the placement of active tables. A low maximum DBSPACES will limit the ability to assign one table to each DBSPACE.

The *computed values* describe the maximum potential size of the database. It should be remembered that *shadow pages* also require resources and the maximums for user data are actually lower than the

SHOW DBCONFIG command calculates. The number of DIREC-TORY blocks generated is a very significant parameter. Each 128 pages in a DBSPACE requires two directory blocks to map logical pages to physical pages: one for the current page and one for the *shadow page*. To calculate the maximum number of data pages that can be added to the database and which will be available for user data in the above example, multiply the number of DBSPACE blocks left (9135) by 64 (128 / 2—to allow for *shadow pages*).

SUMMARY

One of the major purposes of a database is to make the storage of data independent of the hardware used and to free the users of these concerns. Rows of data are added to logical tables that are created in logical DBSPACES that are assigned to logical storage pools made up of one or more physical DBEXTENTS. Adding an extent is a relatively trivial process; removing an extent is impossible.

A procedure must be executed to inform SQL/DS that a DBEX-TENT has been added and assigned to a storage pool. The SQLADBSP EXEC or procedure is used to add DBSPACEs to the pool. DBSPACEs must be acquired to be used. The DBA can greatly exaggerate the space requirements during database generation without having to provide the physical space. The only cost of exaggerating space requirements is eight bytes of directory space for each logical page.

There are three types of DBSPACES:public, private, and internal. The DBSPACE and its characteristics are defined using the ACQUIRE DBSPACE command. A DBSPACE contains data pages, header pages, and index pages.

It is often useful to be able to distribute known *high volume of data* tables among available disk packs. There is no way, however, to determine where a data page or row will be physically stored.

A *shadow page* is the original copy of a page that was modified. The system is aware that a *shadow page* exists by checking the *shadow page* directory block.

Each row in the table is uniquely identified by a tuple-id (TID). Once an address (TID) is assigned to a data row, the TID address is never changed until the row is deleted. When a row is enlarged and it no longer fits into the data page assigned, SQL/DS will move the data to a new page but will **not** change the TID. There will only be one *overflow* page for any one row.

Deleted data pages are not returned to the storage pool. They remain assigned to the DBSPACE. Deleted index pages are not available to other tables but are reserved for the same table and the same range of keys that they previously held. With ever-increasing key values, the reserve of index pages will rapidly be exhausted even though old values are deleted on a regular basis. The way to release the index pages is to drop the index and re-create it.

The SHOW DBCONFIG command provides information that reflects the parameters used at database generation time. The values specified at the time that the database is generated need to be carefully considered because if the values are too low, they may limit the ability of the DBA to tune the database.

RECOMMENDATIONS

1. Adding DBEXTENTS should be planned with care because once they are added they cannot be removed without regenerating the database.
2. The DBSPACE should be defined large enough to satisfy all future expansion needs.
3. Enough directory space should be allocated at generation time to satisfy all future needs.
4. The default DBSPACE values should rarely be used.
5. Table placement manipulations should be avoided where possible.
6. DBEXTENTS should be distributed among as many non-active DASD devices as possible. The entire database should **NOT** be placed on one disk drive.
7. When calculating storage requirements, the shadow page mechanism must be taken into consideration.
8. Deleting of large numbers of rows and dropping of tables should be avoided during peak on-line hours.
9. Care should be taken that the access modules are not automatically re-created after the index is dropped and before the index is re-created.
10. Date values and sequential values are considered poor candidates for indexes but, when they must be used, the indexes should be periodically dropped and re-created.

11. All reorganization should be done in single-user mode after peak on-line hours.

FREE SPACE

Minimizing I/O by eliminating free space and writing as many rows as possible in each data page is a crucial component of SQL/DS performance tuning. Setting aside free space so that newly inserted rows of data can be placed in the same data page as other rows with the same or successive keys (clustering) reduces I/O. This section will discuss the trade-off between these two contrasting concepts and offer suggestions on how to make the best performance decision.

When a new DBSPACE is acquired, the PCTFREE parameter is specified to define the percentage of space in each data page which should be left empty during the initial data load. When additional rows are inserted via the INSERT or INPUT commands, or existing rows are expanded via the UPDATE command, the availability of free space enables SQL/DS to maintain the clustered property of the table and to avoid data overflow. It is important to emphasize that the free space is not automatically available after initial load. **The user must reduce the PCTFREE value BEFORE this free space can be used for new rows.** In the event that the user forgets to alter the percentage of free space to a lower value, the free space will **NEVER** be used for inserting new rows into the data page.

FREE SPACE OR NOT FREE SPACE

When free space is defined, unused space **is reserved on every single data page.** Empty data page space degrades performance because there are fewer rows of data stored on every page. Fewer rows will be retrieved or written with each I/O to the data base and fewer rows will be stored in each data buffer. To reach acceptable levels of performance, **free space should be kept to an absolute minimum.**

When data is physically stored in the sequence corresponding to the sequence of an index, the index is designated as a clustered index. When SQL/DS uses a clustered index, the volume of I/O accessed will be potentially reduced because there will be a strong probability that many of the rows that will satisfy the query conditions will be found in the same data page or buffer. When new rows are inserted into the table, this *clustered* property will be maintained by the use of the free space reserved during the table load. It is important, therefore, that sufficient free space be allocated to satisfy the need for the insertion of new data rows.

The decision to define or not to define free space for inserts has to be based on an additional consideration. New rows will be inserted in the sequence of the **FIRST index** created whether or not this first index is, or ever was, clustered. When there is no index or when the first index has been dropped, no other index, except a new primary key index, will be designated as the **first,** and new rows will be inserted at the *end* of the table as described later in this chapter.

When taking into consideration that free space is left on every single page, it follows that free space is ONLY justifiable when there are many inserts with *random keys.* If the **first** index columns are dates, sequence numbers, or any other ever-increasing or decreasing values, the free space on the vast majority of the pages will be wasted and **PCTFREE = 0 should be specified.**

Defining Free Space

When a DBSPACE is acquired, the percentage of each page to be reserved for later usage is defined. If a value is not specified, the **free space default is 15 percent.** The unused space will be reserved to be utilized when updates expand existing null or variable fields or when new rows are inserted.

The command to set aside at least 15 percent of each page for a private DBSPACE is:

```
ACQUIRE PRIVATE DBSPACE NAMED ATARA1.EXPDBSP (PCTFREE = 15)
```

The general rule is that using a default value is **usually the worst choice.** If 15 percent is the correct percentage of free space, it should be explicitly defined. Experience has shown that most tables would benefit from 0 percent of free space. It is best to specify the minimum percentage of free space required for inserts and updates. If no free space is needed, specify:

```
ACQUIRE . . . . . (PCTFREE=0).
```

To determine if the PCTFREE has been modified to zero, the DBA can issue the following command:

```
SELECT DBSPACENO, NPAGES FREEPCT
    FROM SYSTEM.SYSDBSPACES
        WHERE FREEPCT > 0
        ORDER BY 1
```

The output might be:

DBSPACENO	NPAGES	FREEPCT
15	256	15
16	5120	15
17	1024	15
18	1024	15

This type of output usually signifies that the default values were used and that the DBA never modified the free space to zero.

EXCESSIVE I/O

One method of avoiding excessive I/O on inserts when sufficient free space is not available, is to drop the FIRST index and re-create it. As mentioned previously, when a FIRST index exists, SQL/DS will always try to insert a new row so that this FIRST index remains clustered. If there is no space available in the page that the row should be inserted on, a search will be made to find the nearest page with enough free space to hold the new row.

To avoid scanning every page for free space, free space information is maintained, via a class-code, in each page entry in the directory. This class code enables SQL/DS to scan 128 pages with one directory I/O but can result in excess free space being left unused, as explained later in this chapter. When large tables are involved, this search for free space can be very time consuming.

When this FIRST index is dropped and re-created it is no longer designated as the FIRST index and no FIRST index will exist. When there is no FIRST index, the row to be inserted will be placed in the *last* page of the table as indicated by the CLUSTERROW column in the SYSTEM.SYSCATALOG table. This column, however, is not updated automatically. When this column is not updated periodically via the UPDATE STATISTICS command, the same inefficient procedure of searching for free space in pages near the end, as was discussed in the previous paragraphs, will be followed.

The existence of a FIRST index can be determined by a check of the CLUSTER column of the SYSINDEXES catalog table. The values 'F' and 'W' indicate a FIRST index. 'F' also indicates that the index is clustered:

```
SELECT INAME, CLUSTER FROM SYSTEM.SYSINDEXES
      WHERE TNAME='PERSONNEL_TBL'
```

The output might include:

INAME	CLUSTER
PERSONNEL_IX1	F
PERSONNEL_IX2	N
PERSONNEL_IX3	N

When inserts are requested in a program, the optimizer determines how to perform the insert based on the information it has at the time of preprocess. This means that if the optimizer determines that it must use the default insert rule, the value of CLUSTERROW at the time of preprocess is stored in the access module. When many inserts have been made and the table expands, a re-preprocess should be done.

EXCESSIVE FREE SPACE

If the DBA finds that a table has too much free space, the free space value in the DBSPACE can be altered and an UNLOAD / RELOAD of the table can be performed. It should be realized that the PCTFREE value that is specified is the **minimum** value that SQL/DS sets aside in each page. The actual free space may be quite a bit larger. The actual space left unused depends upon the FREE CLASS code and the size of the data rows.

Readers who are not curious about how many 100 byte rows will fit into a 4K page when PCTFREE = 50, may skip the following example. The FREE CLASS code is used to determine if sufficient space to insert a new row in a data page exists. The code is not precise and this lack of precision may lead to strange results. Fifty percent free space means that a little over 2000 bytes should be left free in each 4K page. A class table having the following values in the higher classes is used:

CLASS	MINIMUM	MAXIMUM
. .	. . . .	. . . .
9	1000	1999
10	**2000**	4017
11	4018	4077
12	**4078**	4078

If the page is empty, the directory entry for that page indicates a free class of 12 which means that 4078 bytes are unused. Before the first 100-byte row will be inserted into the data page an evaluation will be made to determine if enough free space exists to hold the new row **and** to satisfy the 50 percent free space parameter value. The algorithm used requires that the row length + (40 * PCTFREE value) be less than or equal to the MINIMUM free value for the class listed in the table.

To determine if the first row can be inserted, the following calculation is made. The value (40 * 50) represents the approximate amount that must be left free (2K per page or 50 percent):

$$100 + (40 * 50) \text{ must be } \leq 4078$$

4078 is the minimum free space value of class 12 and indicates the approximate space remaining in the page. The value 2100 is less than or equal to 4078, so the first row will be inserted. After the insert, the new class of this page is 10 because 3978 (- control bytes) are still free and free class 10 indicates that there are between 2000 and 4018 free bytes.

Before a second 100-byte row can be inserted, that calculation will again be performed to ensure that the result will be less than or equal to the new class *low value* (2,000) listed in the table. 100 + (40 * 50) now has to be less than or equal to 2000. The result, however, is 2100 and a second 100-byte row cannot be inserted in the page.

The correct answer to how many 100-byte rows may be inserted in a 4K page with 50 percent free space is 1. This exercise shows that the imprecise nature of the class code may lead to distorted results, especially when PCTFREE is greater than 50 percent.

FREE SPACE REORGANIZATION

When a row is deleted, the remainder of the rows in the 4K data space are NOT moved and the updating of slot pointers with the new displacement addresses is avoided. If a new row is to be inserted, however, and there is enough total free space but not enough contiguous space at the end of the page, all of the existing rows will be shifted, if necessary, to free the unused space between them. This may impact performance if it occurs too often. To reduce performance delays caused by this shifting of data, tables with large numbers of random deletes should be reorganized during off-hours.

ADDITIONAL USE OF FREE SPACE

There are instances where, to reduce retrieval time, rows from two tables which are usually used in a JOIN should be interleaved in the same DBSPACE, so that they share the same physical pages. This is possible because when two or more tables are created in the same DBSPACE and free space is available on a data page holding rows from one of the tables, the rows from other tables will be inserted into the data page. The DBA should, however, be aware that there is **no** way to control which rows are inserted on which pages and that this attempt to improve performance may actually degrade performance when additional pages will have to be read in order to retrieve each of the parts of the join rows.

To interleave data rows from two tables:

1. Acquire a DBSPACE with PCTFREE equaling approximately 30–40 percent.
2. Load the first table.
3. ALTER PCTFREE to zero.
4. Load the second table.

INDEX FREE SPACE

Free space for indexes should **only** be defined if new keys will be added randomly or if many new keys will be added. **Free space should be defined = 0** when date or sequential identifying numbers are used as keys. The greater the percent of free space, the fewer the keys on each index page and the greater the number of I/Os required for a search of an index.

Free space is needed, however, to avoid wasting space and increasing I/O when many new key values are **randomly** added to the index. When the lowest level leaf page of an index is full and a new key must be inserted on the page, a new index page is acquired and the key pairs (TID address and key value) are divided equally between the two pages. The now empty half of each of the two new index pages will **never** be used unless keys which follow in sequence are added. This division of index pages will cause additional overhead of pointers on nonleaf pages being updated and will lead to increased I/O because there will be fewer keys on each page.

Data rows need not be stored sequentially but index values must be. When a key is deleted its space will **not** be reused unless a key that logically fits into its sequential location is added. If new keys are always inserted in ascending or descending order, rather than randomly, the space of deleted keys **will never be reused** until the index is dropped.

The PCTFREE parameter of an index does **not** have to be altered (as does the PCTFREE parameter for a DBSPACE). The system automatically modifies the value to zero after the index is created. Be aware that the catalog continues to list the PCTFREE value with the value originally defined and this often leads to undue concern.

NULLS

Each blank or zero fixed length column requires space in a row. If columns are nullable but are located between non-nullable columns, they will **always** occupy space whether or not they contain any data. When the nullable columns are located at the right end of the table, however, the reserving of space for them will depend upon how they are loaded. This implies that if the last column in a table is not-null, space will always be reserved for all null columns in the table. Space will **not** be reserved for nullable columns **only** when the NULL columns are the **rightmost** columns in the table **and** the NULL column names are **not** specified in the INSERT command **or** the DATALOAD command.

SQL/DS will handle not-null columns more efficiently than nullable columns. Null columns should **only** be used when there is a need to distinguish between the absence of any value and a zero or a blank value. In a banking application, for example, zero is a valid value and the user will often need to know whether or not a value was ever entered into the column. If the column were to be non-nullable and would contain a zero, the user would not be able to distinguish between an unfilled column and a zero value column. In this instance, nullable columns are necessary.

The default, unfortunately, is nullable columns. This default should **not** be used unless it is really needed. Nullable columns require the additional definition of indicator variables in application programs to receive the indicator that the column was null:

```
FETCH . . . . .    INTO    :NULLCOL :COLINDVAR
```

The only situation where nullable columns save space and are practical is when the data is inserted once, is rarely updated, and is not reorganized. If these conditions do not exist, to avoid performance problems it would be best to ensure that space is reserved for all nullable columns by placing a non-null column at the end of the table.

When a table or DBSPACE UNLOAD command is executed, space **will** be reserved for nullable columns because the DBSU specifically itemizes all of the columns in the table. If space was not reserved prior to the UNLOAD, the RELOAD will fill more data pages and may result in the DBSPACE or storage pool becoming short on storage.

To utilize the option of **not** reserving space for nullable columns, the design of the table should place the columns in the following sequence:

fixed	**not null**
variable	**not null**
fixed	**nullable**
variable	**nullable**

The fixed and variable null columns should be placed in the sequence of the probability that they will contain data. It should be noted that this type of design is **only** worthwhile with very large tables.

SUMMARY

If sequential keys are used and deleted, drop and re-create the index at regular intervals. This will avoid the use of all available index space even when most or all of the entries in the index are deleted. If the index is a FIRST index, refer to the information on how to retain a FIRST index elsewhere in the chapter.

The specification of PCTFREE requires analysis and it should **never** be defined by default. DBSPACES should not contain a mixture of tables, some of which need free space for rows to be inserted and some which do not. Specify PCTFREE = 0 when acquiring all DBSPACES where modification and inserts are not random. The overhead saved by compacting more rows on each data page will outweigh the occasional overhead of added pages, lack of clustering, or overflow. These tables should, of course, be monitored to determine when clustering is lost or when too many overflow rows exist and reorganization is required.

Remember, when the default or PCTFREE = 15 is specified, **EVERY** data page will have at least 15 percent free space. If only a small number of pages receive inserts, all the rest of the pages will have wasted space and the retrieval of a specified number of rows will require additional I/O.

RECOMMENDATIONS

When the exact insert/update use of a table is uncertain, define PCTFREE = 0. Monitor the overflow column in SYSTEM. SYSCATALOG. Remember that even when PCTFREE = 0, most data pages will contain some free space because rows do not fit exactly. This space is available for row expansion or small row inserts. When, of course, it is known that there will not be many inserts, random keys, or expanding rows, PCTFREE should = 0 when the DBSPACE is acquired.

When there will be **many random inserts and updates** which enlarge the size of rows and a clustered FIRST index exists, PCTFREE should be set at a high value when the table is loaded and reduced to a lower figure soon after. It should not be reduced to zero so as to reserve some additional space for enlarged rows.

When there will be **many random inserts** and there is a clustered FIRST index but few updates which enlarge the rows, load the table with a relatively high PCTFREE value and reduce the value to zero after the load.

When there will be **many updates** which enlarge the rows **and few random inserts** or no FIRST clustered index, load the table with a relatively high PCTFREE value. There will not be any need to reduce the PCTFREE value because updates **will** use the free space even when the PCTFREE value is not changed.

If the FIRST index is dropped and re-created, all newly inserted rows will be placed at the end of the table. There will no longer be any first index, even when other indexes exist, as explained elsewhere in this chapter.

Remember, the PCTFREE default is 15 percent. Do not use the default unless it is really suitable. Modify it, after the table load, to zero so that the free space can be used.

Nullable columns should usually be avoided.

UPDATE STATISTICS

SQL/DS commands are either dynamic or static. Dynamic commands can be used in ISQL, in the DBSU, or in application programs. Static commands are used in preprocessed application programs. When SQL/DS commands are prepared, the optimizer will use the information available in the SQL/DS catalogs to determine the best access path. It will check which indexes are available, estimate the number of I/Os that will be needed for many of the access paths, and estimate how much CPU processing will be involved. When the statistical data stored in the SQL/DS catalogs is accurate, the OPTIMIZER will choose the most efficient method of retrieving the data requested by the user.

Minor changes to the contents of a table do not significantly affect the optimization process. If SQL/DS would update its statistics automatically for every change to a table, the performance degradation would be unacceptable. To avoid excessive overhead every time a row is updated, deleted, or inserted, the statistics are not updated automatically. Instead the user is provided with an SQL/DS command and can decide when to perform the updating of the statistics. The format of the command to update the statistics of a DBSPACE is:

UPDATE [ALL] **STATISTICS** FOR DBSPACE DBSPACENAME

The UPDATE STATISTICS command without the ALL option updates the statistics for every column of a table used in an index. Statistics on those columns not found in an index are not updated. Statistics are also updated automatically each time CREATE INDEX is run on a table. The UPDATE STATISTICS and CREATE INDEX commands also update some general information in SYSTEM.SYSCOLUMNS and other catalog tables. The columns updated in SYSCOLUMNS include:

COLCOUNT. The number of unique values in the column.

HIGH2KEY. The first 8 bytes of the second highest value in the column.

LOW2KEY. The first 8 bytes of the second lowest value in the column.

AVGCOLLEN. The average column length (for a single column index).

ORDERFIELD. 'Y' if rows are ordered in this column sequence.

The columns updated in SYSTEM.SYSCATALOG are: CLUSTERROW, AVGROWLEN, ROWCOUNT, NPAGES, and PCTPAGES. The entire SYSTEM.SYSCOLSTATS table is updated. The columns updated in SYSTEM.SYSINDEXES include: KEYLEN, CLUSTER, FIRSTKEYCOUNT, FULLKEYCOUNT, NLEAF, NLEVELS, and CLUSTERRATIO. The updating of all of these columns in these system catalogs can cause serious contention problems. The UPDATE STATISTICS command in any of its formats, can significantly impact response time, and should **not** be executed during on-line processing hours, unless absolutely necessary.

UPDATE STATISTICS FOR DBSPACE requires one scan through all of the data pages for each table and one scan through all of the index pages for each index. UPDATE **ALL** STATISTICS gathers data about all of the columns in the table or DBSPACE and involves an additional scan of each table to gather statistics on non-index columns. If there are three tables in a DBSPACE, for example, UP-DATE ALL STATISTICS for that DBSPACE would require six DB-SPACE scans.

Many installations schedule the UPDATE STATISTICS to be run in the evening after the reorganization of the tables. A cycle of weekly or monthly offload / reload (with automatic UPDATE STATISTICS) is run, rotating the DBSPACES handled each evening.

In general, UPDATE ALL is **not** recommended. The command takes substantially longer to run than without the ALL option and the statistics it gathers are only used by the optimizer when joins are done on columns that do not have an index. The optimizer needs to know the characteristics of the JOIN column in order to determine whether to do a merge scan or a nested loop scan. When a nested loop scan is chosen, the optimizer must decide which table should be the inner join table and which the outer join table.

If an installation has a situation where no index is the obvious choice to be used and the optimizer's defaults will not lead to the same choice as when the ALL parameter is used, then ALL may prove helpful. The path the optimizer chooses should be checked (with the EXPLAIN command) before and after UPDATE ALL to determine if ALL is needed. At one installation, the reason for using UPDATE ALL on every DBSPACE was, *"as it is, the night shift only has three hours of work."*

START-UP PARAMETERS

During SQL/DS start-up processing, the operator or DBA may specify several parameters to control the operation of the database management system. These parameters include: the number of directory and data buffers to be allocated, the number of lock request blocks to be available, the number of concurrent users to be permitted to access the database, and the frequency of checkpoint processing. All of these have a significant impact on system performance. Each parameter value is variable because it impacts system and database performance and should contain the value which best suits the particular system environment and processing load in which it operates. When some of the parameters are not specified, as shown in the example, the system will utilize default values:

SQLSTART DBNAME(PROD1) **PARM**(STARTUP=W,LOGMODE=A)

These default values are usually not suitable for a production system and should **not** be used. Defaults are useful when the DBA has no experience in SQL/DS or knowledge of the applications to be used. Even in these instances several of the parameters should be modified (NDIRBUF, NPAGBUF, and NCUSERS). Many parameters, once chosen, do not need to be changed and they can be stored in a file and used for each start-up. In VM/SP, for example, the parameters may be specified in a CMS file with the filetype of SQL-PARM. A parameter file called SQLPROD1 SQLPARM might contain the following:

CMSFILE - SQLPROD1　　SQLPARM　　A1

LOGMODE=A, NPAGBUF=30, STARTUP=W,
NCSCANS=32, NDIRBUF=60

The SQLSTART command would specify the filename SQLPROD1 in its PARMID parameter to tell the instruction to retrieve the parameters from the CMS file. The DBA can override the values in the CMS by specifying them in the SQLSTART command as in the following example:

SQLSTART DBNAME(PROD1) PARM(**PARMID=SQLPROD1**,NDIRBUF=**90**)

The SQLSTART above, for example, will first retrieve the necessary parameter values from the PARM in the start-up command, will then check the CMS file for any of the parameters **not** specified in the command, and will finally use the default values for the parameters that are not specified in either the command or the CMS file. In this example, the SQLSTART command will override the parameter in the CMS file for NDIRBUF, will use LOGMODE, NPAGBUF, STARTUP, and NCSCANS from the CMS file, and will allow all of the remaining parameters to default. When SQL/DS initiates, a list of the start-up parameters appears on the console. The DBA should ensure that the proper values are being used. The following is an example of the console listing for a VSE/SP start-up:

```
F5 005 / / JOB SQLSTART PRODUCTION
F5 005 * ****************************************
F5 005 * ARISLIBP: SQL/DS LIBRARY
F5 005 * ****************************************
F5 005 * ****************************************
F5 005 * ARISUSDB: SQL/DS USER DATABASE
F5 005 * ****************************************
F5 005 ARI0025I THE PROGRAM ARISQLDS IS LOADED AT 47008
F5 005 ARI0025I THE PROGRAM ARICMOD IS LOADED AT 15CD08
F5 005 ARI0015I DSPLYDEV PARAMETER IS B
F5 005 ARI0015I ACCOUNT PARAMETER IS N
F5 005 ARI0015I DUMPTYPE PARAMETER IS P
F5 005 ARI0015I LOGMODE PARAMETER VALUE IS L
F5 005 ARI0015I STARTUP PARAMETER VALUE IS W
F5 005 ARI0015I SYSMODE PARAMETER VALUE IS M
F5 005 ARI0015I EXTEND PARAMETER VALUE IS N
F5 005 ARI0015I CHARNAME PARAMETER VALUE IS ENGLISH
F5 005 ARI0015I PARMID PARAMETER VALUE IS SQLP
F5 005 ARI0015I TRACDBSS PARAMETER VALUE IS 00000000000
F5 005 ARI0015I TRACRDS PARAMETER VALUE IS 00000000
F5 005 ARI0016I ARCHPCT PARAMETER VALUE IS 90
F5 005 ARI0016I CHKINTVL PARAMETER VALUE IS 100
F5 005 ARI0016I NCSCANS PARAMETER VALUE IS 30
F5 005 ARI0016I NCUSERS PARAMETER VALUE IS 9
F5 005 ARI0016I NDIRBUF PARAMETER VALUE IS 1000
F5 005 ARI0016I NLRBS PARAMETER VALUE IS 6778
F5 005 ARI0016I NLRBU PARAMETER VALUE IS 1500
F5 005 ARI0016I NPAGBUF PARAMETER VALUE IS 500
F5 005 ARI0016I SLOGCUSH PARAMETER VALUE IS 95
F5 005 ARI0016I SOSLEVEL PARAMETER VALUE IS 10
F5 005 ARI0016I DISPBIAS PARAMETER VALUE IS 7
F5 005 ARI0025I TRACDBSS PARAMETER VALUE IS 00000000000
F5 005 ARI0016I THE PROGRAM ARIXRDS IS LOADED AT 4EF000
F5 005 ARI0016I THE PROGRAM ARIXSXR IS LOADED AT 607000
F5 005 ARI0283I LOG ANALYSIS COMPLETE
F5 005 ARI0282I LOG UNDO COMPLETE
F5 005 ARI0060I SQL/DS INITIALIZATION COMPLETE
```

Real storage size, generated database size, and the frequency and size of transactions are the major considerations in determining start-up parameters. This data should be collected and should be re-evaluated every time frame (month, three months, etc.) to ensure that the parameters chosen are still the most efficient.

REAL STORAGE

Real storage, of course, will be used by the entire environment and SQL/DS will have to compete for this resource when there is not enough available for all of the system users. When a user requests a page of real storage and it is not available, a page fault will occur and the contents of the last used storage page will be discarded or, if it has been modified, it will be written back to disk. This *paging* **should be avoided** when possible.

The number of buffers allocated should be directly related to the quantity of real storage available. When a large amount of real storage is available, the number of buffers should be increased until it results in paging. The number of buffers should then be reduced until the paging stops. The maximum number of directory buffers is 28,000 and the maximum number of page buffers is 3,500. Very few installations have a sufficient amount of real storage available to allow the DBA to assign these maximum values, but if storage is available, use it. Keep in mind, however, that 3,500 * 4K is 14M.

When the system is storage constrained, a small number of buffers should be allocated. The absence of an adequate number of buffers results in additional I/O to the data base but **database I/O is more efficient than paging I/O.** This is true because when database I/O occurs, only the agent requesting the I/O is placed in a wait state while the remaining agents may continue to work. When paging I/O occurs, however, the entire VM/SQL machine or VSE/SP partition waits and all of the users are prevented from continuing.

BUFFERS

Buffers are used to store the data and directory information previously fetched on the assumption that the same information may be needed again in the near future. These buffers serve to reduce the number of I/Os and they greatly improve the response time of a transaction. Buffers also reduce channel and device contention and CPU usage. They reduce the length of time that one user ties up an agent and the resources needed by other users.

Each 4K page buffer may hold data pages, index pages, log pages, or internal DBSPACE pages. Each 512 byte directory buffer holds database control information which maps the logical database to the physical DASD storage used.

When a buffer is modified it is **not** written to disk until the buffer is required by some other transaction. The algorithm used by SQL/DS frees for reuse the least recently used buffer. This is to avoid the use of a buffer which has just recently been used and may soon be needed again. The buffers are allocated by the DBA in the start-up parameters NDIRBUF (directory buffers) and NPAGBUF (data page buffers):

SQLSTART DB(PROD1) PARM(**NDIRBUF**=60, **NPAGBUF**=40)

When real storage is constrained, a decision must be made on whether to increase data buffers or directory buffers. Despite the smaller size of directory buffers, the I/O overhead expended to read directory blocks is almost as great as the I/O overhead required to read the data pages from the database. This implies that it is equally important to increase both types of buffers. The contents of directory buffers, however, are usually required more often than specific data rows are and the directory buffers consume much less real storage than do data buffers.

It is usually worthwhile, therefore, to specify many more (four or five times as many) directory buffers than page buffers in a memory constrained environment. The DBA should not use the default values and should review the use of the buffers to ensure that the value specified is not too large or too small. The SHOW BUFFER command can be used to display the buffers that are currently being used. The following is an example of a partial list of the output:

```
ONLY USED BUFFERS ARE DISPLAYED
```

DBSPACE PAGE BUFFERS	REC	ADDR	FLAGS	FIX CNT
29	0001F9	008A8000	00	0
156	000145	008A9000	80	0
89	00008A	008AF000	00	2
1	0005C7	008B3000	80	0
1	0021A1	008B4000	00	0
0	000622	008B5000	00	1
5	00032F	008B9000	80	0

An additional source of buffer usage information is the COUNTER command. This command will display a count of the number of page reads and the number of looks into the directory or page buffers. When the number of looks into the buffer is equal to the number of page reads, there is a problem because it means that for every page requested by the transactions an I/O to the database was needed. The ratio should be at least five looks in the buffer for every I/O to the database. The ratio is often 10 to 1 or 20 to 1 or even 100 to 1 but should never be 1 to 1.

Buffer allocation should be monitored during peak production periods. The larger the allocation of buffers, the higher the ratio should be between reads from buffer and I/O to disk. The DBA may also tune the system by slowly increasing the number of buffers assigned until additional buffers no longer significantly improve the ratio. Keep in mind that real storage is a critical constraint and buffers should NOT be added if the result is increased paging.

Buffers are added to reduce I/O and improve the *Hit Ratio* and performance. Some workloads, because of their data mix and characteristics, may unavoidably result in low *Hit Ratios* but they are the exception. It should be remembered that at times even a small reduction in I/O activity may be significant. For additional information, refer to Chapter 7.

CONCURRENT USERS (NCUSERS)

This parameter designates the number of active users that can use SQL/DS simultaneously. The parameter value will specify the number of real agents that should be allocated. Each agent requires approximately 200K bytes of storage and potentially generates database and resource contention. To avoid making end-users wait, the systems programmer or DBA should allocate as many agents as the resources will allow. To avoid contention, paging, and locking, the systems programmer or DBA should allocate as few agents as is reasonable. Like most database parameter decisions, there is a trade-off and a need to estimate requirements and to continually monitor the system. In lower powered CPU models, the number of concurrent users should be kept to a minimum (three or four). If more than that number of users would try to access the database they would be placed in a WAIT queue and would be prevented from starting their transaction.

VSE/SP only has real agents. The NCUSERS parameter specifies the maximum number of users that can link simultaneously to the database partition. If more than the maximum try to link, the CICS users will be queued by the Online Manager and batch users will be queued by XPCC until a real agent is available.

In VM/SP, the systems programmer can also define pseudo-agents. The MAXCONN parameter indicates how many minidisks **and** connected users are possible. If the MAXCONN parameter is increased and no additional minidisks are added, more users can be attached to pseudo-agents. The user's VM machine issues an IUCV CONNECT and the user is connected to a pseudo-agent which only requires 300 bytes. These pseudo-agents are placed in a WAIT queue until a real agent has ended its previous *logical unit of work* and is available. If the user who just issued the end LUW tries to start a new LUW, the user is placed at the end of the pseudo-agent WAIT queue and must wait until a real agent is available. To achieve the best overall response and to be fair, users should end their LUWs as quickly as possible and release their real agents.

The CIRB transaction of CICS will reserve several agents for the exclusive use of CICS users and will establish the links to the SQL/DS partition. These agents will no longer be available to other CICS or batch partitions until they are released via the CIRT transaction. Be aware that when VSE/SP is using a VM/SP SQL/DS database in guest sharing mode, the CICS communication links specified during initialization will be connected with pseudo-agents to which real agents will be permanently assigned.

The CIRD transaction can be used to display elapsed time information and to list the transactions that are holding an agent or that are waiting for agents (queued by online resource manager). It, however, does not show batch applications working with SQL/DS agents. The following displays a CIRD output example:

STATUS OF ONLINE SQL/DS APPLICATIONS:

TRANSACTIONS WAITING TO ESTABLISH A LINK TO SQL/DS:

TASKNO	TRANID	TERMID	USERID	USERDATA	WAIT TIME
000013	ST01	L043	DOV1		00:04:01

TRANSACTIONS HOLDING A LINK AND NOW ACCESSING SQL/DS:

TASKNO	TRANID	TERMID	USERID	USERDATA	TIME USED FOR CURRENTTIME ACCESS	TOTAL LUW
000011	ST01	L043	DAN2		00:01:05	00:01:30

TRANSACTIONS HOLDING A LINK TO SQL/DS AND NOT USING IT:

TASKNO	TRANID	TERMID	USERID	USERDATA	TIME SINCE LAST ACCESSTIME	TOTAL LUW
000002	CISQ		DAV3	L041	00:02:31	00:15:03

TRANSACTIONS PREVIOUSLY ACCESSED SQL/DS(NOT HOLDING A LINK)

TASKNO	TRANID	TERMID	USERID	USERDATA	TIME SINCE LAST ACCESS
000007	ST09		AVI7	L042	00:05:53

TIME = 12:15:32   DATE = 09/15/90

The number of agents CICS will acquire is dependent upon the CIRB transaction. If five agents are required, the CIRB command will state:

```
CIRB ,5
```

If there are only 5 real agents allocated, none remain to be available to CMS users or other CICS or batch partitions. If there are less than 5, fewer are assigned and a message is returned to the DBA or operator who issued the CIRB transaction.

In systems with adequate CPU and real storage, the DBA must decide the trade-off between allowing as many users as possible to receive SQL/DS services and between the resource contention which may be generated by a large number of users. If transactions are short and well written, overall response time might be improved if the DBA were to allow only a small number of users at a time and thus avoid resource contention. On the other hand, if applications are not well designed and long LUWs tie up all of the available real agents, the wait imposed by specifying a small number of concurrent users might not be acceptable.

To determine how many links are active or free, use the SHOW ACTIVE command or SHOW USERS command, as shown in Chapter 7. When the DBA finds that real agents are usually free during peak processing periods, the number of available agents should be reduced to conserve the storage for additional buffers.

LOCK REQUEST BLOCKS

SQL/DS uses many locks to maintain database integrity. Each request for a lock usually requires two or more lock request blocks. The DBA can specify the maximum number of request blocks each individual user may request and the maximum number of lock request blocks available to all users at any one time:

NLRBU. Maximum available per user.

NLRBS. Maximum available for the database.

The following example shows an allocation of a maximum of 5,000 lock request blocks per individual user and 20,010 locks for all of the users combined:

```
SQLSTART DBNAME(PROD1) PARM(NLRBU=5000,NLRBS=20010)
```

When the maximum number of locks has been reached SQL/DS will escalate the user to DBSPACE locking. It does not matter if the user was using row, page, or table locking; escalation will **always** be to DBSPACE locking with no intermediate steps. Lock escalation will reduce concurrency by locking more data than the user had intended. The escalation may result in a deadlock which would not have occurred if the lower level locking had continued.

When too few locks are specified, escalation may occur often. Escalation will begin when the number of locks in use reaches the individual limit for a user or exceeds:

(NLRBS - (NCUSERS * 2))

Each lock request block requires only 24 bytes and, if real storage permits, as many blocks as are needed should be defined. The DBA can use the COUNTER command to determine if too many, too few, or just enough blocks have been allocated. To display the number of times that the system was forced to escalate, the DBA should issue the following two commands:

COUNTER ESCALATE

LOCK ESCALATIONS   **ESCALATE: 4**
            COUNTER LOCKLMT
MAXIMUM LOCKS EXCEEDED   **LOCKLMT : 1**

This sample output indicates that the system escalated successfully four times and unsuccessfully one time for a total of five lock escalations. If these occurred in a short period of time it is a sign that more locks need to be allocated. To view statistics on lock usage issue the command:

SHOW LOCK MATRIX   (MATRIX is the default)

This command will display information detailing the maximum number of locks used by any one LUW and the number of lock request blocks that were allocated, that are currently in use, and that remain free. If Max Used By LUW is zero, it implies that an LUW has recently been escalated and that the escalation process set this value back to zero. SHOW LOCK MATRIX also displays the lockwait table which lists the current users and indicates who is holding or waiting for locks. The output might contain the following information:

LOCK REQUEST BLOCK (LRB) AND LOCK STATUS:

NLRBS	IN USE	FREE	NLRBU	MAX USED BY LUW
6778	48	6730	1500	488

*** THE LOCKWAIT TABLE ***

ENTRY = DBSPACE NUMBER ON WHICH THERE IS LOCK CONTENTION
THE PRESENCE OF AN ENTRY SHOWS
THE AGENT REQUESTING THE LOCK AND
THE AGENT HOLDING OR CONTENDING FOR THE LOCK

AGENT   AGENT **HOLDING** OR CONTENDING FOR THE LOCK
REQUESTING
LOCK

	1	2	3	4
1	. . . . SQL070B
2	. . . .
3	. . . .
4 SQL070B	. . . .

When escalation is caused by one or two specific applications the problem can usually be solved by an increase in the NLRBU parameter value which will increase the number of locks available to the individual user. When escalation is caused by combinations of applications and by an insufficient number of system-wide lock request blocks, the situation may be alleviated by increasing the NLRBS parameter value. The alternative to increasing the number of lock request blocks might be to further tune the application programs to require fewer locks by adding more frequent COMMIT WORK or ROLLBACK WORK commands, by ensuring that predicates are sargable, or by specifying table locking in the application program instead of using row or page locking.

CHECKPOINTS

A checkpoint snaps a *picture* of the current state of the database and is taken periodically to synchronize the SQL/DS log and the database. It writes modified buffers to the database, marks each current page as the *shadow page,* releases the old *shadow page,* writes a checkpoint log record, and, when LOGMODE = Y, frees log space.

The increased I/O resulting from an excessive number of CHECKPOINTS can impact performance significantly and, in general, **the fewer the checkpoints the better.** The major impact of infrequent checkpoints is that warm start recovery will take a long time.

This should not be a factor in most installations where SQL/DS does not ABEND frequently. The negative performance impact of frequent checkpoints usually far outweighs any positive gain and checkpoints should be avoided especially during on-line peak processing periods. To determine how many checkpoints were taken the user can issue the command:

```
                       COUNTER   CHKPOINT
      SYSTEM CHECKPOINTS TAKEN         CHKPOINT:   754
```

When sufficient log space and extra pages in the storage pools exist during on-line hours for shadow pages, it would prove beneficial to use a very large value for checkpoint interval so as not to allow **any** checkpoints during peak transaction hours. It should be kept in mind, however, that when the checkpoint does occur under these circumstances, it will take a long time to complete.

Each database system has its own characteristics and the DBA has to make the trade-off decisions. Checkpoints are usually caused when the number of pages written to the log matches the CHKINTVL value specified in the SQL/DS start-up procedure. In a production system, this value should be large and there should be a sufficient allocation of log space. In systems where there is a great deal of on-line update activity, it may not be possible to avoid checkpoints but steps should be administratively set up to force checkpoints during lunch periods or coffee breaks.

Aside from reaching the CHKINTVL value, checkpoints are forced when:

- COMMIT WORK is specified after UPDATE of a row or rows of a table in a nonrecoverable storage pool. Avoid placing tables that are updated on-line in nonrecoverable storage pools.
- The LOG is full.
- DROP DBSPACE is specified for any DBSPACE.
- The number of free pages of any storage pool falls below the minimum SOS level specified.
- A COMMIT WORK is issued in single-user mode with LOGMODE = N. When long-running batch jobs are executed in single-user mode, and correctly, LOGMODE is set to N, make sure that the program does **not** issue COMMIT WORK at regular intervals. When running in multi-user mode, an application should COMMIT WORK regularly but in single-user mode each COMMIT WORK will trigger a checkpoint

and will result in excessive overhead. This emphasizes one of the differences that needs to be considered when application programs are written for single-user versus multi-user modes.

- The database is normally started or ended.
- Before and after an ARCHIVE.

When a checkpoint is scheduled all new DBSS operations must wait until the checkpoint is ended. The checkpoint cannot be initiated unless all of the DBSS operations currently running are completed. This process forces all new users to wait for long-running operations to complete. This checkpoint process can seriously impact SQL/DS response and should be severely limited or completely avoided, if possible, during peak on-line processing periods.

LOGS

The log will be used to record changes made to the database. To determine the size of the log, the percentage used, the percentage remaining before an ARCHIVE, and the number of pages remaining before a checkpoint, the SHOW command can be used:

SHOW LOG

The result might show:

```
LOG STATUS:
     LOG SIZE IS 21237760 BYTES
     LOG USED IS 7 PERCENT 1543520 BYTES
     LOG REMAINING BEFORE IMPLICIT ARCHIVE IS 82 PERCENT
          17570410 BYTES
     LOG PAGES REMAINING BEFORE CHECKPOINT IS 25
```

Mass updates, inserts, and deletes require LOG space and *shadow pages* and should be avoided during peak processing hours. Mass updates, inserts, and deletes should be run in single-user mode both to enhance performance and to avoid filling the log and triggering checkpoints and archives.

DISPATCHER BIAS

When more than one agent is ready to execute, the SQL/DS dispatcher selects one of the agents to begin work. The DISPBIAS parameter specifies for the dispatcher the criteria for choosing the agent to be dispatched. As DISPBIAS is set closer to 1, the dispatcher will select each agent in turn (*round robin*) without considering the level of resources it will need to consume. The closer the DISPBIAS is set to 10, the more priority given to short running low-resource usage agents (*priority dispatching*). The following is an example of a start-up specifying the default DISPBIAS of 7:

```
SQLSTART DBNAME(PROD1) PARM(DISPBIAS = 7)
```

Changing the DISPBIAS does **not** usually greatly impact response time. The default of 7 should be used unless the users begin to complain. If users running short LUWs (ISQL, etc.) complain, increase the DISPBIAS one or two values. If those running long LUWs complain, decrease the DISPBIAS one or two values. Unfortunately there is no indicator of priority problems other than user complaints so if neither type of user complains or both complain do **not** change the DISPBIAS.

SINGLE USER MODE

It is usually more efficient to run bulk batch jobs in single-user mode. The main advantages are:

- LOGMODE = N may be used to eliminate most logging overhead. (Reduces I/O)
- There is no IUCV overhead in VM/SP or XPCC overhead in VSE/SP when transferring data from the user machine or partition to SQL/DS and back. (Reduces CPU usage)

The disadvantage is that only one batch application program can operate at a time. On-line users and other batch applications cannot share the database with the single user. Batch applications that only SELECT and produce reports can be run in multi-user mode simultaneously with other similar batch applications.

CHOOSING A LOGMODE

In multi-user mode the DBA has the choice of specifying whether or not archiving and automatic forward recovery should be available.

The LOGMODE is specified in the start-up command. The following example specifies a LOGMODE of L:

SQLSTART DBNAME(PROD1) PARM(**LOGMODE = L**)

LOGMODE may be 'A', 'L', 'N,' or 'Y.' The 'A' specifies that an automatic ARCHIVE of the database should be executed when the ARCHPCT parameter value is reached. The archive can only be directed to tape (under VM/SP). A LOGMODE of 'L' specifies that an automatic LARCHIVE of the log should be executed when the ARCHPCT parameter value is reached. The log archive can be directed to tape or to disk.

LOGMODE 'N' is only applicable to single-user mode. Application modifications to the database are not logged but the system still uses the logs for internal operations.

When LOGMODE = Y is specified, the logs are maintained, and they wrap around when they run out of space, but no forward recovery is possible. The major **dis**advantage of this mode of operation is that should there be a disk crash of the database disk, all the work done after the previous user backup or archive will be lost. This does not mean to imply that SQL/DS cannot recover from a power failure or system ABEND. In the case of a power failure or system ABEND, an SQL/DS warm start is performed and the SQL/DS system will use the log to recover. This mode will **not** trigger an archive when the log runs out of space. LOGMODE=Y should **only** be used in test systems, when very few updates or inserts are performed on-line, and when it would be fairly easy to re-update, delete, or insert the day's transactions should a hardware failure occur.

In general, it is much safer to use LOGMODE = L (or A) which specifies that a LOG archive (or full archive) should be taken when the log is running out of space and that full forward recovery should be available in case of a DASD failure. It is also important to specify dual logging and to place each of the logs on a different DASD device. There is a bit more overhead with this type of logging and, if the log is too small, peak time processing may trigger an archive.

LOG FULL CONDITIONS (ARCHPCT)

The ARCHPCT parameter specifies at which point an on-line archive or log archive needs to be scheduled. If the ARCHPCT is 80, when the LOG is 80 percent full the operator is notified and an archive is scheduled. It is very important to avoid on-line archives because they tie up the system and are prone to occur during peak processing time. The DBA should make sure that the log is large enough to avoid automatic archives. The ARCHPCT is specified in the start-up PARM parameters:

SQLSTART DBNAME(PROD1) PARM(**ARCHPCT**=80)

LOG CUSHION (SLOGCUSH)

Very often the log will become full because the checkpoint was unable to free sufficient space in the log. Long running transactions often prevent the checkpoint from taking place because all transactions must stop before a checkpoint can be initiated. If a long running transaction continues to fill the log, the log will eventually run out of space and trigger an archive.

There is another parameter which may prevent automatic archiving in the situation described above but the DBA must decide what is more important. SLOGCUSH is a start-up parameter which will invoke a log overflow procedure that will try to allow a checkpoint to run **by rolling back the longest running transaction:**

SLOGCUSH = 90

Popular wisdom says that the long running transaction has used so many resources that *it should be allowed to run to completion* and it should **not** be rolled back. It is better, therefore, to trigger an archive and not to trigger the SLOGCUSH rollback. In that case the ARCHPCT value should be lower than the SLOGCUSH value so that an archive is triggered before a rollback. If experience dictates otherwise, the values can be reversed.

The SLOGCUSH parameter specifies the point at which the system should begin to take action to prevent the log from becoming completely filled. Additional checkpoints will be initiated by the system and the longest running LUWs will be rolled back in order to free log space. This may cause a job that was almost complete after running for more than an hour, to ABEND. It might really irritate the user and should be avoided. Be aware that ARCHPCT and SLOGCUSH are prone to be reached during peak processing periods. To stipulate a cushion of 90 percent, the DBA would specify:

SQLSTART DBNAME(PROD1) PARM(**SLOGCUSH**=90)

The logs should be large enough to avoid on-line archiving and to avoid reaching the SLOGCUSH value. Long-running LUWs of an hour or more should be run in single-user mode when possible, especially if they modify many database rows.

SHORT ON STORAGE (SOSLEVEL)

As current pages and *shadow pages* proliferate, the available pages in some of the storage pools will become allocated to specific DBSPACES which will result in fewer and fewer pages being free. To prevent a storage pool from running out of pages, the DBA should specify an SOSLEVEL parameter value that specifies when the system should trigger a checkpoint. The following example specifies that when less than 9 percent of the pages in any storage pool remain free, a checkpoint will be forced:

SQLSTART DBNAME(PROD1) PARM(**SOSLEVEL=9**)

Each time the number of available pages in the storage pool reaches the SOS level, a checkpoint will be triggered and it may occur numerous times. When it does occur, the operator will receive a message and should notify the DBA. The DBA must decide whether or not the situation warrants the addition of a DBEXTENT to the storage pool. If a DBEXTENT needs to be added, the SQL/DS system will have to be terminated. Care should also be taken to assign internal DBSPACES to a separate storage pool so that they do not cause a pool with production tables to reach the SOSLEVEL.

MULTIPLE START-UPS

Database operation should be monitored to provide a basis for tuning modifications. There may be different start-up needs for different times of the day, month, or year. It is fairly easy to bring SQL/DS down and start it up again with a different set of start-up parameters for different times. These changes may have a dramatic positive impact on performance. The SQL/DS start-up parameters needed for on-line transactions are definitely not the ones needed for night-time batch runs. At night there are fewer users and many additional buffers can be allocated. It is recommended that the needs of each period of the day be carefully reviewed and the proper parameters be used.

ARCHIVING

To protect a database from hardware failures or software corruption, SQL/DS provides archiving and logging facilities. The function of a database or log archive is to copy the current contents to tape or disk so as to have an undamaged, complete, and consistent copy of the database or log. Using these facilities, the user can recover from most hardware and software failures. Archive, however, requires vast amounts of system resources and directly affects system performance and should be carefully planned to be run during non-peak transaction time.

ARCHIVE TYPES

There are three types of archives available to the DBA or systems programmer: a user archive using **non-SQL/DS** software (full archive), a database archive using **SQL/DS** facilities (full archive), and a **log** archive. The full SQL/DS archive is a complete copy of the database from the *begin archive checkpoint.* The log archive is fast and efficient because it only backs up the log of database modifications and not the entire database. The log archive should be used in conjunction with a user or a database archive. The recommended procedure is to execute a user or database archive once every four to seven days and a log archive once or twice a day.

Archiving the database or the log during peak on-line processing periods can seriously impact transaction response time. It makes little sense to archive during peak transaction time when the database is generally in an inconsistent state.

There are several start-up parameters which may lead to the automatic triggering of an archive. **The automatic triggering of an archive or log archive should be prevented at almost any cost.** This in no way means to imply that automatic archiving should not be specified to protect against the unusual events that may occur at an installation. Automatic log archiving should definitely be specified in a production system but steps to ensure that the log will be large enough to prevent an automatic archive should be taken.

Log or Database Archive

There are trade-offs in deciding whether to take log archives or database archives. It is much easier to restore from a database or user archive because only one process and one set of tapes is involved. The data, however, is usually at least a day old and, should a problem occur, a great deal of work may have to be redone manually. The full database archive will usually not be scheduled as often as a log archive would be because it would take too much time to execute.

The log archive copies the log to disk or tape but does not copy the SQL/DS directory or the DBEXTENTS. The use of log archiving will be much faster than full archive. The only drawbacks are the need for administrative maintenance of a series of tapes or disk files and the need to restore an old archive and all of the log archives, sequentially, before the database would be returned to its current state. If one of the log archive tapes is misplaced or unreadable, subsequent log archive tapes cannot be restored. The format of the tape is not easy to decipher, which will make user-written restore applications difficult or impossible to write.

The restore from a log archive may be further complicated by the fact that using the log implies the re-execution of **every** command issued by every application. Restoring from the log may require less elapsed time than the actual execution but it may require the same net time. This is a major reason why full database user or SQL/DS archives should also be executed regularly when log archiving is used. A full database archive obviates the need to keep old log tapes but the tapes should be preserved for at least two cycles.

When log archiving is in effect, starting an archive or a user archive will trigger a log archive first to ensure continuity of log archives.

User or SQL/DS Archive

The reason many installations employ the user archive facility instead of the SQL/DS archive facility is because the SQL/DS archive may be relatively slow. The SQL/DS archive is DASD independent and does not exploit the specific characteristics of the disks being archived. It is **not** slower than user archives, however, when large DBEXTENTs are assigned to the database but the data pages are not as yet allocated. The user archive cannot differentiate between allocated pages and unallocated pages and will, therefore, have to back up everything. The SQL/DS archive facility will only back up allocated pages.

Another advantage of the SQL/DS archive facility is that applications, while temporarily slowed by an archive or log archive, may continue to access the database. User archives do **not** permit continued database access by end-users because processing has to be terminated before the user archive is executed.

Systems programmers who wish to migrate a VSE/SP SQL/DS database to a VM/SP system must utilize the SQL/DS archive facility.

The migration obviously cannot be done with the user archive facility.

The log archives may be used to skip a full database archive tape which is found to have errors. This assumes that all of the log archive tapes from the archive to be restored to the present are intact and available.

REQUESTING AN ARCHIVE

The computer operator may specify that an archive is to be taken at the termination of SQL/DS processing. The operator might specify the command example below which indicates that the operator will be taking a user backup after SQL/DS terminates. SQL/DS must be notified that a user archive will be taken so that it can issue the required log archive and checkpoint:

SQLEND   **UARCHIVE**

After informing the system that a user archive will be taken and after SQL/DS terminates, the user should run VMBACKUP, DDR, VSE/FASTCOPY, or any other backup product that will copy the entire contents of the disks.

As an alternative, an archive using the SQL/DS facilities might be requested. The operator could specify that an archive should be taken without terminating SQL/DS or that it should be taken after SQL/DS has ended:

ARCHIVE   or
SQLEND   **ARCHIVE**

The ARCHIVE command will start the process immediately and will permit SQL/DS to continue operation after the ARCHIVE checkpoint has completed. The SQLEND ARCHIVE command will terminate SQL/DS after the ARCHIVE is complete. The same procedure may be used for log archive. The operator may request that the log archive be taken while the system continues to function or may request that SQL/DS terminate after the log archive has been completed:

LARCHIVE   or
SQLEND   **LARCHIVE**

If the operator specified SQLEND LARCHIVE, the following may appear on the console:

ARI0028I SQL/DS IS TERMINATING
ARI0065I SQL/DS OPERATOR COMMAND PROCESSING COMPLETE
ARI0293I ARCHIVE STARTING
ARI0239I EXTERNAL LABELING OF THIS ARCHIVE IS:
      TYPE: LOG ARCHIVE
      TIMESTAMP: 01-03-90 03:32:37
ARI0299A READY ARCHIVE OUTPUT VOLUME. REPLY CUU
490
ARI0292I ARCHIVE COMPLETED
ARI0032I SQL/DS HAS TERMINATED
ARI0043I SQL/DS RETURN CODE IS 0

TEST THE RESTORE PROCEDURE

It is highly recommended that two backup copies be made and that periodic tests of the restore procedure be made. Many installations take backup every day and have never needed to restore. They also have not as yet tested the restore procedure to see that it works. It is also recommended that the DBA and systems programmer take the time to practice restoring from archives and log tapes on the test system in order to be prepared for emergencies. Experience gained in an emergency is rarely forgotten but it usually is very expensive.

The high reliability level of SQL/DS is another argument for log archives instead of daily full archives. It should be realized, however, that log archives must be sequential and cannot be skipped. If one tape in the sequence is unreadable, all of the remaining tapes cannot be restored. Two copies of every tape should be kept. If a log tape is found to be defective, a full archive, if possible, should be immediately taken to preserve the backup capability.

In view of the above, it is easy to answer the question as to whether or not to use full archive or log archive. The answer is *yes!* Both should be used on a regular basis.

To determine if a log archive is imminent, the SHOW LOG command can be used to display log status. It indicates the log size and the space remaining before a checkpoint or archive. This command may be issued from the SQL/DS operator's console or from an ISQL terminal:

LOG STATUS:
    LOG SIZE IS 7229440 BYTES
    LOG USED IS **2 PERCENT** 204721 BYTES
    LOG **REMAINING BEFORE IMPLICIT ARCHIVE IS 87**
            PERCENT 6301739 BYTES
NO non r/o AGENTS BEGAN BEFORE THE LAST CHECKPOINT
LOG PAGES REMAINING BEFORE CHECKPOINT IS 7

The log display shows that only 2 percent of the log has been used and that a log archive is, most probably, not imminent.

After an archive has been requested, monitoring of the database using the SHOW command can only be done from the operator's SQL/DS console. This is because the checkpoint agent requests a DB lock to prevent new transactions from starting. Existing transactions are allowed to terminate and when there is a long-running transaction, the checkpoint may be delayed and all of the users locked out. The SHOW command can be used to see which user is delaying the checkpoint and that user can be contacted or forced off. An example of the SHOW USERS command might display:

SHOW USERS

STATUS OF CONNECTED SQL/DS USERS:
  2 USERS ARE CONNECTED TO SQL/DS
  2 SQL/DS USER(S) ARE ACTIVE
          VM-ID = SQLUSER1 SQL-ID = DOV1
          VM-ID = SARA   SQL-ID = MARTHA NOT PROCESSING

Checkpoints, full archives, and log archives negatively impact performance and should be carefully planned and scheduled. The operator should also be aware that if an ARCHIVE or LARCHIVE is requested and it takes five or ten minutes to mount the tape, the users will **all** have to wait. The operator should first mount the tape and then request the archive.

SUMMARY

When SQL/DS commands are prepared, the optimizer will use the information available in the SQL/DS catalogs to determine the best access path. Minor changes to the contents of a table do not significantly affect the optimization process. If SQL/DS would update its statistics automatically for every change to a table, the performance degradation would be unacceptable. The user is provided with the UPDATE STATISTICS command to perform the updating of the statistics. The command usually requires one or more scans of all of the pages in the table or in the DBSPACE.

Start-up parameters control the operation of the database management system. Parameters can be stored in a file and used for each start-up. The parameters depend upon real storage size, generated database size, and the frequency and size of transactions. SQL/DS will have to compete for real storage when there is not enough available for all of the system users. The number of buffers allocated should be directly related to the amount of real storage available.

Buffers are used to store the data and directory information on the assumption that they may be needed again in the near future. Each 4K page buffer may hold data pages, index pages, log pages, or internal DBSPACE pages. I/O overhead expended to read directory blocks is almost as great as the I/O overhead required to read the data pages. Directory buffers, however, are usually required more often and consume much less real storage. *Hit Ratio* is calculated by dividing the number of buffer looks by the number of read requests.

NCUSERS designates the number of active users that can use SQL/DS simultaneously. Each agent requires approximately 200K bytes of storage. VSE/SP only has real agents. VM/SP also has pseudo-agents. The CIRB transaction of CICS will reserve agents for the exclusive use of CICS users. In systems with adequate resources, the DBA must make the trade-off between allowing many users and between the resource contention they cause.

Many locks are needed to maintain database integrity. Each request for a lock usually requires two or more lock request blocks. The DBA allocates the maximum number of request blocks to be available. When the maximum number of locks has been reached, SQL/DS will escalate the user to DBSPACE locking.

A checkpoint snaps a *picture* of the current state of the database to synchronize the SQL/DS log and the database. It writes modified buffers to the database, marks each current page as the *shadow page,* releases the old *shadow page,* writes a checkpoint log record, and frees log space. When a checkpoint is scheduled, all new DBSS operations must wait. The checkpoint cannot be initiated unless all of the DBSS operations have terminated.

DISPBIAS specifies the criteria for choosing the agent to be dispatched. DISPBIAS = 1 means *round robin;* DISPBIAS = 10 means *priority dispatching.* Changing the DISPBIAS does **not** usually impact response time.

It is usually more efficient to run bulk batch jobs in single-user mode. The disadvantage is that only one application program can operate at a time.

The LOGMODE, which specifies the type of logging required, is specified in the start-up command. Another start-up parameter, ARCHPCT, specifies at which point an on-line archive or log archive needs to be scheduled. Very often the log will become full because the checkpoint was unable to free sufficient space in the log. SLOG-CUSH is a start-up parameter which will ROLLBACK the longest running transaction. To prevent a storage pool from running out of pages, the DBA should specify an SOSLEVEL parameter value that specifies when to trigger a checkpoint to release the *shadow pages*. There may be different start-up needs for different times of the day, month, or year.

Archiving and logging protect a database from hardware failures or software corruption. There are several start-up parameters which may lead to the automatic triggering of an archive. The three types of archives are: a user archive, a database archive, and a log archive. The log archive copies the log to disk or tape but does not copy the SQL/DS directory or the DBEXTENTS. The use of log archiving will be much faster than full archive. When log archiving is in effect, starting an archive will first trigger a log archive.

The SQL/DS archive is DASD independent and does not exploit the specific characteristics of the disks being archived. It is not slower than user archives when large DBEXTENTs are assigned to the database but the data pages are not as yet allocated. User archives do not permit continued database access by end-users. To migrate, the SQL/DS archive facility must be used. The operator may issue ARCHIVE or LARCHIVE from the operator SQL/DS console at any time, but it should never be done during peak transaction time.

RECOMMENDATIONS

1. The UPDATE STATISTICS command should **not** be executed during on-line processing hours.

2. UPDATE **ALL** STATISTICS is *not* recommended.

3. The start-up default values are usually not suitable for a production system and should not be used.

4. Specify many more directory buffers than page buffers.

5. Do not use the default buffer values. Monitor buffer use during peak processing periods.

6. The DBA should slowly increase the number of buffers until additional buffers no longer significantly improve the *Hit Ratio*.

7. Buffers should **NOT** be added if the result is increased paging.

8. The DBA should monitor lock usage to avoid escalation.

9. Checkpoints should be avoided during on-line peak processing periods.

10. Steps should be administratively set up to force checkpoints during lunch periods or coffee breaks.

11. Mass updates, inserts, and deletes require log space and *shadow pages* and should be avoided during peak processing hours.

12. It is recommended that programs that perform mass updating, deleting, or inserting should be run in single-user mode.

13. It is much safer to use log or full archive in order to be able to recover from a failure.

14. Specify dual logging and place each of the logs on a different DASD device.

15. Avoid on-line archives.

16. ARCHPCT should be lower than SLOGCUSH.

17. Different start-up parameters should be used at different times in the day.

18. Automatic archiving should be specified but automatic triggering of an archive should be prevented at almost any cost.

19. Log and full archives should be used on a regular basis. Log archives should be taken once or twice a day; full archives should be taken every few days.

20. It is highly recommended that two backup copies be made of archive tapes and that periodic tests of the restore procedure be made.

21. ARCHIVE or LARCHIVE should never be executed during peak transaction time.

CHAPTER 9

Operating System Parameters

Tuning the VM/SP or VSE/SP operating systems for effective performance of the SQL/DS data management system is very similar to the standard tuning process for all systems. There are several tuning techniques that have a significant impact on SQL/DS performance and these will be covered in this chapter. VM/SP parameters and the use of VMMAP will be discussed in the first section and VSE/SP parameters and VSE Performance Tool (VSE/PT) will be discussed in the second section. The third section will cover I/O tuning in both environments and the final section will discuss the new VM/VSE SQL/DS guest sharing feature.

This chapter is intended for systems programmers and assumes a knowledge of the respective operating systems. The term VM/SP will be used to signify all of the VM systems including VM/SP, VM/HPO, and VM/XA. The information was tested on VM/SP and VM/HPO but in most instances it also applies to VM/XA. The monitoring tools should be used to detect the potential bottlenecks by comparing the values received, to the *rule-of-thumb* values. Those values that exceed the recommended values are not necessarily problematic but they should be the first candidates for tuning.

VM/SP

There are many tuning parameters possible in a VM/SP system but only a few specific ones will be mentioned. The systems programmer should be aware that every time a parameter is tuned to improve SQL/DS processing it may negatively impact the performance of a non-SQL/DS user and every change should be carefully monitored before and after implementation.

Unlike SQL/DS running in a VSE/SP environment where only one database machine can be operating, under VM/SP many database machines can be defined to all operate simultaneously. Each database machine can have its own function and it can be totally independent of the other databases. One SQL/DS database, for example, can be used as the *test database* while another one can be used as the *production database*. Each database machine can be accessed by those users who have been granted authority to use it. When the volume of SQL/DS queries is high, the workload should be spread among several SQL/DS machines. This multi-database capability has a distinct advantage over the single database and users in an installation operating VSE/SP as the transaction guest system under VM/SP should carefully consider using the new guest sharing feature and placing at least the test database under VM/SP. The new guest sharing feature discussed later in this chapter will permit VSE/SP users to access an SQL/DS database operating in the host VM/SP system.

Defining the SQL/DS Database Machine

When installing SQL/DS for the first time, the default starter database should be used to simplify the task of learning the installation process and use of SQL/DS. The production database, however, should definitely **not** use the default values. The size of each minidisk should be carefully calculated. The most important calculation is the size of the directory disk. It determines the maximum size of many of the resources that can**not** be modified once the database is generated.

The service disk (193) and the production disk (195) may be shared among multiple databases. The production minidisk contains the IBM programs shipped with SQL/DS and it is updated when the database starts up, is generated, or a DBEXTENT is added. An installation that wants to avoid any possible contention may define multiple production minidisks but the possibility of contention seems very minimal and may not justify multiple minidisks. The database itself should be distributed among as many extents as possible to reduce I/O contention.

The database machine directory entry might contain the following:

```
USER SQLPROD1 SQLPW 8M 8M G
ACCOUNT 123456
OPTION MAXCONN 30
IUCV ALLOW
IUCV *IDENT SQLPROD1 LOCAL
IPL CMS
CONSOLE 009 3215 T SYSOPX
SPOOL 00C 2540 *
SPOOL 00D 2540 A
SPOOL 00E 1403
```

```
LINK MAINT 190 190 RR
LINK MAINT 19D 19D RR
MDISK 191 3380 200 015 MDK191 W
MDISK 193 3380 215 050 MDK191 R RSQL WSQL
MDISK 195 3380 265 012 MDK191 RR RSQL WSQL
MDISK 200 3380 300 034 PROD01 R RSQL WSQL
MDISK 201 3380 300 015 PROD02 R RSQL WSQL
MDISK 202 3380 100 400 PRDSQL R RSQL WSQL
MDISK 403 3380 100 300 PRD2QL R RSQL WSQL
```

Defining a User Machine

To be able to access SQL/DS, the CMS user must have a virtual machine with sufficient storage and the necessary authority to link to the SQL/DS machine. The following is an example of a user machine definition:

```
USER DOV1 DOV1PW 2M 2M G
ACCOUNT 654321
IUCV SQLTEST1
IPL CMS
CONSOLE 009 3215
SPOOL 00C 2540 *
SPOOL 00D 2540 A
SPOOL 00E 1403
LINK MAINT 190 190 RR
LINK MAINT 19D 19D RR
MDISK 191 3380 185 015 MDK191 W
```

Communication Authority

To initialize each VM/SP user's access to the database machine, the SQLINIT EXEC must be invoked. The user must have the authority to communicate with the database machine via IUCV or APPC/VM. To initialize communication with the TEST001 database machine, the user would specify the following command:

```
SQLINIT DBNAME(TEST001)
```

This command will copy the following two bootstrap modules to the user's A disk:

```
ARISRMBT MODULE A - Resource manager
ARISISBT MODULE A - ISQL bootstrap module
```

The user can check to which database he or she is connected by issuing the following command:

SQLDBID

Explicit Connect

The EXEC should also explicitly CONNECT to the SQL/DS database desired. If it does not, the default user-id is the VM/SP userid and the default database is the last database accessed.

Saved Segments

SQL/DS code not stored in saved segments will run in the DMSFREE area (or in the VM/XA user free storage area). The code of ISQL, DBSS, DSC, RDS, and the resource manager can be stored in saved segments by updating the DMKSNT table's DEFSEG command. When the code is not stored in saved segments, each virtual machine will load its own copy of each system and application program into its own virtual storage. This process will increase the working set, increase the need for real storage, and increase the paging potential of the user. The use of saved segments will reduce excess resource utilization and will reduce transaction start-up time. Frequently used application programs which can be coded in a re-entrant fashion could also be stored in the saved segments.

SQL/DS is a heavy user of several VM modules which should be placed above DMKCPE in the CP Load List prior to regenerating the CP Nucleus. The modules include: DMKBIO, DMKIUA, DMKIUE, and DMKIUL.

Saved segments can also be made to retain SQL/DS resident in the system by the execution of a program using DIAGNOSE 64 to invoke the shared program. The user issuing the DIAGNOSE 64 would then be DISConnected until the end of the processing day thereby keeping the pages resident. Care should be taken not to disrupt the processing of other users when this technique is implemented.

Free Storage Extensions

The control program (CP) routines use the free storage area for dynamic control blocks and work areas. When the free storage area is filled, the *free storage extend* process is invoked and frames from the dynamic paging area are borrowed. Dynamic extensions of CP free storage should be carefully monitored and kept to a minimum. These extensions usually represent totally unnecessary overhead.

The CP activities are suspended during this extension and, at each call for free storage, CP will try to avoid using the extended page. CP will continually check to try to unextend and return the frames to the dynamic paging area. This process will generate significant overhead and should be avoided.

The VMMAP listing should be checked to ensure that the average number of extensions is **zero.** If extensions are zero, free storage should be reduced until the average is greater than zero. Free storage should then be adjusted upwards until the average returns to zero. The manipulation of the free storage size is done by increasing or decreasing the free parameter of the SYSCOR macro in the DMKSYS.

The need for extending the free storage might be reduced if users were encouraged to log off their virtual machines when they were finished using them. The systems programmer might also set up a procedure to force nonactive users off the system.

SET PRIORITY

The user priority value is utilized by the CP scheduler to calculate the user machine's deadline priority. The deadline priority is used to determine which virtual machine to dispatch first. The lower the priority value, the more CPU time allocated to the user. This parameter should be changed very carefully and the results monitored to ensure that other important system applications are not negatively impacted.

SET QDROP

To eliminate the overhead of scanning page and segment tables and of moving resident pages to the VM flush list when the SQL/DS machine enters the idle wait status issue, the SET QDROP parameter is used. The format of the command is:

SET QDROP SQLMACHINE **OFF**

The use of this command will improve the chances of the pages referenced by the SQL/DS machine to remain in memory even though the user has been dropped from the queue. Its use will prevent the resetting of the reference bits for the resident pages when the user is dropped and the pages will only be replaced when page stealing becomes necessary.

When the word USERS is added after the word OFF, the application machines communicating with the SQL/DS machine via IUCV or VMCF will also benefit from similar treatment. Their referenced pages will not have the reference bit reset for as long as the communication is in effect. The command format is:

SET QDROP SQLMACHINE OFF **USERS**

When the word NOQ3 is added to the SET QDROP command, VM/SP will not place the SQL/DS machine into the lowest queue and it will be dispatched more quickly. When VM/HPO is being used, NOQ2 can be specified to keep SQL/DS in the Q1. This parameter should be used with care:

SET QDROP SQLMACHINE OFF USERS **NOQ3**

SET FAVOR

The SET FAVOR command might be used to ensure that the SQL/DS machine remains dispatchable, in the run list, and not placed in the eligible list, whether or not the real storage it needs is available:

SET FAVOR SQLMACHINE

It is recommended that both SET QDROP OFF and SET FAVOR be used for the SQL/DS machine.

SET FAVOR with a percentage value can have a dramatic impact upon the system and should be used with great care. The parameter will definitely improve the availability of the CPU to the user but it may significantly disrupt the response to other users. SET FAVOR with a percentage modifies the *fair share* mechanism of VM/SP which allocates a percentage of CPU time to each user. Setting the percentage is a double-edged sword. VM/SP will try to ensure that the user receives the favored amount but it also ensures that the user will **not** receive any more than the favored amount.

Why Priority and Favor?

When the production SQL/DS applications run in only one or two virtual machines, they consume most of the system's resources. VM/SP's CP scheduler algorithm uses a fair share scheduler scheme because of which these critical virtual machines may **not** be able to receive the allotment of resources that they need. When I/O is not a bottleneck, this *fair share* scheduling can cause major delays in SQL/DS response. SET PRIORITY will increase the CPU allocated to these users and SET FAVOR will increase the real storage allocated. The systems programmer should be aware that if the system is already overloaded, favoring SQL/DS will have a very serious negative impact upon other VM/SP users.

SET RESERVE

SET RESERVE reserves several page frames in the dynamic paging area for a specific user and usually improves the response time of that user. SET RESERVE might be used to keep the SQL/DS working set in storage but it should usually **not** be used because in VM/SP only one user can use it. In VM/HPO more than one user can issue the SET RESERVE command and it **is** recommended for use with SET MINWS instead of SET QDROP. It should be issued after the SQL/DS machine has begun executing. The impact on non-SQL/DS users should be carefully monitored. The format of the command is:

> **SET RESERVE** SQLMACHINE nnn

SET MINWS

SET MINWS is a VM/HPO parameter that sets the minimum working set size for the virtual machine. It is only useful if swap areas are allocated on disk and the workload is not stable. In VM/HPO, SET RESERVE and SET MINWS are equivalent to issuing SET QDROP OFF in VM/SP. There is more flexibility in using the two SET statements rather than one and it is therefore recommended. The command format is:

> **SET MINWS** SQLMACHINE nnn

LOCK

It usually does not pay to use the LOCK parameter to lock specific real pages in memory.

Limiting ISQL Users

Unlike VSE, there is no easy way to limit the number of users who can sign on to ISQL. The systems programmer might set up a standard

ISQL EXEC on a system disk which every user would be required by administrative regulations to use. It could maintain a count in a CMS file and refuse to start ISQL when, for example, a maximum value (of 2) was reached, but any knowledgeable user would be able to bypass this.

CMS Work Unit Support

While it is still not possible to join two tables from different databases or to issue a subquery involving a table in a database different from the database of the table in the main query, using newer versions of SQL/DS it is now possible to access tables from different databases without ending the *logical unit of work* (LUW). VM/SP Release 6 has introduced the concept of CMS work units which allows SQL/DS applications to establish more than one independent path to one or more SQL/DS databases. This function is only available in VM/SP Release 6 or a later version when running SQL/DS in multiple user mode.

In SQL/DS version 2.1, applications running under CMS could switch between different SQL/DS database machines but only after the current *logical unit of work* had completed. An application could **not** concurrently read from two different database machines.

Recent versions of SQL/DS, utilizing the CMS work units function of VM/SP, will allow multiple LUW's to be actively accessing the same or different SQL/DS database machines. CMS will maintain all of the necessary control blocks and data pertaining to the different work units. When an application switches between work units, CMS will restore all of its pointers and storage in such a way that it will seem to the user that it is the only work unit active. VM/SP Release 6 provides the necessary routines in its Callable Service Library (CSL) to establish and manage the CMS work units. The routines include EXTRACT, GET, PUSH, POP, and RETURN functions.

Work units can only be switched by entering or leaving the CMS subset or by explicitly handling the work units from within an application program. When a work unit is switched, the application will remain within the new work unit until explicitly switched back. This limits SQL/DS usage and prevents the overlapping of SQL/DS requests in different work units. A user cannot, for example, start a long-running query in one work unit and then switch to another work unit to start another SQL/DS query while waiting for the first to complete. This is because the application or EXEC does not regain control **until** the first query has completed. Asynchronous processing is, therefore, still not possible.

Work Unit Switching Example

An application can, however, SELECT a row from a table in one database and write that row to a table in another database. An example of a procedure, using pseudo code, to accomplish this follows:

```
            Establish Work Unit 'A'
            Connect TO DATABASE FIRSTONE
            DECLARE CURSOR cursone FOR SELECT FROM FIRSTONE
            OPEN CURSOR CURSONE
            Establish Work Unit 'B'
            Connect TO DATABASE SECNDONE
            DECLARE CURSOR CURSTWO FOR SELECT FROM SECNDONE
            OPEN CURSOR CURSTWO

            PERFORM LOOP1 UNTIL no more records to FETCH

            CLOSE CURSOR CURSONE
            COMMIT WORK
            Establish Work Unit 'B'
            CLOSE CURSOR CURSTWO
            COMMIT WORK
            RETURN
    LOOP1     Establish WORK UNIT 'A'

            FETCH CURSONE INTO :HOST VARIABLES

                IF SQLCODE = 100
                    LEAVE
                END-IF
            Establish WORK UNIT 'B'
            PUT CURSTWO FROM :HOST VARIABLES
            END-PERFORM
```

Work Units and Performance

Maintaining more than one work unit will often result in holding resources and locks in **both** databases for longer periods of time than might be otherwise done. This may negatively impact performance in both databases. This feature is very useful but care should be exercised when it is implemented. The DBA or application developer should investigate alternate ways of achieving the same results, such as:

1. Maintaining a copy of the table in both databases.
2. Selecting the entire table to a CMS file and ending the first CMS work unit before starting the second.

The use of CMS work units from ISQL without first ending queries **should usually be avoided.** This is especially important when AUTOCOMMIT is set OFF and/or the option *repeatable read* is in effect. It should also be avoided when UPDATEs or DELETEs are being executed.

In general, for good performance, the user should COMMIT WORK and release the SQL/DS connection before switching CMS work units (but then there is no point in starting a new work unit because once an LUW is completed, a second database can be accessed from the same CMS work unit). This new function can and should be used when needed but the performance aspects should be carefully planned.

The user should exercise care not to tie up too many agents, locks, and buffers and should be aware of the *potential deadlock* situations which cannot be detected or handled by SQL/DS:

*   When **one user** starts a work unit to SELECT a row from a table in a database and then switches work unit to UPDATE a row in another database.

*   While **another user** has SELECTed the row that the first user wants to UPDATE in the second database and starts a new work unit to UPDATE the row that the first user has SELECTED in the first database.

The **result** will be an undetectable **infinite deadlock**. Both users will WAIT until one gets tired and cancels one of the transactions.

Using an EXEC

EXEC and XEDIT files used with SQL/DS should be placed on specific minidisks that do not contain other files. This will prevent CMS from searching large directories for them and will improve response time.

The ADDRESS COMMAND should be used, where appropriate, to inform the REXX interpreter that commands will be prefixed with an identifier of the environment being invoked (MACRO, XEDIT, etc.) to prevent file searching for CMS commands. This can reduce file searching and improve EXEC performance.

Terminating an EXEC

When executing an application program via a CMS EXEC or when accessing SQL/DS from an EXEC the user should explicitly terminate the *logical unit of work*. This is important for several reasons as will be explained next.

When an application finishes its processing and returns to CMS, CMS will free the communications link and issue a COMMIT WORK when the application completed normally, or a ROLLBACK WORK when the application completed abnormally (in CMS terms). When an application runs via an EXEC, however, it returns to the EXEC processing when it completes and not to CMS (unless it ABENDS). The EXEC processor does not issue a COMMIT WORK or a ROLLBACK WORK but rather continues executing the next statements in the EXEC. If neither the application program nor the EXEC issues an explicit COMMIT WORK, any commands or applications processed by the same EXEC will be part of the same *logical unit of work*.

The most effective way to handle this problem is to **always** terminate the *logical unit of work* in the application. If for some reason this is not desirable or practical, REXX now includes an EXEC which will end an SQL/DS LUW. The SQLRMEND EXEC should be included in the application EXEC to terminate the LUW. The EXEC will accept several parameters:

SQLRMEND   RELEASE

will end an LUW, and will release the link to SQL/DS. The use of this format is highly recommended when the application has completed but there is additional non-SQL/DS processing that is required from the same EXEC. The RELEASE parameter will free the SQL/DS link for use by others. When the application does not explicitly end the LUW and the user wants to decide from the EXEC how to end the LUW, the EXEC may specify:

SQLRMEND COMMIT

or

SQLRMEND ROLLBACK

Without SQLRMEND, when the application does not explicitly end its LUW, the LUW will continue until the EXEC terminates or until another application which terminates the LUW, executes.

If the first application does not end its LUW and there is no SQLRMEND COMMIT, then:

1. If the second application commits its work, the first applications' LUW will also be committed.

2. If the second application rolls its work back, the first applications' LUW will be rolled back.

3. If the subsequent CMS code in the EXEC results in an error, the SQL/DS LUW will be rolled back (even though the SQL/DS application finished with no errors).

4. If the second application tries to issue a CONNECT, it will receive an SQLCODE -752 which specifies that a CONNECT may not be issued from within an LUW.

If the first application has a CONNECT or was implicitly connected and SQLRMEND was not included in the EXEC after the first application, then the second application will be using the **same** CONNECT as the first. This is also true if:

SQLRMEND   KEEP

was issued between the two applications. If we assume that the default userid is DOV1 and the following EXEC (in pseudo-code) is run:

```
CONNECT TDBAUSER IDENTIFIED BY TDBAUSERPW TO proddb
Start APPLICATION one
SQLRMEND KEEP
Start APPLICATION two
SQLRMEND RELEASE
Start APPLICATION three
```

then application two will use the same CONNECT and database as application one and application three will use the DOV1 userid and DOV1's default database.

ISPF

The Interactive System Productivity Facility (ISPF) is widely used in VM/SP installations for the development and execution of interactive applications known as ISPF Dialogs. ISPF makes it easy to access, display, and save data by storing the data in ISPF variables. ISPF provides services to make it easy to invoke EXECs and application programs and provides a HELP facility and a tutorial service. When a performance problem exists and SQL/DS is used with ISPF, it is sometimes difficult to determine exactly where the performance bottleneck is. The variable and table functions of ISPF, for example, may slow down the response time and they should be checked to ensure proper usage.

SUMMARY

Tuning with SQL/DS is very similar to the standard tuning process for all systems. The monitoring tools should be used to detect the potential bottlenecks. Those values that exceed the recommended values are not necessarily a sign of trouble but they should be the first candidates for tuning.

Many database machines can be defined under VM/SP. The CMS user must have sufficient storage and the links to SQL/DS minidisks. The VM/SP user must have authority to communicate with the database machine via IUCV or APPC/VM.

Every time a parameter is tuned it may negatively impact the performance of other users. Frequently used re-entrant application programs can be stored in shared segments. Dynamic free storage extensions usually represent totally unnecessary overhead. The lower the PRIORITY value, the more CPU time allocated to the user. SET QDROP OFF will improve the chances that the pages referenced by the SQL/DS machine will remain in memory. USERS can also benefit from similar treatment.

The SET FAVOR command is used to ensure that the SQL/DS machine remains dispatchable.SET FAVOR with a percentage value will improve the availability of the CPU to the SQL/DS machine but it may significantly disrupt the response to other users.

SET RESERVE reserves several page frames in the dynamic paging area for a specific user and improves the response time of the user, but it is not recommended.

SET MINWS will set the minimum working set size for the virtual machine and should be used with SET RESERVE in a VM/HPO environment.

It is possible to access tables from different databases without ending the *logical unit of work* using the concept of CMS work units. Work units can only be switched by entering or leaving the CMS subset or by explicitly handling the work units from within an application program. Asynchronous processing is, however, still not possible. Maintaining more than one work unit will often result in holding resources and locks in both databases for longer periods of time than might be otherwise done.

ISPF is used for the development and execution of interactive applications.

RECOMMENDATIONS

1. If ISPF is used, ensure that the variable and table functions are not responsible for poor response time.

2. The EXEC should explicitly CONNECT to the SQL/DS database desired.

3. Every change should be carefully monitored before and after implementation.

4. In order to reduce paging, SQL/DS modules should be stored in the shared segment area.

5. The discontiguous shared segment area should be used to contain active application programs if possible.

6. The VMMAP listing should be checked to verify that the average number of storage extensions is zero.

7. To reduce the extension of free storage, users should be encouraged to log off.

8. It is recommended that both SET QDROP OFF and SET FAVOR be used for the SQL/DS machine.

9. SET RESERVE should usually not be used in VM/SP.

10. In VM/HPO, SET RESERVE and SET MINWS should be used instead of SET QDROP.

11. The use of CMS work units from ISQL should usually be avoided.

12. EXEC and XEDIT files used with SQL/DS should be placed on specific minidisks that do not contain other files.

13. The ADDRESS COMMAND should be used.

14. Explicitly end the *logical unit of work*.

VMMAP

The VM/MONITOR facility will collect data on system activity and VMMAP can be used to produce summarized reports from the data collected. This chapter will highlight only a few of the categories of information available from VMMAP and similar performance tools. It is important to reiterate that any explicit values mentioned are derived from specific environments and from the author's experience and should serve **only** as a guide.

Resource Availability Index (RAI)

A major indicator of how well the system is performing with the resources it has available is the Resource Availability Index (RAI). It specifies the probability that users will be able to acquire the system resource they need when they are ready to execute. The general rule is:

RAI of 1.00. Users will not have to wait for any resources. This is the optimum but it might also indicate that too many resources are available and are not necessary.

RAI of 0.80. This is usually the minimum acceptable and indicates that 80 percent of the time the users do not have to wait for resources.

RAI < 0.80. This is usually **not** acceptable. The system bottlenecks should be identified and relieved.

VMMAP also provides an RAI for each virtual machine. The RAI for the SQL/DS machine and for production end-users should be greater than 0.80.

Percent CPU (PCTCPU)

The PCTCPU value indicates the percentage of the CPU utilized by the entire system. Its value should usually be less than 80 percent. Many systems run without difficulty when this value is higher but it usually implies that CPU capacity is reaching a critical level. If any workload growth is anticipated, CPU power should be increased.

The usual values that almost always indicate a CPU bottleneck for the specified workloads are:

Batch workload	95 percent
On-line SQL/DS	80 percent
CMS users	90 percent

QUEUES

To further determine whether or not virtual machines are active yet waiting for system resources, the user can check the following values:

PCTPAGEQ	Percent of active users waiting for **paging**
PCTCPUQ	Percent of active users waiting for **CPU**
PCTIOQ	Percent of active users waiting for **I/O**
PCTSTGQ	Percent of active users waiting for **storage**

Each of these values should be less than 7 to 9 percent. The overall storage utilization STGUTIL should be less than 50 to 55 percent and the paging rate should be lower than the manufacturer's recommended maximum average rate for the model.

Privileged Instruction Simulation (PRIVOP)

When system utilization is high and RAI is low, check to ensure that the privileged instructions simulated by CP per second (PRIVOP) and the number of interruptions simulated by CP per second (PG-MINT) are not too high. PRIVOP should be less than 150. When these values are high, a CP trace may have to be used to determine which user machine is causing the high CP activity. The rescheduling of this machine to non-peak hours, when possible, should reduce I/O, CPU, and storage utilization. A value in the thousands may indicate that a microcode assist function may **not** be operating correctly.

Eligible Lists

The E1 and E2 eligible list values show the number of users who are ready to run but are waiting to enter the CP dispatcher run list. This value should **always be zero.** Non-zero values indicate a storage problem. VM/SP only uses these queues when real storage is unavailable. When it is not zero, the real storage needs should be reduced by rescheduling applications, by greater use of shared segments, or by the reduction of SQL/DS buffers. In VM/HPO, the systems programmer should check the size of the trace table. If allowed to default, the trace table size can reach 512K in a 32M CPU. 16K is more than enough for a trace table.

TVR Value

The OUTUSER report provides data concerning individual virtual machines. The TVR value is a ratio of the total CPU time to the virtual machine's CPU time. When VSE/SP is running under VM/SP this value should be less than 1.5. This value indicates that most of the CPU power is being used by VSE and not by CP. The higher the value, the **less** CPU is being used by the virtual machine. A ratio of 2.5 to 3 is acceptable for the SQL/DS database machine. The paging rate of the SQL/DS machine and other users should be monitored and kept to a minimum.

Paging Rate

The paging rate can be one of the main bottlenecks in an SQL/DS system. **Even a low paging rate of the SQL/DS virtual machine can be devastating to response and performance.** This occurs because of the high percentage of time that will be wasted in a page wait state. As an example, it can be assumed that the process from the beginning of a page fault until the SQL/DS machine is re-dispatched can take approximately 40 milliseconds. If the virtual machine's page fault rate is 10 per second, the page waits will consume almost 400 milliseconds or 40 percent of the time. This is totally **un**acceptable. It is recommended that **the paging rate for the SQL/DS machine be less than four per second** in higher-powered CPUs and even less in the lower range of CPUs with slow DASD devices.

When VSE/SP is running as a guest machine under VM/SP, the paging rate of the VSE/SP machine should also be kept very low.

Page Dataset

It is crucial to distribute the paging activity across several disk devices. These disks should be attached to different channels and the DASD I/O should be balanced.

DASD I/O

Channel utilization should not go above 30 to 35 percent, which translates to approximately 70 I/Os per second on 4381 CPUs with 3380 DASD and to 36 I/Os on the 9370 CPUs. The average I/O on any actuator should usually not be greater than 5 per second (with a maximum of 11-14) and the utilization rate should be less than 25 to 30 percent. The average length of queues for each device should be low (.3 or .4) and this value should be considered along with the percentage of time that the device had a queue. The impact of the average length of a queue that reaches 1.0, for example, is that the response time of an I/O will double.

The OUTDASD report contains I/O rate values, average queue length values, and the time it takes to execute an I/O. The balance of these values should be monitored to ensure that I/O bottlenecks do not develop.

VMMAP does not report on all potential bottlenecks. I/O bottlenecks for SQL/DS databases or for any other virtual machine using BLOCK I/O system services will **not** be reported nor will internal SQL/DS queue information be reported. Dedicated DASD and internal queue information of VSE/SP guest machines will **not** be reported nor will VSE/SP paging when VIRTUAL = REAL. There are other tools that can be used to gather this information.

Some of the following may be helpful depending on whether the system is a VSE/SP under VM/SP or a VM/SP system without VSE/SP:

CICSPARS and GPARS—CICS tools

VM/SP and VSE/SP Accounting records

TRACE data from VTAM, CP, Hardware, CICS, SDAID, CP, PER, and so on

VM/SMART—On-line display of system and user activity

CP INDICATE—By comparing the values received from two or more CP INDICATE commands, the systems programmer can check CPU usage for an individual machine (VTIME) and for CP (TTIME), TVRATIO (TTIME/VTIME), I/O's issued, resident working set, and pages read and written.

SUMMARY

It is important to reiterate that any values mentioned are derived from specific environments and from the author's experience and should serve only as a guide when your system's performance values differ significantly:

- RAI is an indicator of how well the system is performing with the resources it has available.
- The PCTCPU value indicates the percentage of the CPU utilized by the entire system.
- PRIVOP is an indication of the privileged instructions simulated by CP per second.
- PGMINT is the number of interruptions simulated by CP per second.
- Nonzero E1 and E2 eligible list values indicate a storage problem.
- The TVR value is a ratio of the total CPU time to the virtual machines' CPU time.
- The paging rate can be one of the main bottlenecks in an SQL/DS system.

RECOMMENDATIONS

1. RAI of 0.80 is optimum.
2. PCTCPU value should usually be less than 80%.
3. Each of the following queues should be less than 7 to 9 percent: PCTPAGEQ, PCTCPUQ, PCTIOQ, and PCTSTGQ.
4. The overall storage utilization STGUTIL should be less than 50 to 55 percent.
5. PRIVOP should be less than 150.
6. In VM/HPO the size of the trace table should be reduced to 16K.
7. When E1 and E2 eligible list values are not zero, the real storage needs should be reduced.
8. When VSE is running under VM/SP the TVR value should be less than 1.5. A ratio of 2.5 to 3 is acceptable for the SQL/DS database machine.
9. The paging rate for the SQL/DS machine should be less than four per second.
10. Distribute the paging activity across several disk devices.
11. Channel utilization should not go above 30 to 35 percent.
12. The average I/O on any actuator should usually not be greater than 5 per second and the utilization rate should be less than 25 to 30 percent. The average length of queues for each device should be .3 or .4.

SQL/DS UNDER VSE/SP

The VSE/SP system will only allow the operation of one SQL/DS database at a time. This forces installations to place both test and production tables in the same database. Any priority given to the production tables in this system will also be given to the test tables. When both sets of users are running from the same CICS/VS system, they also have the same priority. This makes tuning VSE/SP native systems even more important and a lot trickier than tuning VM/SP systems.

The standard solution is to run VSE/SP as a guest system under VM/SP. This allows the systems programmer to define two VSE/SP virtual machines and to maintain an SQL/DS database machine in each. An alternative can be used when VSE/SP version 4.1 is installed. The database can be placed under VM/SP, yet it can be accessed from the VSE/SP guest machine. When VSE/SP is running as a guest machine under VM/SP, the systems programmer should also refer to the first part of this chapter.

Tuning VSE/SP to run efficiently requires a knowledge of the system, of VSAM, and of CICS/VS, and the system should be monitored to pinpoint the system bottlenecks. The major IBM monitoring tools include VSE/PT (performance tool), CICSPARS, and the Display System Activity (DSA) function of the Interactive Interface (II). There are also many non-IBM products on the market for monitoring the system that do an excellent job.

There are several differences between monitoring a VSE/SP system running native and a VSE/SP machine running as a guest system under VM/SP or VM/HPO that will be discussed later in this chapter.

VSE System Tuning

The areas that particularly affect SQL/DS performance are partition priority, system file placement, VSAM buffer definitions, real storage, and CICS/VS and IPL parameters.

Partition Priority

The VSE/SP priority algorithm determines that the partition with the highest priority will be dispatched first, assuming it is ready to do so. The application in the partition will continue to execute until an interrupt occurs. The system will then return control to the highest priority partition ready to run.

SQL/DS should usually receive the priority directly below that of the CICS/VS partition using it. This will reduce the probability that SQL/DS will impact other CICS/VS users when a high resource utilizing SQL/DS function is executed. It should be realized, however, that CICS/VS attempts to hold the CPU for as long as it possibly can. When there are many non-SQL/DS users in CICS/VS, CICS/VS will **not** release the CPU and SQL/DS transactions may be delayed because the SQL/DS partition will **not** receive control.

It is recommended that when an installation utilizes two CICS production partitions, the CICS/VS partitions be divided in such a way, where possible, that all of the SQL/DS transactions run in one of the CICS/VS partitions and all of the non-SQL/DS transactions run in the other. Partition balancing should usually **not** be specified for SQL/DS or for CICS/VS but the batch partitions can usually benefit from it (even under VM/SP). With POWER having the highest priority (but this is no longer mandatory) the PRIORITY command might specify:

PRIORITY BATCH1=BATCH2, SQL/DS, CICS, VTAM, POWER

DASD Files

The critical DASD files include the SQL/DS extents, the Page Data Set, the Lock File, and the Power Queues. Every attempt should be made to spread these data sets among several disk actuators. Periodic monitoring should be carried out to ensure that "Hot Spots" of high disk activity are kept to an absolute minimum. This is important for non-SQL/DS files as well as SQL/DS files.

An adequate number of buffers should be defined for non-SQL/DS VSAM I/O. BUFND, BUFNI, and STRNO are the VSAM parameters which involve buffers. Adequate VSAM buffers for non-SQL/DS VSAM files will ensure that these files do not negatively impact the overall system thruput. The CI size of 4K or 8K should usually be used with 3380 DASD and a 4K POWER DBLK size is recommended.

NOFASTTR

The FASTTR option will maintain a buffer of the translated CCWs from I/O requests and the system will try to re-use them to satisfy new I/O requests. When applications are being compiled, this option should be used but the FASTTR option should **not** be used with SQL/DS or for CICS/VS because it will usually cause extra overhead and it has been found to be wasteful. The option can be disabled by adding the following JCL to the SQL/DS start-up job:

```
/ / OPTION NOFASTTR
```

If the system default was changed to NOFASTTR and the user wants to specify FASTTR, the following command may be used:

```
/ / OPTION FASTTR
```

ISQL Under CICS/VS

ISQL transactions will usually use more resources than preprocessed application programs because the SQL/DS commands are executed dynamically and an access path will have to be calculated for each command (as explained in Chapter 6). There is also no control possible over the **quality** of the queries a user will enter via ISQL and one user may successfully create a total resource bottleneck by entering a non-efficient query. The standard procedure is to limit the number of ISQL users in a production system to one by assigning the CISQ task to a particular CICS/VS Class and limiting the users to one at a time. When multiple groups of users utilize ISQL, the ISQL transaction name can be changed and a different task name can be assigned to each group of users. Here, too, only one user at a time from each group should be allowed to use ISQL.

ISQL routines are loaded into CICS/VS temporary storage. There should be a balance between the use of auxiliary storage and main storage for this temporary storage requirement to avoid excessive paging and to minimize the impact on response time. Each active ISQL user requires two CICS/VS tasks. The CMXT parameter can be used to further limit the number of concurrent users but the AMXT value usually should be increased.

Virtual Addressability Extension (VAE)

VSE/SP systems running SQL/DS are often VAE systems because more than 16M of virtual storage is usually needed to support VTAM, a large CICS/VS partition or two, and SQL/DS. The overhead of address space switching is costly and the rule is to try to minimize it. This is done by grouping the most active partitions in the same *address space* and assigning the highest priorities to them. Installations that choose VAE, usually do so because they require a huge CICS/VS production partition which cannot be placed in the same *address space* as SQL/DS. When virtual storage permits, however, it is best to place SQL/DS and CICS/VS in the same *address space*.

It is also useful to isolate SQL/DS I/O to DASD devices not used by other partitions. When contention for I/O occurs space switching often increases because partitions in each *address space* are waiting for I/O and a vicious cycle of I/O wait/*address space* switch may be initiated.

VSE/SP Guests Under VM/SP

When VSE/SP is running as a guest machine with SQL/DS, the machine should be given a high priority by specifying a low value to VM/SP. This priority value is used by VM/SP to determine the dispatching priority and a production VSE/SP should have priority over other machines. The VM/SP paging should be distributed among as many independent I/O paths and physical disks as possible. This will help avoid device and controller I/O bottlenecks.

When running VSE/SP under VM/SP it is important to tune both systems. The major performance bottleneck is often I/O and efforts should be made to reduce I/O to the bare minimum. When VAE is used under VM/SP, the supervisor mode = 370 is used and real storage should be allocated to VSE/SP using the Virtual = Real method. When mode = 370, VSE/SP will do its own paging. This is necessary because VM/SP cannot page for a virtual memory greater than 16M and VAE has up to 40M of virtual storage.

When V=R is not specified for VSE/VAE, both VM/SP and VSE/SP will handle the paging. This will result in double paging and very poor performance. When a test VAE is to be set up for a short period of time, double paging may be an acceptable overhead but its use should be only temporary.

When V = R is used the VSE/SP profile should include:

SET STBYPASS VR

to inform VM/SP not to maintain its own shadow tables and:

SET NOTRANS ON

to inform VM/SP not to translate I/O channel programs. By placing these commands in the profile, the systems programmer will ensure that they are invoked each time the VSE/VAE machine is IPLed.

The larger the real storage available to VSE/SP (V = R area) the less paging that VSE/VAE has to do and the greater the number of SQL/DS buffers that can be assigned. The trade-off is that less real storage will be available to CMS and other VM/SP users because once the storage is assigned to VSE/SP, no other VM machine can use it.

SUMMARY

The VSE/SP system only allows the operation of one SQL/DS database at a time. VSE/SP is often run as a guest system under VM/SP and each VSE/SP can have its own database. An alternative is to install the database under VM/SP and to access it from the VSE/SP guest machine.

The areas that particularly affect SQL/DS performance are partition priority, system file placement, VSAM buffer definitions, real storage, and CICS/VS and IPL parameters. The VSE/SP priority algorithm determines that the partition with the highest priority will be dispatched first. The application in the partition will continue to execute until an interrupt occurs. The system then returns control to the highest priority partition ready to run.

The critical DASD files are the SQL/DS extents, the Page Data Set, the Lock file, and the Power Queues. The FASTTR option maintains a buffer of translated CCWs from I/O requests and tries to re-use them to satisfy new I/O requests.

ISQL transactions usually use more resources than preprocessed application programs. The standard procedure is to limit the number of ISQL users by assigning the CISQ task to a particular CICS/VS Class. The CMXT parameter can be used to limit the number of concurrent users.

VSE/SP systems running SQL/DS are often VAE systems. The overhead of address space switching is costly and it should be minimized. It is also useful to isolate SQL/DS I/O to DASD devices not used by other partitions.

When VSE/SP is running as a guest machine with SQL/DS, the machine should be given a high priority. When VAE is used under VM/SP, V=R should be specified. When V=R is not specified for VSE/VAE the result will be double paging and very poor performance.

RECOMMENDATIONS

1. SQL/DS should usually receive the priority directly below that of the CICS/VS partition using it.
2. It is recommended that the CICS/VS partitions be divided in such a way, where possible, that all of the SQL/DS transactions run in one of the CICS/VS partitions.
3. Partition balancing should not be specified for SQL/DS or for CICS/VS.
4. Address space switching should be minimized in a VAE system.
5. An adequate number of buffers should be defined for non-SQL/DS VSAM I/O. BUFND, BUFNI, and STRNO are the VSAM parameters which involve buffers.
6. The FASTTR option should not be used with SQL/DS or for CICS/VS.
7. When V = R is used, SET STBYPASS VR and SET NO-TRANS ON should be specified.

VSE/PT

The use of VSE/PT to monitor SQL/DS operations is not different from monitoring any other VSE/SP system activity. A minimum of 1500 scan intervals is recommended otherwise the results may not be valid. Very short and very long time intervals should be avoided. Reporting intervals of 30 minutes or longer during peak hours are usually the best. The report, however, should be subdivided into 15 minute intervals to get a better picture of system activity. The averages produced when the monitor is allowed to run for four or five hour intervals are usually very low and distorted.

The system should usually be monitored when it is under stress but **not** when it is so overstressed that the resource requirements of the monitoring tool itself will seriously impact the results of the monitoring. VSE/PT removes several pages of real storage from the pool for its use and real storage should not be in such short supply as to make this significant. When DASD I/O is being monitored the trace should be written to tape so as not to distort the results. The systems programmer should limit what is being monitored and avoid, for example, activity SVC tracing and storage monitoring, both of which are heavy users of many resources.

The manuals available for each computer model indicate some of the reasonable values for each device (paging, etc.) and these manuals should be consulted. Experience has shown that the following *rule of thumb* values are acceptable but, as mentioned elsewhere, there is no guarantee that they are appropriate in every environment. The values stated should be used as guidelines to enable the reader to quickly pinpoint areas which might require immediate investigation.

Rules of Thumb

- The **average I/O** rate per second for an individual 3380 disk actuator should be < 6. When SIO reaches 10, a bottleneck may be indicated. Disk device utilization should not exceed 25 percent.

- The disk **channel utilization** should not be above 30 to 35 percent and when the value is below 10 to 15 percent it, most probably, is **not** the bottleneck.

- SQL/DS handles I/O better than VSE/SP handles paging. The **paging rate** for the CICS or the SQL/DS partition should not exceed 6 pages per second on any model. This is because the CICS partition or the SQL/DS partition is stopped when a page fault occurs and it can take 50 to 60 milliseconds for the partition to regain control. When paging is greater than 6 per second, the CICS or SQL/DS partition is idle for more than one third of the time. A high paging rate to a particular disk will degrade response even more. The page data set should be placed on low activity disks. The total space allocated should **not** be greater than the virtual size and the size of each extent should be the same on each disk.

- The **CPU utilization** should not exceed 70 to 80 percent. When it is below 35 percent, it, most probably, is not the bottleneck.

- **System waits** on the DASD devices should not exceed 5 percent and average millisecond wait to SIO should be less than 5 percent. When SIOFAST is in effect this value does not include the hardware level queuing time and even 5 percent may be too high. The average I/O queue length should be .4 or lower. A balanced system should have a high degree of overlapped I/O and CPU activity (at least 70 percent of the time I/O is being done, the CPU should be busy). If this is not the case then the I/O subsystem is **not** powerful enough to fully utilize the CPU.

- If there is any **partition deactivation,** it is a clear sign that the system suffers from a lack of real storage. When there is system deactivation of partitions the resources tied up by the partition are not freed and the application in the partition may be holding many SQL/DS locks. Deactivation also involves a great deal of overhead and should be avoided. The periodic use of the MAP command from the console will also show if any partitions were deactivated. One or more of the partitions should be closed when deactivation occurs so as to redistribute system resources.

VSE/PT Under VM/SP

When VSE/SP is a guest machine under a VM/SP or VM/HPO system, the VSE/PT CPU and storage needs may themselves negatively impact the environment. Care should be taken to ensure that the resource needs of VSE/PT do not distort the measurements. In VM, many functions are simulated and cannot be correctly measured by VSE/PT. VMMAP should be used for many of the measurements. The values that are **not accurate** include:

Channel Activity Level	Average CPU Utilization
LTA Wait Counts	Storage Occupancy
Estimated Breakdown of CPU Utilization	

VSE/PT **is useful,** however, for providing an overview of VSE/SP system activity and may be useful for spotting significant problems but the values reported must be double checked by other means (VMMAP, etc.). VSE/PT is also useful because of the DASD activity report for each partition. The VMMAP report only shows activity for the entire VSE/SP machine. The VSE/PT report is fairly accurate for dedicated disk seek analysis and less accurate for nondedicated disks. It does, however, point out which partition accesses which cylinders on the disks.

Aside from the DASD activity report for dedicated disks, the VSE/PT values that are reported to be **valid** under VM/SP include:

SVC counts	Total seek requests
Total SIO	Unsuccessful seeks and counts
Reserve/Release counts	Average and maximum queue lengths

Display System Activity (DSA)

When the Interactive Interface is available a *display of system activity* may be requested. The contents of this display are derived from the VSE/SP accounting function which must be active. At IPL time the systems programmer must have specified in the automatic start-up:

JA = YES

The following is an example of a *Display System Activity* screen output:

```
IESADMDA    DISPLAY SYSTEM ACTIVITY    23 SECONDS    11:02:01

*---------------SYSTEM---------------*  *------------------CICS------------------*
| CPU      : 39% SIO/Sec: 30 |  | No. Tasks:  97 Per Sec:      * |
| Pages In :  8   Per Sec:  * |  | Active Task: 3 Suspended:   0 |
| Pages Out: 11   Per Sec:  1 |  | Most Active: 5 Pages Avl:  345 |
*-----------------------------------*  *---------------------------------------*
Console Replies: BG

ID  S  JOB NAME PHASE NAME   ELAPSED   CPU TIME   OVERHEAD   %CPU   SIO
                              TIME     PER STEP   PER STEP   TIME   PER
BG  1  BATCH1   STP0001      00:15:01   10.25      1.72       3%   3,124
FB
FA
F7
F8
F9
F6               ETC.
F5
F2
F3
F1

PF1=HELP       3=END        4=RETURN         5=CPU
```

When VSE/SP is operating as a guest under VM, the data available is valid for VSE but the number of events per second is invalid because non-VSE time is not available. CP servicing time (TTIME-TIME) required by the guest VSE is not included in CPU time and no paging activity is shown when VM does the paging. When the VSE/SP guest receives dedicated real storage (V = R), VSE/SP does its own paging and that paging is reflected in the DSA. The VM/SP paging, of course, is not included.

While the DSA is not a monitoring tool and printed reports are not available, it does provide indicators which point to areas requiring further investigation. The main activity display will indicate:

- Where most of the DASD activity occurs.
- The progress of individual partitions.
- Whether or not VSE/SP is utilizing a large amount of CPU.
- The resources currently used by the SQL/DS and the CICS/VS partitions as compared to other partitions.
- Whether or not VSE/SP is doing excessive paging.
- Which partitions other than SQL/DS and CICS/VS are being used. When the operator decides, without consulting the DBA, to run SQL/DS or non-SQL/DS batch jobs during peak on-line activity, the display will indicate this. This will usually explain the sudden worsening of response time.
- Changes to partition priorities which also greatly effect response times.

An I/O display panel is also accessible and may serve to indicate excessive I/O to one or more individual devices. Be aware that all of the DSA values are based upon short time intervals, are rounded and exclude most VSE/SP system I/O operations (operator console control, paging I/O, error recovery, etc.) in the device I/O counts. These displays are meant to serve as performance indicators for further investigation and verification.

SUMMARY

The system should usually be monitored when it is under stress. VSE/PT removes several pages of real storage from the pool for its use. **Rule of thumb** values are acceptable but there is **no** guarantee that they are appropriate in every environment.

When VSE/SP is a guest machine under a VM/SP or VM/HPO

system, the VSE/PT CPU and storage needs may themselves negatively impact the environment. In VM, many functions are simulated and cannot be correctly measured by VSE/PT. VMMAP should be used for many of the measurements. The VSE/PT report is fairly accurate for dedicated disk seek analysis and it points out which partition accesses which cylinders. Valid VSE/PT values include: SVC counts, total seek requests, total SIO, unsuccessful seeks and counts, reserve/release counts, and average and maximum queue lengths.

RECOMMENDATIONS

1. A minimum of 1500 scan intervals is recommended for VSE/PT. Use a reporting interval of at least 30 minutes.

2. When DASD I/O is being monitored the trace should be written to tape.

3. Avoid SVC tracing or storage monitoring.

4. The **average I/O** rate per second for a 3380 disk should be < 6. When SIO reaches 10, a bottleneck is indicated. Disk device utilization should not exceed 25 percent.

5. The disk **channel utilization** should not be above 30–35 percent.

6. The **paging rate** for the CICS or the SQL/DS partition should not exceed 6 pages per second.

7. The **CPU utilization** should not exceed 70–80 percent.

8. **System waits** on the DASD devices should not exceed 5 percent and average millisecond wait to SIO should be less than 5 percent. The average I/O queue length should be .4 or lower.

9. **Partition deactivation** is a clear sign that the system suffers from a lack of real storage.

I/O TUNING

I/O is usually the major bottleneck in a database system. The reasons for this situation include:

- Installations often do not have sufficient actuators and channels to match the CPU power.

- Disk usage is not distributed and *hot spots* are generated.
- Too many active data sets are on too few devices.
- BLOCK and control interval sizes are not correct for the disks being used.
- Too many I/O bound applications are executed during the same time frame.

The performance monitors should be used to identify the most active data sets and the systems programmer should distribute the data sets to as many different devices as possible. When several active data sets have to be on the same actuator, it is recommended that they be clustered together to reduce arm movement on that particular device.

Major System Files

The major VM/SP high volume files include SQL/DS extents, spooling files, page and TEMP areas, and the 190 and 19E CMS minidisks. In VSE/SP, the SQL/DS extents, the page data sets, the label area, the lock file, the POWER files, and the VSAM catalogs are the major high volume active data sets. These files should be distributed among as many disk actuators as possible.

Alternate Paths

Another tuning method is to assign alternate paths to the DASD actuators, when possible. The 3880 controller, for example, may be attached to two channels and should be assigned to two consecutive channel addresses. There is a difference in the way alternate path assignment is done in VSE/SP and VM/SP. VSE/SP will alternate between the two channels and try to balance the I/O activity. It is sufficient to specify to VSE/SP in the ADD command that an alternate channel exists. If the first channel assigned is Channel One, and an alternate channel assignment is indicated, the VSE/SP supervisor knows that the alternate channel is Channel Two.

VM/SP does **not** alternate between the primary and the alternate channel. It always checks the primary channel and **only** if that channel is busy will it try the alternate channel. Most installations balance the I/O artificially by assigning the disks to different primary channels. It is best, of course, to know which are the most active channels and to assign them in a balanced manner. When this is not possible and there are six disk actuators, three are assigned to one channel and three to the other as shown in the following example:

```
RDEVICE ADDRESS = (150,3), DEVTYPE = 3380, ALTCU = 250
RDEVICE ADDRESS = (253,3), DEVTYPE = 3380, ALTCU = 150
```

Block Size

The block size of the many files in the system can also be tuned to better utilize the DASD devices attached and to reduce the number of I/Os. Block size should not be made too large because real storage buffers are required to hold the I/O blocks of data. There should be a balance between the real storage constraints and the need to reduce the number of I/Os. It should be noted that reducing the number of I/Os in a VM/SP system will also reduce the CPU needs because CCW translation for virtual machines consumes a great deal of CPU power. Care should be exercised to ensure that the reduction of I/O due to the increase of block size is not offset by an increase in paging.

As a rule of thumb, 4K blocks are recommended for most modern DASD devices. VSAM control intervals (CI) should usually be 4K for data but for indexes the CI size should be 2K. The POWER data file size (DBLK) should be 4080 or 6128 and the ICCF DTSFILE should be 8K. CMS minidisks should usually be 4K and most application files should be 4K. These suggested blocking factors are, of course, dependent on the allocation of sufficient real storage to prevent paging.

I/O Priority

There is no way to prioritize the I/O in a VM/SP environment but in VSE/SP there is a new Attention Routine command which may help prioritize the I/O from the SQL/DS partition. PRTYIO allows the systems programmer to specify which partition's I/O request should be placed in the wait queue for the device ahead of the I/O requests of the other partitions. The default priority is *first come, first served.* To indicate that partition F3, for example, should have the highest priority, followed by F2 and F5, and all other partitions should have equal priority, the systems programmer should specify:

PRTYIO   F3, F2, F5

This command should be used with great care and the results monitored to ensure that other critical applications are not negatively impacted.

Batch I/O

The I/O intense batch applications should not be run during peak on-line processing periods. The PRTYIO command will be of no value with batch applications because all of the I/O to the database is requested from the database partition. Heavy I/O intense system workloads such as disk initialization, backup, recovery, and the printing of large reports should also be avoided during peak on-line processing periods.

SUMMARY

I/O is usually the major bottleneck in a database system. The major VM/SP high volume files include SQL/DS extents, spooling files, page and TEMP areas, and the 190 and 19E CMS minidisks. In VSE/SP, the SQL/DS extents, the page data sets, the label area, the lock file, the POWER files, and the VSAM catalogs are the major high volume active data sets. VSE/SP will try to balance the I/O activity and VM/SP does not alternate between the primary and the alternate channel.

The block size of files can be tuned to utilize the DASD devices attached and to reduce the number of I/Os. Reducing the number of I/O in a VM/SP system also reduces the CPU needs. PRTYIO allows the VSE/SP systems programmer to prioritize the I/O.

RECOMMENDATIONS

1. Active data sets should be distributed among as many different devices as possible.
2. Assign alternate paths to the DASD actuators.
3. In VM/SP artificially balance the I/O by assigning the disks to different primary channels.
4. Care should be exercised to ensure that the reduction of I/O is not offset by an increase in paging.
5. 4K blocks are recommended for most modern DASD devices. VSAM CISIZE should be 4K for data and 2K for indexes. CMS minidisks should usually be 4K and most application files should be 4K.
6. I/O intensive applications should not be run during peak processing periods.

VM/VSE GUEST SHARING

Many VSE/SP installations use VM/SP to enable them to run more than one 16M VSE/SP machine on one CPU. Often a test system, an on-line production system, and a batch production system all share the same CPU. In the past these VSE/SP machines were unable to share the same database. Either the contents of the database were stored in three separate copies or on-line and batch production were unable to run at the same time. The latest versions of SQL/DS have introduced an interesting new concept for VSE/SP (version 4.1 or higher) users. When VSE/SP executes as a guest machine both VSE/SP and VM/SP may share the same SQL/DS database machine.

It is not recommended that batch and on-line SQL/DS run at the same time against the same database machine unless the batch is designed to be able to continually release the resources it locks. Batch production applications are usually unable to release resources because the COMMIT WORK command automatically closes all of the *cursors* in the application. Batch applications should not be, but often are, written without taking the total environment into consideration.

In today's environment, while peak on-line and batch do **not** run simultaneously, there are increased demands for round-the-clock on-line access to the database even at the cost of degraded response time during off-hours. There is often a need for batch and on-line to run against the same database when night batch runs do not complete on time. The introduction of SQL/DS Guest Sharing has made it possible for VM/CMS users and multiple VSE/SP machines (including CICS and batch users) to all access the same database machine. It is now also possible for two CICS partitions in the same VSE/SP machine to access two different VM/SQL machines. One, for example, might access the test SQL/DS while the other accessed the production SQL/DS machine.

The potential uses of this feature are enormous. VSE/SP users migrating to VM/SP can continue to run the old production jobs under VSE while the new production applications can run under CMS and both can access the same VM/SQL database. End-users can access SQL/DS from their applications in CICS/VS while the DBA who prefers REXX can monitor and tune SQL/DS from the CMS environment.

The major question about guest sharing is how serious the impact is upon performance because the performance for VSE/SP users of SQL/DS under VM/SP cannot be allowed to deteriorate to unacceptable levels. **The good news is that early performance tests have shown** that while CPU utilization tended to slightly increase, the response time in VSE/SP running against a VM/SQL database was at least as good, if not better, than when running against a SQL/VSE database. This may be difficult to believe, but there are some possible explanations which will be discussed later.

It can be assumed, therefore, that the average response time for VSE on-line applications will not be significantly different when running against a VM/SQL database. This is especially true when blocking is used to reduce the row-by-row communication via the VM/SP IUCV function to the VSE/SP machine.

There are **significant advantages** to using VM/SQL even if there is some response time penalty:

- Removing SQL/DS from VSE will reduce the virtual storage requirements. If SQL/DS previously existed in multiple VSE machines, having only one or two SQL/DS machines will reduce overall system storage requirements and will reduce paging.
- VSE will only allow one SQL/DS database. Both the test CICS and the production CICS have had to use the same database. With guest sharing, each CICS can run against its own VM/SQL database.
- With *guest sharing,* a *test* or a *production* VM/SQL machine can be accessed from one or more VSE/SP guest machines. In addition, each database can also be accessed by CMS users writing in REXX, COBOLII, or COBOL, and other languages, or by using QMF, CSP, AS, ISQL, and similar VM products.
- VM/HPO with more than 16M of real storage may allow many more buffers than could be defined under VSE/SP.
- When running in dual-processors, the SQL/DS machine can utilize one CPU while VSE/SP utilizes the other CPU.

Users of CPUs running at 85 to 95 percent of CPU capacity may have to defer a move to guest sharing because of the potential increase in CPU utilization. It is **not** recommended that the native VSE user install VM/SP just to be able to utilize guest sharing. Those who already run under VM/SP, however, should carefully evaluate the use of this feature.

Most of the recommendations in this book are applicable to SQL/DS guest sharing. Those that apply to application performance should be used in the CICS/VSE environment and those that apply to the database should be used in the VM/SP environment.

Be careful to ensure that the SQL/DS machine under VM/SP is defined with the following option:

SET QDROP OFF USERS

This option significantly reduces CPU utilization. Under VM/HPO this option may not be necessary. To monitor CPU and I/O usage in the guest sharing environment utilize the tools described in this chapter.

The use of BLOCKing, especially in the batch environment, is usually beneficial, and the decision on whether or not to increase the number of buffers is based on the same parameters of paging and real storage discussed elsewhere.

The SQL/DS database machine should be defined in VM/SP with the parameter:

IUCV *IDENT DBNAME **LOCAL**

When using VM/SP release 6, VTAM and AVS connected via an SNA gateway or connected via TSAF to other systems which need to connect to the database machine, specify:

IUCV *IDENT DBNAME **GLOBAL**

This authorizes the SQL/DS machine to connect to the *IDENT CP system service and identifies the database as a LOCAL or GLOBAL resource. During SQL/DS start-up, the operator may decide, for databases defined as GLOBAL resources, whether the database will be used locally or globally:

```
SQLSTART DBNAME(DBPROD1) PARM(PARMID=PARMPRD1, DBMODE=G)
SQLSTART DBNAME(DBPROD1) PARM(PARMID=PARMPRDL, DBMODE=L)
SQLSTART DBNAME(DBPROD2) PARM(PARMID=PARMPRD2)
```

DBPROD2 is defined as a LOCAL resource and may only be started with DBMODE=L. It might always be useful to define the database as a GLOBAL resource in the VM directory because it can be modified at start-up time by specifying the DMODE parameter.

The MAXCONN parameter should be set high enough to include the VSE/SP connections. A sample VM/SP directory entry for an SQL/DS machine in a *guest sharing* configuration might be:

```
        USER SQLPROD passwrd1 6M 6M G

        ACCOUNT
        OPTION MAXCONN 40 ACCT ECMODE
        IUCV ALLOW
        IUCV *IDENT DBPROD1 GLOBAL
        IUCV *IDENT DBPROD2 LOCAL

        IPL CMS
        CONSOLE 009 3215 T OPERATOR
        SPOOL 00C 2540 READER
        SPOOL 00D 2540 A
        SPOOL 00E 1403

        LINK MAINT 190 190 RR
        LINK MAINT 19D 19D RR
        LINK MAINT 19E 19E RR
        MDISK 191 3380 1024 020 DSK191 W
* Libraries for SQL/DS
        MDISK 193 3380 0150 050 SQLSRV R RPW WPW
        MDISK 195 3380 0200 020 SQLSRV RR RPW WPW MPW
* Database Minidisks
        MDISK 200 3380 0060 040 SQLPRD R RPW WPW
        MDISK 201 3380 0100 020 SQLPR1 R RPW WPW
        MDISK 202 3380 0120 240 SQLPR2 R RPW WPW
        MDISK 203 3380 0220 150 SQLSRV R RPW WPW
```

The value for MAXCONN should include the number of mini-disks and virtual machines to be connected. The parameter ACCT will allow the use of the SQL/DS accounting facility.

The minidisks are placed on different physical devices in order to balance the active I/O load among the disks and channels. All too often the entire database is temporarily placed on one physical disk during initial generation and *there is nothing so permanent as these temporary assignments.* Plan the balancing of the I/O **before** installation and database generation.

VSE IPL for Guest Sharing

During the IPL of the VSE/SP supervisor, the

SET XPCC TARGET SYSARI TO APPCVM TARGET DBPROD1

command informs the VSE/SP supervisor to utilize VM/SP resources for XPCC commands to SYSARI (the default SQL/DS database resource) by issuing APPC/VM requests. All Batch SQL/DS requests will go to this database. This TARGET for Batch cannot be changed without re-IPLing the VSE system. Without the above SET command, Batch SQL/DS commands can only be used on the VSE/SP SQL/DS database. With the above SET command a VSE database cannot be used by Batch applications.

The CICS CIRB command has a new parameter that allows the DBA to specify which database will be accessed by all the users in the CICS partition. When this new parameter is not used, CICS accesses the database specified in the XPCC command for TARGET SYSARI. If the SET XPCC command was not used, the default will be the VSE/SP database:

CIRB CIRBPSW, 6,,,,**DBPROD2**	(uses DBPROD2)
CIRB CIRBPSW, 6	(uses default)

SUMMARY

When VSE/SP executes as a guest machine under VM/SP both may share the same SQL/DS database machine. It is now possible for two CICS partitions in the same VSE/SP machine to access two different VM/SQL machines. VSE/SP users migrating to VM/SP can continue to run the old production jobs under VSE while the new production applications can run under CMS and both can access the same VM/SQL database. End-users can access SQL/DS from their applications in CICS/VS while the DBA who prefers REXX can monitor and tune SQL/DS from the CMS environment.

Early performance tests have shown that while CPU utilization tends to increase, the response time in VSE/SP running against a VM/SQL database is at least as good, if not better, than when running against a SQL/VSE database.

The CICS CIRB command has a new parameter that allows the DBA to specify which database will be accessed by all users in the CICS partition.

RECOMMENDATIONS

1. Batch and on-line SQL/DS should not run at the same time against the same database machine.
2. The SQL/DS machine under VM/SP should have SET QDROP OFF USERS.

CHAPTER 10

Translating Theory
into Practice

Some readers begin with Chapter 1 and some start at the end of a book. If you have reached this point by starting at Chapter 1, it is hoped that you have derived a great deal of benefit from this book. If you are starting from this chapter, read it first to see if you agree with the author as to which chapters will interest you most. This last chapter will provide several guidelines to each of the members of the *performance tuning team* to help them actually start the process of performance tuning.

THE APPLICATION DEVELOPMENT STAFF

The systems analyst and the application programmer make up the application development staff. Each has a crucial role to play in **preventing** poor performance.

The process of performance tuning begins with the **systems analyst** who is primarily responsible for the *prevention* phase in performance tuning. He is responsible for defining the:

Input. Raw data, tables, and other files.

Processing. How the input will be used and what output will be produced.

Output. Data, tables, and reports.

The analyst must determine how the data will be used so that the tables can be designed for performance and efficiency. Working with the database administrator (DBA), the analyst should design the tables using normalization techniques to reduce redundancy and denormalization techniques to improve performance. A major task, therefore, of the analyst is to correctly design the application so that system performance is not impacted by the inefficient use of the data. He or she should design the table structure, indicate the format of each column in each row, designate primary and foreign keys, prepare the test data environment, and document the required *joins* and subqueries. Only the analyst has sufficient information from the user department to properly make the necessary decisions about table design.

The analyst might also use the EXPLAIN facility to test suggested queries, updates, deletes, and inserts to validate as best as possible that the design is feasible and efficient. (This task, however, might be accomplished by a programmer/analyst.) The analyst should also estimate for the DBA and for the systems programmer what quantity of data will be inserted into the tables so that sufficient storage media can be made available when needed.

The chapters that should be of special interest to the systems analyst are:

Chapter 1   Introduction
Chapter 2   Basic Concepts
Chapter 4   Table Design Considerations
Chapter 5   Some New and Useful functions
Chapter 6   Application Development

It is recommended that the following chapters also be reviewed:

Chapter 3   The Optimizer
Chapter 7   Resource Contention

The **application programmer** will accept the design from the analyst and will code and test the programs. The programmer must cooperate with all of the other members of the *performance tuning team* to provide performance feedback, request assistance, and update the team as to the status of the application.

The programs should be written after the application programmer has mastered the techniques for efficient coding found in the manuals and in this book. When the application programs are completed and a test data environment created, the programmer, in cooperation with the DBA, must examine each SQL command in the programs using the EXPLAIN facility.

The following procedure should be carried out as part of application testing to ensure that the programs perform efficiently:

1. Inspect each SQL command in the application to verify that:

   (a) **It cannot be made logically more efficient.** An example was noted by the author in an application that had to check a code in a very complex query. The programmer issued the SELECT statement seven times, once for each code value, instead of using the *GROUP BY* and *ORDER BY* clauses. These clauses might have made the query a bit more complex but the command would have required only one access and one set of internal DBSPACES instead of seven. When these clauses were added, the application ran significantly faster and did not run out of internal DBSPACES.

   (b) **Each command is in its simplest form** and contains no, or a minimum of, UNIONs, joins, subqueries, scalar functions, and so on.

   (c) **The indexes it needs are available.** To check the indexes from ISQL, the programmer can use the following commands:

   ```
   SET VARCHAR 100
   SET ISOL CS
   SELECT INAME,INDEXTYPE,CLUSTER, KEYTPE,COLNAMES
       FROM SYSTEM.SYSINDEXES
       WHERE TNAME = 'TABLENAME' AND
           CREATOR = 'CREATORNAME'
   ```

2. Review the definition of each table to ensure that the definitions of the columns in the application exactly match the definitions in the database. To view the column definition, the application programmer can use a command similar to the following example:

   ```
   SELECT CNAME,COLTYPE,LENGTH,NULLS,SUBTYPE
       FROM SYSTEM.SYSCOLUMNS
       WHERE TNAME = ' TABLENAME'
   ```

3. Confirm that indicator variables are used with **every** nullable column and that dynamic SQL commands are only used where necessary.

4. Verify that the test data is appropriate and that the volume of data is similar to that of the production environment (at least for the final system testing).

5. Prepare a stripped-down copy of the application and add the EXPLAIN clause to appropriate SQL commands. (see

Chapter 6). The results of the EXPLAIN tests should be reviewed with the DBA.

6. Check that *blocking* and/or *cursor stability* are being used where appropriate.

7. Remove COMMIT WORK commands from applications executing in single-user mode and add COMMIT WORK to all other programs, where applicable.

8. Identify segments of code which may generate contention problems and discuss possible alternatives with the DBA.

9. Verify that *cursors* are not being excessively opened and closed.

The chapters that should be of special interest to the application programmer are:

Chapter 1   Introduction
Chapter 2   Basic Concepts
Chapter 3   The Optimizer
Chapter 4   Table Design Considerations
Chapter 5   Some New and Useful functions
Chapter 6   Application Development

It is recommended that the following chapters also be reviewed:

Chapter 7   Resource Contention
Chapter 8   SQL/DS Data Management

The initial concern for efficient performance is in the hands of the application developers. They must design and prepare the data and applications for minimum resource utilization. They must cooperate and consult with the DBA and systems programmer to verify that the environment is conducive to maximum performance efficiency. The DBA can only correct a problem that already exists; the application developer can prevent the problem from occurring in the first place.

THE DATABASE ADMINISTRATOR (DBA)

The DBA is accountable for the overall database environment and for the performance of the many applications that access the data. His responsibility is to:

1. Generate the test and production databases.
2. Choose effective startup parameters.
3. Cooperate with the systems programmer to distribute the data across a sufficient number of data paths.
4. Plan for future expansion.
5. Monitor database activity to be able to identify periods of performance degradation.
6. Review application design and programs.
7. Establish standards.
8. Prepare guidelines.
9. Grant and revoke authority.
10. Allocate resources.
11. Provide a user-friendly environment for production and application development.

The DBA should carefully avoid unilateral and arbitrary regulations which only serve to make it more difficult to utilize the database environment. The DBA should provide service to developers and end-users and promote the effective use of SQL/DS.

The following steps should serve as a guide for a DBA to identify the cause(s) of degradation in response time. They have proven useful to the author but cover only a few major recommendations. Additional suggestions for action may be found in the other chapters of this book.

Prior to taking any action, the DBA should corroborate the accuracy of the complaint that response time has deteriorated. This will require the maintenance of up-to-date response time statistics for key applications. Once the increase in response time has been verified, the following steps should be followed:

1. Consult with the operations department to determine if any nonscheduled (batch) applications have been executed. Pressure by management upon the operations department often forces the staff to execute unscheduled applications that seriously impact on-line response time. Also verify that the system is not waiting for an operator response or that a hardware failure is not being handled by the technicians.
2. Verify that no new applications have been added. New applications may be accessing tables needed by existing

applications and are a primary cause of sudden performance degradation.

3. Check the system console to verify that an ARCHIVE
has not been triggered. Use the COUNTER command to
ensure that an excessive number of checkpoints has not
been executed.

4. Use the SHOW commands to check catalog contention. An
ISQL or QMF user may have accessed the catalogs or a DBA
user may be creating an object and locking out other users.
Precompilations are also a main source of system catalog
contention. Check if anyone is doing precompiles to the production system. These activities are the major performance
degredation culprits in a test system but they should **not** be
permitted in a production system during on-line processing
hours.

5. Ask the systems programmer to examine the system using
VMMAP, VSE/PT, or another measurement tool to verify
that there is **no** system-wide bottleneck. Ensure that a change
has not been made recently to any system parameters.

6. Question the end-users to confirm that they are not executing any nonscheduled on-line applications which may involve mass updates, deletes, or inserts.

If the problem involves a specific application, the follows steps
should also be taken:

7. Contact the application developer to verify that programs
have not been modified. *"Nothing important has been
changed"* and *"the program was **only** recompiled"* are standard indications that the problem was caused by the *unchanged* program. Check it out and examine the output.

8. Verify that indexes have not been modified or dropped.
Examine the SYSTEM.SYSUSAGE table as described in
Chapter 6.

9. Check that primary or foreign keys have not been added or
deactivated.

10. Ensure that huge amounts of data have not been recently
added or deleted from the tables.

11. Check with the user department to verify that no additional
users are using the application and that no unusual data is
being used.

12. If the problem has still not been found, run the EXPLAIN facility to try to find what is causing the degradation.

13. If there still is no clue, check again from Step 1 and request additional monitoring assistance from the operations and systems staff.

The role of database administrator is a crucial one and the task should not, in most installations, be relegated to a very part-time one (unless the environment is very stable with no new applications or major modifications under consideration). After an application is in production the primary responsibility for performance belongs to the DBA just as it is the responsibility of the application development staff before it is in production.

Every chapter of this book should be of special interest to the DBA.

THE SYSTEMS PROGRAMMER

The systems programmer is responsible for the overall system environment. Critical applications not using SQL/DS may be executing in the system and may require resources and priority. The systems programmer generates the system environment, allocates system resources, establishes installation standards and operations guidelines, authorizes users, manages change management, and handles system problems. The systems programmer should carefully avoid unilateral and arbitrary regulations which only serve to make it more difficult to use the system. The systems programmer should provide service to all of the system users.

When response problems occur, the systems programmer should use the standard tools available (VMMAP, VSE/PT, and similar products) to pinpoint the bottleneck (or to ensure that it is not a system problem). The systems programmer should review the specific parameters mentioned in Chapter 9. If any new system components have been added or upgraded, the systems programmer should verify that all applicable PTFs have been installed.

The systems programmer will mainly be interested in:

Chapter 9   Operating System Parameters
Chapter 7   Resource Contention
Chapter 8   SQL/DS Data Management

but will gain a much better understanding of the impact of SQL/DS by reading:

Chapter 1   Introduction
Chapter 2   Basic Concepts

A FINAL WORD

There are no magical reasons for good or poor performance. Once the SQL/DS professional has mastered the concepts of performance tuning, it should be relatively easy to produce efficient applications and to successfully tune the database system. GOOD LUCK !

Index